MARBLE

the history of a culture

Luciana and Tiziano Mannoni

MARBLE
the history of a culture

Facts On File Publications
New York, New York ● Oxford, England

Contents

Acknowledgements

The Authors and Publishers wish to thank all those who collaborated to collect written, oral and iconographic material for this book, and in particular: Augusto C. Ambrosi, Aldo Andrei, Ilario Bessi, Pietro Boni, Carlo A. Del Giudice, Enrico Dolci, Antonio Frova, Stanislaw Kasprysiak, Ugo Lagomarsini, Silvia Lusuardi, Cesare Piccioli, Ennio Poleggi, Maria Pia Rossignani, Sergio Scavezzoni, Dodo Torri, the Marble Institute of America, the Conventions and Visitors Bureau of Boston, the friends of the Institute of History and Material Culture for many invaluable ideas that were the result of a common research, the quarrymen, marble workers and inhabitants of Carrara who with their enthusiasm helped and encouraged us with this book.

The pictures of chapter six are by:
Agenzia Fotografica Luisa Ricciarini, Milano, figg. 266, 274, 275
Fiore, Torino, figg. 265, 268, 269
I.C.P., Milano, figg. 264, 272, 273
Pictor International Leo Aarons, figg. 267, 270

Book's original title «Il marmo - materia e cultura»
© Sagep Editrice, Genoa - Italy

Translated by Penelope J. Hammond-Smith

First published in the United States by
Facts On File, Inc.
460 Park Avenue South
New York, N.Y. 10016

ISBN 0-8160-1350-0

Printed in Italy-Genoa - by Sagep Editrice

Foreward

Whoever reads a marble bibliography for the first time is usually astonished by the number of books and periodical reviews published on the subject. However many publications are purely technical, born from specific commercial requirements, since marble (although it has been used for thousands of years), is still very much part of present day life (especially in Italy). There are a few books about the uses of marble in antiquity and different working techniques.

In other fields like geology, scientists study how marble was formed in the crust of the earth, and engineers study the technical data in order to better exploit the physical properties of marble. The bulk of publication however deals with sculpture and architecture throughout history, and lastly a few books are about the social, juridic and enviromental aspects of marble production.

This book however is not meant for specialists, and was not written for commercial or technological purposes. On the contrary it provides an answer to all questions like «what is marble», «how is it produced?», «how important has it been in the history of mankind?» etc. that any layman may ask himself. The Authors have tried to answer such questions without going into too great detail, or deep individual analyses (also there would not have been room for this in the book), but rather follow a «humanistic» trend — in the original sense of the word — that brings together within the same spectrum science, technology, the arts and society. It is an all-embracing historic survey that goes back to the origins of marble within the bowels of the earth hundreds of milions of years ago, up to the history of mankind, his work and achievements; how old and new techniques developed hand in hand with fresh inventions and scientific discoveries, and how products and production methods varied according to when and where and by whom they were made.

Above all it is a history of different places and their inhabitants, where marble had became a vital and irreplceable part of civilization, as in the Apuan Alps where, among other things, the photographs of extraction methods reproduced in this book, were taken.

L. & T.M.

Introduction

The Origins and Meaning of the Word Marble

The meaning of the word «marble» gradually changed as the marble market expanded throughout the Western World.

The modern Italian version *marmo* derives from the medieval *marmore* and the Latin *marmor, marmoris*; the roots of the modern German *marmor* and the French *marbrière* and *marbre* are Latin; the English version *marble* derives from the French. However, the original version is not Latin but Greek, *marmaros*, from old Aegean, and means «a snow white and spotless stone, a rocky mass»; the adjective *marmoreos* means «resplendent», and the verb *marmairo* «to shine».

Originally the word marble indicated an «ornamental stone taking polish», but for centuries, notwithstanding fierce arguments, it has been impossible to establish which ornamental stones are marble and which are not.

Both the Egyptians and the Sumerians knew how to work and polish hard silicate rock; the greater variety of Grecian crystalline calcareous rock was more suitable for sculpture, decorations, and could be coloured: these calcareous rocks were loosely known as marble.

Later the Romans worked all kinds of ornamental rock and named them according to colour and place of origin.

A new genetic classification of rocks was established in the 19th century, and all crystalline calcareous rocks came under the heading of marble. Nowadays in the commercial and industrial worlds the distinction is rarely made: in the past alabaster and ophicarbonate rock, the physical properties of which are similar to crystalline calcareous rock, were thought of as marble, but today all ornamental stones, silicates in particular, and even travertine stones that do not polish well, come under the same heading; the only distinction is that crystalline calcareous rock is marble in the strict sense of the word, while all other ornamental rocks are classified as marble products or marble activities. Under Italian law all exploitation of marble, granite, serpentine, syenite, quarzite, porphyry, alabaster and diorite come under the heading of «marble industry».

Essential Physical Properties of Marble

Marble is one of the rocks that make up the crust of the earth; it weighs from $2\frac{1}{2}$ to 3 tons every cubic metre and is difficult to transport without special equipment and devices. Marble is both resistant and longlasting suitable for architectural decoration and supporting structure, in large and small buildings. Unlike metal that is mined underground, marble can be extracted from open cast mines: some rare types are quarried underground in tunnels called *«gallerie»*, once the surface deposits have been worked out. In short, all rock sharing the following properties comes under the heading of marble: a particular structure and texture that takes polish and can be cut into thin slabs and carved in full relief, colour, pattern and homogeneous surface.

The Importance of Marble in the Western World

Monumental sculpture and architecture make up only a small chapter in the history of civilization

1

1. *Andrea Pisano: «La scultura», a marble slab from the Campanile of Giotto (Florence, middle of the 14th century). Realistic representation of equipment and tools: axes, chisels, wooden and iron mallets, hammers, pegs and a compass etc.*

that began at the dawn of time and developed differently in every part of the world. Marble products from different areas and periods are best evaluated typologically according to where they come from, and with what tools or equipment they were made.

Archeologists and etnographers use typology to establish cultural and chronological orders, dates and places of origin for museums. Unfortunatly too many scientists are interested only in this aspect of civilization and neglect the more human side. Their argument is that scientific certainties are based only on typological evidence, and that hypothesis cannot be proved by concrete facts: however if typology is an end in itself, it is of service to nobody except a small group of archaeologists and etnographers.

Traditionally the history of art has been one of the most reliable means of artistic evaluation: beautiful articles from every period and culture are assessed individually as the work of anonymous or known artists and aesthetic judgement is essential. But the shortcomings of art criticism are well-known: judgement is subjective, and, cultually speaking, art historians are invariably children of their times; and even if it were possible to judge all works of art according to a universal criterion the problem of whether beauty is the most important thing still remains.

For practical reasons in the past works of art were commissioned by private or public buyers who were less interested in the aesthetic side, that depended on the artists' ability, imagination and eccentricity. An artist learnt technique and subject matter from the older generation and eventually would teach them himself: this meant that a work of art mirrored contemporary society. We do not intend to debase the importance of aesthetics, on the contrary, in must be dealt with in detail within the contemporary social framework, bearing in mind the destination, patron, production organization and artists' flair.

Initially many marble articles do not seem to have a practical purpose; during the Middle Ages in order to become a member of the Guild of Stone-cutters and Sculptors (*Arte dei Lavoratori della Pietra*) it was not necessary to have great natural talent, rather a good knowledge of the material (both good and bad points), technique, tools, equipment and a good repertoire of conventional figures and ornamental motifs; above all it was necessary to enjoy the protection of the corporation. If a sculptor possessed good natural talent he could become famous during his lifetime (though usually this happened only after his death) and his work was imitated by other artisans. As Michelangelo said the stone cutter's first lesson is the art of «taking away»: no piece can be put back. Great masters and the most humble stone-cutters — whom they so often despised — were united by the same bond.

Finally it is necessary to explain why marble was used for sculpture, instead of another type of rock that apparently would have done just as well: the reasons were not only aesthetic. The first statues of gods and men endowed with magic power were made in Egypt and Mesopotamia using dark and highly polished marble (silicates), that came from distant mountains. Colour and brightness had a symbolic value. During the Bronze and Iron Age men believed that shiny rock like quarzite were made by the Gods possibly because they shone like the sun. According to an old Apuan legend the crystalline marble of Gorfigliano was made of stars' tears, and in another Christian legend the «*lucciche*» — shiny specks in white Carrara marble — were meant to be the tears of Christ (see Appendix). The first marble statues made in the Aegean were brightly coloured, and traces of colour and gold have been found on statues of the Archaic and Classical periods; this tradition was continued by the Romans who painted the eyes in great detail (see fig. 180). White marble was possibily first used in the Aegean and Greece partly because it was easy to carve and could be extracted in large blocks, and partly because it could be painted without difficulty and the colours did not deteriorate. Statues to ward off evil spirits were painted in bright clashing colours, and the personality of gods and demigods was expressed, like masks for the theatre, by posture, harmonious contours and colour. The rediscovery of classical sculpture and white marble during the Renaissance and the Neoclassical periods stemmed from a contemporary trend, since all the other aspects of classical sculpture were ignored.

Production Organization

Marble production can roughly be divided into two stages: extraction, transportation and manufacture. The first stage is the hardest, where man must wrestle with the rock itself to extract large enough blocks, since marble for small articles is easily available.
Contemporary novelists are largely responsible for the romantic but totally inadequate picture of life in the quarries: a quarryman's job is essentially the same as it was thousand years ago although the equipment is more sophisticated; like miners they become addicted to their way of life, and are incapable of changing it. Craftsmanship is essential to the second stage of production, and, as in the past, varies from mass-produced standard articles to figure and decorative sculpture that come to life as the artisan's idea is put into practice; sculpting requires intense mental and physical effort, and traditionally «lapicidi» (stone carvers) have always been portrayed as completly absorbed by their work (see fig. 1). Competent quarrymen, stone-cutters, stone-dressers, sawers and sculptors all

possess a keen understanding of marble, how it must be handled, which way to cut a block to eliminate flaws and exploit the sound parts. Experience is essential and is only acquired after years of training in marble producing districts. Nowadays few artists are prepared to spend so much time and effort to learn the craft: they prefer to make originals from softer material, consequently the traditional rapport between the artist and marble has changed radically (see fig. 166).
A detailed historical analysis is necessary in order to understand how technique and the socio-economic productive organization has altered in the Western World over the past centuries.

Uses of Marble

Marble was one of the first materials man ever used for building, and for this very reason it is difficult to classify: is beauty, quality, quantity or utility more important? It is impossible to lay down a set of rules so we shall classify marble according to how, and for what purpose it has been used.
In the past marble was mainly used to make monolithic columns and supporting structures for large public, private and religious buildings (see fig. 2); since it has great bearing strength but its resistance to fracture and shearing stress is low, marble has been used only for short and well-proportioned architraves, steps and corbels. It is very expensive and for this reason has never been used for load bearing walls except in marble producing districts (see fig. 3). Carved marble window frames (see fig. 4), jambs and door-jambs were common and had great ornamental as well as functional value; marble was also used for floors (see fig. 5), parapets, small

columns and external facing (see figg. 10, 210, 216). Different shaped slabs of coloured marble were used to decorate as well as protect inside walls (see fig. 14) but coloured marble was mainly used for decorative reasons (see fig. 15). It was also used to construct acqueducts, fountains (see figg. 6, 9), bridges and road-side parapets. In the 16th century marble was used to build syphons for acqueducts because it was the only known material capable of withstanding high pressure (fig. 16). Marble was also used to produce small household articles like semi-transparent window-panes, fireplaces (see fig. 7), bath-tubs (see fig. 8), sinks, washbasins and shelves, thrones and chairs (see fig. 224); in particular elaborate polychrome, plain or inlaid tables were produced. Marble vessels included weights, mortars, (see fig. 13) containers for grocers and spice sellers (see fig. 12); the trend for rare marble ornamental vases (figg. 11, 179) is centuries old: initially marble was used to replace prehistoric stone-ware, but became a luxury after the invention of pottery.

It was also used for cannon balls (see fig. 17), scale weights and glass makers' *marmora* — blocks of polished marble used in glass blowing — and later for electric panels since crystalline calcareous marble is a good insulating material.

Skilled stone-cutters were trained to carve lettering on marble slabs and monuments (see fig. 19): in this way marble was used to express architectural, figurative and written ideas (see figg. 20, 21).

Although the alphabet had been invented, people in the past used to communicate most frequently with drawings; traditionally marble was used to commemorate great and powerful men (see figg. 201, 213, 214), portraying their likeness and telling of their deeds (fig. 20), or depicting scenes of battle, and everyday life and men at work. Aesthetic elements were subordinate to reality: in Egypt skilled artisans were trained to reproduce metal and marble workers and potters accurately (see figg. 115, 127, 163). The columns of Trajan and Antoninus were the ancient equivalent of modern history books, erected to commemorate the Emperors Trajan and Marcus Aurelius' deeds. Sacred sculpture was less straightforward: it had a didactic function and reproduced the contemporary way of life: an artist worked from a traditional fixed model for all essential features of sculpture but produced other everyday articles as well, (that changed in time), and soon acquired a symbolic value: even today many people still believe that icons can ward off the evil eye (see fig. 21).

Statues were as beautiful as possible in order to inspire awe and devotion (see fig. 209) among the congregation, and in time a formal and plastic sculptural style gradually evolved (fig. 263). Nowadays, a trend has developed in the Western World, whereas the meaning of a work of art has become more important than whether it is beautiful or not. The same thing happened in the past when power, from the hands of the aristocracy, passed to the middle classes: the new and more numerous bourgeoisie prefered neoclassical and mythological subject matter, and the most popular were mass-produced (see fig. 215) along with imitation marble statues made using special powders for the benefit of the working classes.

Sources

Science is essential to the history of marble. Geology provides a clear picture of the genesis and structure of

2. Basilica of Santa Maria of Castello in Genoa (1130-1137): the right-hand side aisle is built with granite columns and capitals of white marble originally taken from ancient Roman monuments.

3

4

5

6

3. *Cathedral of Sant'Andrea at Carrara: white marble ashlars from the back façade, (Gothic phase).*

4. *Church of the Madonnetta in Genoa (1696): portal of white marble. The parvis is made of marine cobblestones of white quartz and dark green peridotite (1732).*

5. *Oratory of San Filippo Neri in Genoa (middle of the 18th century): the floor is made of rhomboidal tiles of Languedoc red, Portoro black and white marble of Carrara.*

6. *The Fountain of Bedizzano near Carrara, (17th century): the white marble monolithic basin.*

7. *Palace of the Meridiana in Genoa (16th century): white marble chimney-piece with the emblem of the Grimaldi family.*

8. *Villa of the Peschiere in Genoa (16th century): streaked white marble monolithic bath tub.*

7

8

rock deposits and the different technical characteristics. There are two main historical sources one direct, archaeology, and one indirect, written sources and iconography. The first concerns marble products and the second the means of production, commerce and use.

A lot of research and field-work has been done, including stratigraphic digging and dated typology (that unfortunatly is only too often seen as an end in itself); in the case of individual monuments and works of art, archaeology is usually thought of as a subsidary branch of art history so much so that many art historians are, for the first time, studying the technical side of building materials in view of restoring and preserving palaces and monuments that otherwise would fall into decay. There are still great gaps in the history of civilization that have never been filled because of academic or traditional prejudice; the history of marble monumental sculpture and architecture is more exciting, but the study of the more common and less beautiful domestic and everyday articles is essential to the understanding of man's past.

Typology together with the study of commodities, geochemistry and petrology provides basic information about trade routes and where the raw material came from; in particular submarine archaeology is essential to the salvaging of shipwrecked loads of raw marble and manufactured articles. Another important branch of archaeology deals with marble production: different equipment and working methods leave different traces on marble; the best results are obtained by excavating old production sites and workshops: half-finished articles, tools and rejects can be dated accurately by comparing them to similar known products. On the other

hand there is no connection between blocks of marble found «on site» in old quarries and the «tagliate» — cuts — on the quarry-face: contemporary documents on how a quarry was run, or when it ceased to function, and extraction techniques (that however did not change for centuries) and inscriptions are the only existing reliable data. All traces of activity and equipment dating back to the Industrial Revolution should be analysed and documented and, if possible, preserved for future study: such finds are as important and imposing as the monuments and pieces of sculpture themselves.

Unfortunatly there are two drawbacks: in some countries where this has been put into practice archeologists try to preserve all old buildings indiscriminately for the traditional aesthetic reasons, but do not consider tools and equipment, dating back to before the first part of the Industrial Revolution and after, to be of any value. Infact the commercial and production side, from the beginning of the Modern Age, was organised along capitalistic lines long before any other industry, and the socio-economic effects were felt much sooner than the technological changes, especially in countries like Italy where the Industrial Revolution was not a local phenomena.

Written sources are fundamental to the history of marble: public statutes, laws and by-laws, articles made in standard sizes for taxation purposes, security systems and protective measures for trade, stone-carvers' corporative statutes (that establish what a member of a guild may and may not do), public concessions requesting the exploitation of marble deposits, communal archives compiled by important families and church trusts for purchase and use, private deeds under the seal of a notary concerning the sale of quarries and

9. Villa Mansi at Capannoni near Lucca: swimming-pool and parapet of white marble dating back to the beginning of the 18th century.

10. Cathedral of Sant'Andrea in Carrara: external covering in slabs of streaked white marble with Bardiglio marble with inscription of the 16th century.

9

...OR FVI · ET
...A · SENVI · ET
...VID · IVSTVM
...ICTVM · NEC
...IEN · EIVS
...NS · PANEM

10

mining rights, equipment, semi-finished and finished articles, contract work for building, agreements between apprentices and artisans, and inventories of goods. It is difficult to understand whether the names of marble workers that crop up in notary deeds are derived from the men's jobs or not; parrochial records are helpful in production areas (see Appendix). Most Medieval and Modern sources have never been published, the language is sometimes obscure and can only be understood with the help of dialects and archaeological finds. The ancient sources are better known and have all been published. Tracts on art and architecture and the work of ancient naturalists and geologists that date back from the 2nd century B.C. to the great changes of the 19th century are essential to understand the evolution of the marble industry. Local historical research dating back to the 18th and 19th centuries is an invaluable source of information: however these documents are based on political rather than socio-economic events and are not always reliable: archives are often incomplete or need revising.

Iconography and cartography are indirect sources and provide interesting detail about working methods in production areas. To date an archeological find accurately it is necessary to compare it with known contemporary equipment. Throughout history, from ancient Egypt (see figg. 115, 163) and Roman times (see fig. 153) up to the Middle Ages, craftmen's workshops and tools have been reproduced in great detail. Topographic maps, chorographies and land registers contain invaluable information about quarries, their location, equipment, what material could be extracted, and the means of transport. Usually they were made during the Modern Age but the oldest

11

technical map of a known quarry dates back to ancient Egypt (see fig 90). Finally, other indirect sources come from information carried on by word of mouth for generations, but it is difficult to establish whether the sources are reliable or not. Phonetic changes, (toponyms for instance, can be easily traced by following linguistic developments), make it is possible to ascertain where old quarry transport routes and workshops were located. Information that cannot be backed up by facts («my great grandfather told my grandfather who told my father etc.») is less credible and generally turns out to be local folklore or erroneous scientific hypothesis. However this sort of information is useful in so much that it considerably narrows down the field of archaeological research. The origins of legends have deeper roots and reveal the psychological beliefs of

11. Corsini Gallery in Florence: white marble Roman crater with scenes of Bacchus.

12. Civic Museum of Albenga: medieval public measurements cut in a block of white marble.

13. From the collection of History of Material Culture (ISCUM Genoa): 19th century mortar from Luni.

14. Giotto's Campanile in Florence (14th century): polychrome covering with white Carrara marble, Chianti red, and green serpentinite from Mt. Ferrato.

15. Church of Jesus in Genoa (17th century): internal covering in inlaid work of coloured marble on a background of white marble of Carrara.

16. *Civic acqueduct of Genoa: a segment of a huge tube of white marble, 17th century.*

17. *Sant'Angelo Castle in Rome: white marble cannon balls.*

17

18

21

20

18. *Nanni di Bianco: Four crowned Saints, from the aedicula in Orsanmichele, Florence (1416), detail illustrating sculptors' activities.*

19. *Soprana Gate in Genoa (12th century): inscription for passers-by carved on a slab of white marble.*

20. *Church of San Niccolò of the Boschetto in Genoa: burial slab of white marble for Battistina Doria (1470).*

21. *Marble icon by Pietro of Guido fixed on a house in the town of Carrara (1466).*

22. *Rome, Trajan Column: figurative representation of Roman victories in Dacia.*

pre-scientific primitive and isolated societies. Old marble workers still remember the way of life and working methods used when they were young, and provide a clear picture of pre-industrial and industrial society seen through the eyes of the working men: they also remember the local dialects that are essential to understand records.

Chapter One

The Geology of the Origins of Marble

The Importance of the Geologic Pattern

The crust of the earth known as lithosphere is made up of many different kinds of rock, among which is marble. The life zone of the earth including the lower part of the atmosphere, the hydrosphere, and the upper lithosphere form the biosphere, and compared to what happens every day in the biosphere the developments in the mineral world appear unnaturally slow.

Even landslides and floods are caused by external rather than internal factors, since all other forms of life change their environment to suit their needs. Only a few phenomena depend directly on an internal mechanism within the earth itself and, unfortunatly sometimes disrupt man's daily life: earthquakes and volcanic eruptions.

In ancient times Herodotus and other writers had realised that even the most unexciting rock contained pieces of sea shell even if located high above sea level; Leonardo was the first to voice publicly the opinion that the configuration of the earth had altered over the centuries. Initially people believed the «Flood» to have been the cause, but later, as the natural sciences developed, naturalists established that some fossils were not very old, while others were even five hundred milion years old, but they were all ancestors of contemporary forms of life; so geologic time, that covers a much larger span than human time, was invented. Developments were either too slow for man to notice, or occured within the earth itself where man could not reach; so an empirical explanation of the world was invented and, as scientific means and research developed, the new theories were proved or disproved.

The Crust of the Earth: its Dynamics

In the past twenty years a theory dating back to the beginning of this century has been re-examined. It concerns earthquakes, the configuration of the sea-bed and continental drift. In the past 200 milion years parts of the earth have joined together and other parts have broken apart; this is proved by the existence or non-existence of different species of flora and fauna, and a theory taking into consideration the layout of fossils, the shape of present day continents and chains of mountains, the great fractures and shelves on the sea bottom, (see fig. 23) has been developed (see fig. 24). The lithosphere is made up of large plates that move slowly a few inches a year along the upper mantle made of silicates of iron and magnesium called peridotitic rock.

The lithospere is divided into the continental crust (up to 2000 mt below sea level) and the oceanic crust that is about 4 km thick and made up basically of basalt. The continental crust is thicker (from 10 to 70 km in depth) and is mainly silicates of alluminium (granitic rock). Movement is caused by thermal convection within the earth's covering crust. The plates move away from the hotter areas located in the sea where the crust is continually regenerating oceanic ridges (made of volcanic basaltic rock). Oceans are getting larger as the plates are slowly absorbed by the covering crust along trenches in the cooler areas. The movement of the plates and continental platform within the covering crust causes volcanic eruptions and earthquakes. The upper part of continents is continually eroded by natural forces but the remains soon settle again round the

23. Model of the tectonic plates of the crust of the earth. a) is a section of the earth, how it was about 100 milion years ago and shows the migration of the Indian continent. b) the continents grouped together in the Pangea about 200 milion years ago. c) the position of the continents showing the oceanic ridge and the subduction zones about 65 milion years ago. (from R.S. Dietz and J.C. Holden).

24. Vertical model of the tectonic plates showing the different areas of genesis of the main rocks frequently used as ornamental stones: 1: Calcareous rock, Conglomerates, Sandstone, Ardesia. 2: True marbles. 3: Alabasters. 4: Travertines. 5: Serpentinites, Ophicarbonate rock, Gabbros and Basalt. 6: Granite. 7: Porphyry. 8: Diorites and Syenites. 9: Trachyte, Andesite, etc. 10: Basalt. 11: Gneiss, Quartzite.

25. The Basilica of Saint Mark in Venice: transennae and iconostasis (14th century). There is a large quantity of exotic and local marble, among which huge slabs of Portasanta (Holygate) and antique green marble.

26. The Arch of Constantine in Rome: the column is made of antique yellow marble from Numidia.

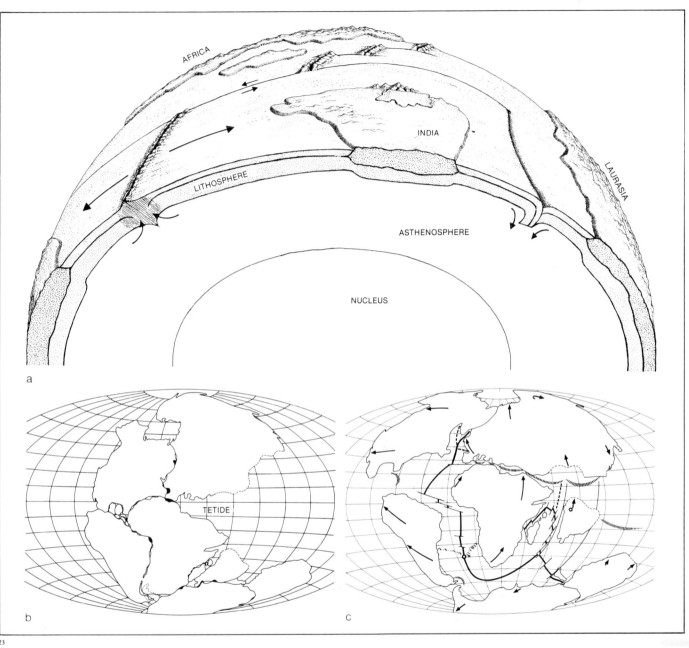

a

b

TETIDE

c

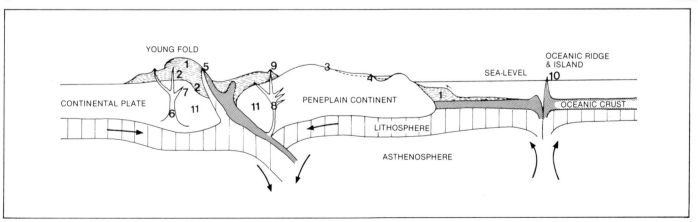

YOUNG FOLD

OCEANIC RIDGE
& ISLAND

SEA-LEVEL

CONTINENTAL PLATE

PENEPLAIN CONTINENT

OCEANIC CRUST

LITHOSPHERE

ASTHENOSPHERE

25

27

27. Church of the Annunciata in Genoa: from top to bottom: mandorlato marble; inlays of Sienna yellow, red and variegated jasper on a background of Belgium black; inlays of France red, Ligurian peridotites and white marble of Carrara on alabaster (16th century).

28. Church of Jesus in Genoa: Portoro marble columns (17th century).

28

29

30

31

29. *Church of Our Lady of the Vines in Genoa: baroque medallion with a panel of lumachella marble.*

30. *Church of Our Lady of the Consolation in Genoa: baroque altar with pilaster strip and spiral columns of polychrome breccia or Seravezza mischi.*

31. *Church of Jesus in Genoa: columns of Sicilian red marble of the 17th century.*

35

32

bases of the continents. In areas where continents collide the sediment is thrust upwards and creates chains of mountains that in turn are easily eroded (Orogenetic Cycle).
The crust of the earth is thicker under folds where magmatic and sedimentary rock is metamorphosed by pressure or heat, or melted and transformed into granitic magma.

The Classification of Marble

Strictly speaking, only metamorphic rocks of recrystallised calcite and dolomite can be classified as marble, but, since recent industrial and commercial developments all ornamental rocks, including limestone and dolomite, that take polish come under the same heading. This classification includes all types of marble.

First of all it is necessary to make a distinction between marble derived from sediment and marble derived from magma, that is produced by the solidification of the magma after the fusion of the continental crust or upper mantle, and marble that has undergone a structural metamorphosis; the components of these three groups of marble have similar structure, physical composition and working behaviour.
Other classification methods are based on: colour, that changes from one deposit to another, or even in different parts of the same deposit; use; distinguishing marble that was used in the past, and has been worked-out, from the more numerous kinds that are excavated today; for obvious reasons it is impossible to mention all kinds of marble in this book, and details concerning use, place of origin and commercial names can be

32. Archeological digs in Luni (La Spezia): Roman column of Cipollino of Karystos.
33. Collina di Castello in Genoa: baroque columns of France red from the church of San Silvestro that was destroyed during the War.

found in any catalogue.
This book is about the different types of marble that have similar origins and physical structure, including the most important past and modern examples. In the Appendix there is a more detailed list of places of origin and other relevant information.

Limestone

Limestone is a sedimentary rock formed in the sea and sometimes in lakes by the compression and cementation of white granules of calcium carbonate from the shells and skeletons of animals and algae, directly in the water or occasionally in acquatic chemical deposits.
In different quantities limestone contains granules of silica, clay, ferric hydroxide, that gives a yellow or pink colouring, and organic substances that give a grey or black colouring.
The movement of the earth has gradually caused limestone deposits to shift and come to light in mountainous areas, and the limestone is extracted like any common building material. Usually the layers are only a few inches thick, fractured by corrugation, and it is practically impossible to obtain large uniform blocks.
Limestone can be polished and used as ornamental rock only if the layers are both compact, extensive and homogeneous («Belgium black» [see figg. 27, 45], «Biancone»), and if the fractures and interstices are cemented with pure calcium carbonate or mixed with clay and ferrous hydroxide («Portoro» [see fig. 28], «Lumachella», «Ammonitic red» [see figg. 27, 42], «Broccatello» [see fig. 207], «Limestone Breccia» [see fig. 179], «Lunel», «German red»). Any impurities, especially clay, cause limestone marble to stand up to weather badly, so it is best used inside rather than out.

34. Catacombs of San Callisto in Rome: detail of Santa Cecilia by Stefano Moderno in Apuan statuario marble (17th century).

True Marble

Calcite and dolomite are radically transformed either under pressure of a few thousand atmospheres or at a temperature of about 400 degrees centigrade. These changes take place either at great depth within the original basin, (regional metamorphosis, i.e. Apuan marbles), or because the deposits are near hot magmatic masses (contact metamorphosis, i.e. Pyros marble); the original granules of calcium carbonate are reorganised into perfectly adherent white calcite crystals larger than the initial ones, (from one hundredth of a millimetre to a few millimetres). All impurities are transformed into stable materials: silica and clay into white or colourless quartz crystals, albite and mica; carbon, derived from organic substances, into black graphite lamelle; ferric hydroxide into red hematite crystals; graphite and hematite occasionally migrate creating new colour zones.
Metamorphic calcareous marble has a more compact and homogeneous structure, good technical and aesthetic qualities (saccharoidal structure); it is easy to work in detail even with primitive tools because calcite is not very hard, and is translucent because of the uninterrupted structure of transparent crystals. It stands up to changes in weather and mechanic stress better than calcareous rock. The original layers occasionally disappear giving place to cleavage planes (metamorphic schistosity) that coincide with microfractures in the marble, the so-called «peli» — hairs — that can only be detected by an expert hand: however the microfractures can be exploited in such a way as to separate large individual blocks even with rudimentary tools.
True marble can also be classified

CECILIA McBRIDE OF

according to whether the colours are homogeneous or not: the bianchi, white marble, are the purest (see fig. 45), and some types of *statuari* (see fig. 34) contian 99.9% calcite in large or small homogeneous crystals; the *bianchi venati*, (veined white marble), are veined in places with streaks of grey (see fig. 8), that become widespread in the *nuvolati* (clouded), more intense in the *Bardigli* (see fig. 188), and with streaks of white on a grey background in *Bardiglietto* marble; the arabesque (see fig. 169) pattern, white polygonal shapes surrounded by grey links, is more simple than the *brecce* or *mischi* marble where the fractures and links, are more obvious, and the calcitic cement is brightly coloured with combinations of blacks and yellows, reds and greens, (*Paonazzetto* and *Breccia Medicea*). The *cipollini* (onion shaped) (see fig. 32), have some impurities — up to 10% minerals other than calcite — and derive from calcareous rocks that contain large quantities of clay, later transformed into parallel planes of isolated grey-green or gold mica.

Colour basically depends on ferrous hydroxide decorated with different coloured veins and links, (*Giallo Antico* [Antique yellow, see fig. 26], *Giallo di Siena* [Siena yellow, see fig. 27], *Fior di Pesco* [Peach blossom], *Portasanta* [Holygate, see figg. 35, 188, 25], *Rosso Antico* [Antique red, see fig. 37], *Rosso di Francia* [French red, see fig. 33], *Rosa di Portogallo* [Portoguese pink]).

Limestone Alabaster and Travertine

Limestone alabaster also known as «limestone onyx» or «stalactite» (see figg. 27, 45) is another type of ornamental rock; its structure is perfectly uniform and the calcite crystals are generally large, up to several centimetres long.

Usually alabaster is found only in small quantities in karst zones near caves or streams, and is formed by chemical deposits of calcium carbonate in over saturated waters. It is either striped or decorated with concentric rings and unusual contrasts of colour: yellow and pink and sometimes green due to ferrous oxides. Alabaster is translucent, can be polished easily, but is not suitable for sculpture and does not stand up to bad weather — in ancient times thin slabs were used to make window-pane.

Limestone alabaster is classified as false marble, and although it is similar to crystalline limestone, it has different origins and use (Egyptian alabaster, Algerian onyx, Marocco onyx, Pakistan onyx).

Although its origin is similar to limestone alabaster, «travertine» or «tufa limestone» is still known as false marble (see fig. 43); it is formed in continental waters, streams or lakes, that lack carbon dioxide but contain large quantities of calcium carbonate. It is not a very compact rock, and due to vegetable residue in the waters it is occasionally porous and consequently does not take polish well. It is frequently used in architecture partly for its warm uniform colour and partly because it is easy to cut and stands up well to weather.

Sedimentary Mechanic Rocks

If the residue of rocks destroyed by erosion is not entirely consumed mechanically or chemically by the movement of water, it accumulates in alluvial planes or near river mouths. Here, buried by other material, compacted and cemented by the

35

35. *Giacomo della Porta,
fountain in Piazza Colonna
in Rome; the basin is made
of Portasanta (Holygate) of
Chios.*

36. *Giacomo della Porta,
fountain of the tortoises in
Rome: the shell is made of
polychrome breccia of Theos
(16th century).*

36

41

weight of the above waters, it is transformed in geologic time, into clastic rocks, classified according to their component elements: shale (one 1000th of a millimetre), sandstone (millimetres), puddingstone and conglomerates (centimetres): They differ from breccias that are polygonal shaped, since they have been rounded by the movement of water. Clastic rocks are made of more than one kind of stone, (monogenic or polygenic); but only when the material in conglomerates and puddingstone can be polished, is resistant and many-coloured and cemented by crystalline minerals, is it known as marble and used as an ornamental stone (African, African green [see figg. 36, 188], Breccia, *Ceppo*).

Although it cannot be polished and the colours are not striking, sandstone is successfully used for buildng if cemented with calcium carbonate; it only takes polish if metamorphosed as in the case of Egyptian graywacke (*Basanite*) (see fig. 39); and if the level of regional metamorphosis is high sandstone is transformed into crystalline schist.

Shale can not be used either for sculpture or building unless it has been previously fired and transformed into ceramics: colour and shine are merely the result of technique, and have nothing to do with the properties of marble. A slight metamorphosis can transform shale into a more consistent rock, «ardesia» a kind of slate that contains 40% calcium carbonate, takes polish and can be sculpted, but is not suitable for external masonry (see fig. 38).

Serpentine and Ophicarbonate Rock

Up until now serpentine and ophicarbonate rocks have been classified as true marble possibly because their origin was unknown, and only outward similarities were taken into consideration (fine, soft grain, green uniform or striped surface with breccias); ophicarbonate rock and serpentine, however, have nothing to do with true marble. Geology has shown that serpentine comes from certain types of peridotites that is present in large quantities in the upper mantle. Peridotites (see fig. 44) is found in the continental crust because of folds on the sea bottom caused by the collision of lithospheric plates. It is mainly made of ferrous and magnesium silicate (olivine), that becomes hydrous on its upwards journey and is embellished with snake-like ribbons of colour. Colour ranges from dark to pale green occasionally streaked or criss-crossed with more recent white veins of calcite that lessens mechanic resistance (black jasper, Genoa green [see fig. 41], Alpine green, Tinos green).

Ophicarbonate rock is breccia rock similar to serpentine but cemented by crystalline calcium carbonate, occasionally coloured with red ferrous oxide (hematites) and criss-crossed with white veins of calcite. Ophicarbonate rock is produced by fractures in the upper crust of peridotites on the sea bottom where it is mixed with calcium carbonate and cemented with ferrous oxide. Ophicarbonate rock takes polish well and is beautifully coloured with reds, greens and white; however since it is made of so many different materials it is very fragile and not suitable for sculpture (Antique green [see fig. 25, 40], Levanto red [see fig. 44]).

Magmatic Rocks

A large number of magmatic rocks, commercially known as granite, are

37. *National Museum of Luni (La Spezia): pilaster strip capital in Tenaro red marble (1st century B.C.).*

38. *Graveglia Valley (Genoa): local ardesia doorjamb (18th century).*

39. *Louvre Museum in Paris: torso of an Egyptian statue of black graywacke or Basanite (8th century B.C.).*

40

41

42

40. Basilica of Saint John in Lateran in Rome: ophicarbonate marble or antique green of Thessaly columns. (17th century).

41. Church of San Siro in Genoa: ophicarbonate marble Polcevera green holy water stoup, (18th century).

42. XX Settembre street in Genoa: pilaster strip in mandorlato or Nembro of Verona. (12th century).

43. Lorenzo Bernini: fountain of the Rivers in Rome (1651): white marble figures emerging from travertine «grottoes».

44. Cathedral of San Lorenzo in Genova: detail of the main door (13th century). The columns are made of ophicarbonate marble (Levanto red) and Ligurian peridotite.

45. Church of Jesus in Genoa (17th century): column dado with the Durazzo family emblem. Inlays of Belgium black, Sienna yellow, red jasper and lapislazuli on statuario of Carrara.

43

used as ornamental stones and take polish well. Most granite is large grained (from a millimetre to a few centimetres long) and multicoloured, although at a distance the colours merge together and appear uniform. Magmatic rocks and true marble not only have different genesis, but also a different mineral structure (silica and silicates) harder than crystalline calcite limestone; granite is difficult to work especially with rudimentary tools, and it is very difficult to carve in bas-relief. On the other hand, granite is neither stratified or schistose, and its texture is homogeneous even in large blocks, unless regional tectonic thrusts or changes of temperature have caused fractures.

Ornamental magmatic rocks are classified according to the composition of the magma: they contain large amounts of silica, alluminium, iron and magnesium; the structure depends in what part of the terrestrial crust they were formed: granular (crystals of the same size) in large slow-cooling masses at great depth, or porphyric (large crystals in a small crystal based-masses in quick-cooling dike-like injections). Effusive rocks are not ornamental but they are used as common building material. They are formed at great depth by the fusion of the limbs of the continental crust as it descends towards the lower mantle. The purer the continental crust, the greater the amount of silica and alluminium. They are formed by the following minerals: achromic quartz, white or coloured feldspar (generally orthoclase), yellow, rust, pink and white or occasionally black mica, (red granite, Egyptian syenite [see fig. 46], Swedish red granite [see fig. 49], Baveno pink granite, Cornish grey granite).

The fusion of polluted limbs of the continental crust with minerals containing large quantities of iron and magnesium form syenites and diorites; unlike granite, syenite does not contain quartz, but large amounts of black mica (biotite), and hornblend, a dark green and black amphibole. Feldspar (plagioclase) is generally coloured, usually a pinky purple (syenite of Balma), and sometimes sprayed with (see fig. 47) turquoise-grey (labradorite). Plagioclase is generally white in diorite; biotite and hornblend are more common and the colour scheme is white spots on a dark background, (green granite, granite of the Forum, [see fig. 50], black diorite of Anzola).

Gabbros are formed in the earth's mantle like serpentine: they are richer in iron and magnesium but contain only small amounts of silica and alluminium (euphotide, ophite, granite *della Sedia*). Gabbros contain large grains of white plagioclase and dark green or black lamella shaped pyroxyne. Some varieties contain olivine, a light green mineral. In a broad sense rock with a porphyric structure formed in dike-like injections is called porphyry.

The largest crystals are prisma-shaped, usually white, but occasionally red or pale green prismatic feldspar, while the structure of the smaller crystals varies according to the composition of the magma.

The mineral structure of quartz porphyry is the same as granite, although it looks like syenite and diorite.

The ground colours vary from grey (black and white) to black, pink, brick-red and green: the last two match the colours of phenocryst, and produce a fairly uniform coloured rock (Antique red porphyry [see fig. 48] or Antique green porphyry, serpentine [see fig. 51], Egyptian green phorphyry or jeracite black phorphyry).

Crystalline Schists

Both sedimentary and magmatic rocks are inwardly and outwardly transformed by radical changes of pressure and temperature (high-grade metamorphosis); this new variety of rock called crystalline schist shares the following characteristics: the componing minerals are recrystallised, and more stable minerals are formed, and the new surrounding structure is compacted. The planes of flattened rock are re-orientated creating schistosity and a tendency to cleavage planes. Crystalline schists have always been used as sheets for covering in building, or tiling, but do not take polish. The more compact variety can sometimes be polished and used for ornamental purposes. Metamorphosis also alters some varieties of gneiss (*Sarizzo* for instance), but its structure is similar to that of granite.

Quarzite originates from clay cemented quarzitic sandstone, and contians achromic quartz and a small quantity of hard and very resistant white or pale yellow mica (garnet mica schist like *Pietra Braschia*, Braschia stone).

Ornamental Minerals

Even in a short survey of ornamental stones it is impossible to ignore the existance of other minerals that share similar physical properties, colour, pattern and take polish. The main reason why these minerals are not classified as marble, even in the broadest sense, is because they are much more rare and only found in small deposits: it is impossible to mine blocks larger than one cubic metre, and consequently the commercial value is extramely high.

Semi-precious stones, more valuable than marble and less than precious stones, are used for small pieces of sculpture, inlay and marquetry, together with valuable marble to obtain rich chromatic effetcs.

Malachite is a deep green striped, copper carbohydrate; it is extracted in copper mines where it has been transformed by water.

Calchedonis and opals (agatha, corniols, cats' eyes etc.) range from white to pale blue, hazel and red; they contain large quantities of silica, and are formed in nodule shaped deposits in sedimentary rocks. In tropical areas they can occasionally be found laying on the ground, or near springs that contain large quantities of colloidal silica. Jaspers are monogranules of sedimentary silica: the colour schemes range from red, yellow to green and violet. Lapislazuli is a silicate-based volcanic stone: it is blue with white spots and pyrate crystals (see fig. 45). Before concluding this brief survey it is necessary to add that some names of marble have a double meaning. The scientific names have been used in this book, and although the traditional names have been used where possible, a certain amount of confusion is inevitable. For instance syenite was the name given to a certain variety of magmatic rock coming from Egypt, and the first geologists called all similar rocks syenites: recent studies have shown that syenite of Assuan was a kind of granite. Porphyry gets its name from porphyra — purple — and comes from Mons Porphyrites in Egypt: different coloured porphyry was known by another name; Grecian green porphyry was known as or serpentine like all marble with peridotitique origin. Basalt, a black effusive rock, derives from the Egyptian Basalt: but now it is known to be a metamorphic sandstone, and some varieties are granitic (see comparative table in Appendix).

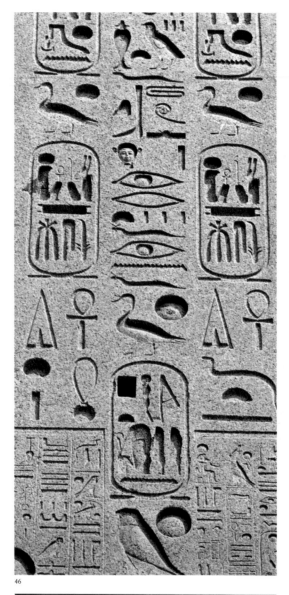

46

48

46. *Piazza del Popolo in Rome: obelisk of Rhames II of red granite of Assuan inappropriatly called syenite (13th century).*

47. *Genoa: statue dedicated to the soldiers who died fighting for the Resistenza, in syenite of the Balma.*

48. *Basilica of Saint Mark in Venice: figures of thetetrarchs in Egyptian red porphyry (4th century).*

49. *Head office of the Banca Popolare of Novara in Genoa: Swedish red granite external covering.*

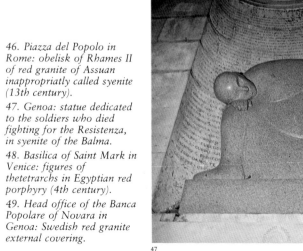

47

49

50

Naturalistic Methods of Study

Initially it is essential to examine marble in its natural setting: a geologist can only establish whether a deposit is usable or not on the spot, or accurately assess the different series of stratification in chronological order, the movements caused by the tectonic thrusts of the lithosphere that update the deposits, and hypothetically reflect all movement within the earth, or find the necessary information for the location and orientation of new quarries. The specimen of rock taken from certain clearly marked places is brought to mineralogical and petrographic laboratories and examined with special methods: microscopic examination of transparent sections (300th of a millimetre thick), to trace each individual component mineral, original, or generated by metamorphosis, dimension and ratio within the rock itself (see fig. 52); chemical analyses of all elements found both in large and small quantities or merely traceable; the structure of the magma, in the case of magmatic rocks, and the degree of purity in the case of sedimentary ones.

50. Fountain of the Quirinal in Rome: monolithic basin of Egyptian granodiorite, called granite of the Forum or Claudiano.

51

Mineralogical anlyses with X — rays to identify impurities and alterations or colouring; analyses with a stereoscope or an electron microscope to study natural or worked surfaces (see fig. 53).

These analyses are also useful to foresee the behaviour of marble during working processes, its resistance to stress, wear and tear, and weather; also to a subsidary branch of archeology to trace the history of the uses of marble, a way to gain information backwards: instead of examining a marble deposit to draw a picture of its structure, the structure of an unknown piece of marble is examined to try and identify the original deposit. This is more difficult than it seems: the same genetic mechanism and lithospheric structure are repeated in different parts of the world, far away from each other.

It is possible to reconstruct the pattern of trade and the propagation of finished products in the light of these discoveries (sarcophagi and architectural decorations for instance), and in the case of exceptionally rare marble, this can be done just by looking at it.

In certain well-known marble production areas quarrymen are so expert that they can tell a glance which quarry each individual block comes from.

Technical and Physical Properties

The structure and nature of different rocks varies tremendously: hardness depends on the component minerals; low weight density and resistence to compression on a non-compact structure; porous rocks crumble away at temperatures below zero.

Builders, as well as having a good knowledge of all technical properties of rocks, stress resistence for instance, that are essential to building, must be well informed on the weight density of rock, like any geologist, naturalist or petrologist, and must have a good understanding of the isostatic balance between different masses of lithospheric rock.

Although man has been building for the past 5000 years, geology as a science is only 100 years old, and dates back to the middle of the past century; unfortunatly builders and engineers were only interested in the physical properties of rock, and never did any research to ascertain the cause of different types of behaviour: breaking point, resistance to weather, to wear and tear, to stress, and a whether rock was suitable for building or not. Nowadays, by law, all experimental testing is done in order to protect consumers from fraud and bad quality. Modern materials, like reinforced concrete and steel, have been thoroughly tested, while traditional ones, like marble, are still used according to the old empirical rules.

The correct exploitation of marble presents three problems: firstly, it is necessary to take into consideration all past tradition and know-how, secondly, to have an accurate and up-to-date knowledge of the technical particular for building and ornamental purposes (a table with all the necessary imformation has been compiled only recently), and thirdly, scientific research to establish the cause of different technical behaviour, what material to extract and how to use it at a low cost. For instance the chemico-physical mechanism that produces polish at a microscopic level is still unknown.

Marble can be classified according to density: the density of each individual componing element is analysed as well as the existance of possible empty in-between spaces. To measure accurately the real weight density, the specimen must be ground to dust to eliminate empty spaces, then it is necessary to work out the relation between the weight and an equal volume of water. A more practical method, bulk density, is given by the relation between the weight and volume of a block of marble. The lower the bulk density in relation to the real weight density, the more empty spaces exist in the marble: the structure can be compact, vacuous — with non-communicating empty spaces — porous — with capillary-like communicating empty spaces — or sponge-like; only travertine has a sponge-like consistency. Occasionally porous-like structure dates back to the genesis of marble caused by microscopic intercrystalline empty spaces — or it happens at a later stage (dislocation, dissolution of minerals in subaereal surroundings, or fractures caused by tightening).

Marble is thus calssified: porosity proper, the difference between the total volume of the solid area, and the block itself; apparent porosity, the percentage of water that is absorbed under pressure of 150 atmospheres; imbibition coefficient, the volume percentage or weight of water absorbed after being submerged for a certain period of time, under normal conditions; permeability against air and water, the amount of time it takes air or water to cross a block of marble of a certain thickness under pressure; hydroscopicity, the amount of water absorbed from the atmosphere; absorption, the amount of water permiating through a block of marble vertically in a certain time.

The thermal properties of marble depend on those of each individual component: if homogeneous — according to the dilatation index — it is more resistant to rapid changes of temperature; if heterogeneous, the bond between granules is more easily broken, and the marble is transformed into sand.

Thermic insulation, as opposed to conductivity, is important for covering; refractory marble is heat resistant.

Marble can be classified according to mechanic resistence: the harder the marble, the more difficult it is to scratch: this partly depends on the componing minerals and partly on the cohesion and compactness of the crystals.

In some cases the surface cannot be scratched, but small chips of marble can be broken away. The harder the marble the more resistant it is to wear; this is measured by sliding friction with a turning wheel and sand, or by rolling resistance. Hard marble is not easy to work: perforation is measured by how far a hollow air-drill can penetrate; cutting, with a wire saw, diamond disk or chain saw; it is easy to carve with a chisel if the texture is homogeneous, and takes polish.

The force required to split a block with gibs, and its resistance to static stress depend on the shape, size and texture of the grain, and on the cohesion and compactness of the structure. They are measured by placing a standard specimen under increasing strain until it breaks; it is noteworthy that small compact grain has perfect stress relief, that is further increased if the main metamorphic schistosity plane is parallel to the pressure surface: this is the original position in which the marble was crystallised (cleavage planes have different names in different areas: «verso», «letto», «falda», «pioda», «seda»). On the other hand resistance is less in other fields: flexure, traction and cutting, since they depend directly on the cohesion of the grain (from 1/5th to 1/50th respect compression);

51

in these cases the resistance is increased if the force is parallel to the cleavage plane (called «*mozzatura*»), but goes against it and is perpendicular to the second cleavage plane («*trincante*», «*rabuffo*», «*recisa*»). In all cases water saturation, chemico-physical wear and prolonged stress are bad for resistance. Finally marble has a high «modulus of elasticity» or «rigidity» which can be translated into the force necessary to double the length of a specimen if it did not break; this must not be confused with «impact strength»; fragile marble has low stress resistance that depends on the shape and texture of the grain, and is measured by dropping a metal ball on a block of marble from an established height. Data concerning physical and technical properties of different marble is included in the Appendix.

Colour

Aesthetically the importance of colour cannot be underestimated, since it increases the ornamental value and consequently the commercial value of marble. It is also important from the

51. Victoria and Albert Museum in London: Byzantine medallion of green porphyry of Greece, wrongly called Serpentine.

52. Microphotographs with a petrographic microscope of thin sections of various ornamental rocks (enlarged 35 times). A1: calcareous rock with organic residue. B1: True marble. C1: serpentinite. A2: olivine diabase. B2: quarzite. C2: sandstone. A3: basalt. B3: porphyritic trachyte. C3: porphyritic andesite. A4: gneiss (Sarizzo). B4: gabbro C4: granite.

a

b

c

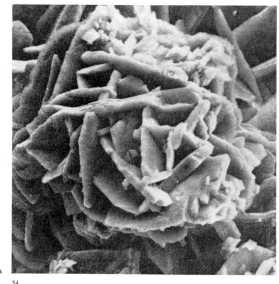

54

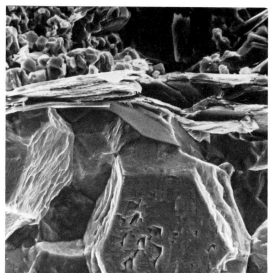

b

53

a

b

55

53. *Superficial microphotograph, done with an electron microscope, of Sienna yellow marble (enlarged 600 times): a) calcite crystals; b) crystals of calcite and mica; c) crystals of calcite and ferrous coloured compounds (from R. Peruzzi and L. Di Capitani).*

54. *Superficial microphotograph done on an electron microscope of chalk crystals that form the «black crust» of altered marble (from G. Alessandrini, R. Peruzzi, and L. Di Capitani).*

55. *Castle of Herten in Westphalia: atmospheric pollution has speeded up the process of decay of sandstone statues of 1702; 1) as they were in 1908; 2) as they were in 1969 (from E.M. Winkler).*

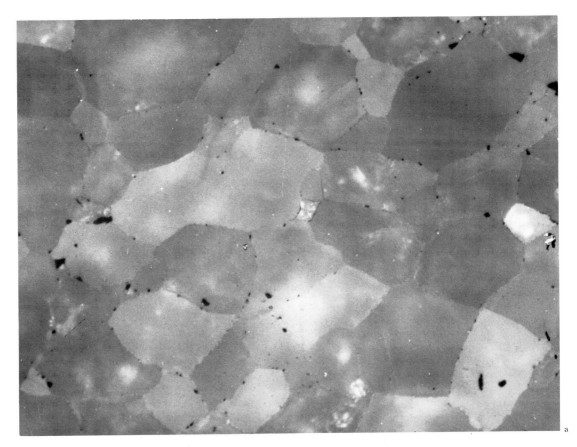

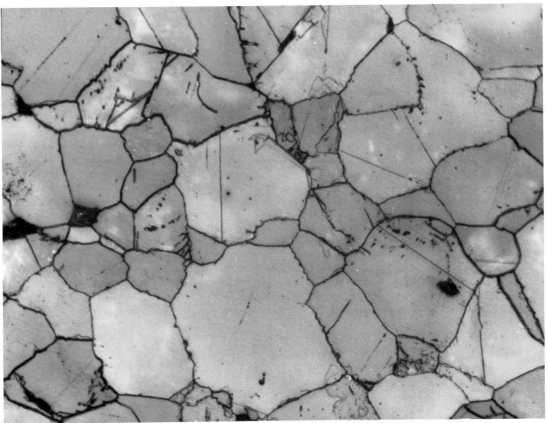

56. Microphotographs of
true marble polished surfaces
done with a light reflecting
microscope and enlarged 300
times; a) calcite crystals after
having been polished; b) the
same, after treatment in a
slightly acid atmosphere
(from R. Peruzzi, G.
Alessandrini and E. Broglia).

56

57

physical point of view: different colours can increase marble's resistance to wear and tear, its durability and resistance to bad weather; some rock, for instance, cannot be used like marble since the original beautiful colouring does not last once it comes into contact with the air.

Marble is either coloured by its component minerals (idiochromatic), or by pigmentation with the minerals themselves in interstices, in cement of sedimentary rocks and in veins that fill possible fractures (allochromatic); the former are more stable and last longer. These minerals vary from white (feldspar, calcite and dolomite) to black (biotite, hornblenda, augite) or green (clorite, epidote, actinote, diallagio, diopsite, olivine and serpentine derivatives); quartz, muscovite and mica are achromic: the gamut of colours from yellow to orange, red and violet do not exist in pure minerals and are always caused by pigmentation. Iron oxides are ususally red (hematite); if hydrous, marble changes from brown to yellow (limonite); green iron oxides are rarer, and are formed in places that lack oxygen (bivalent iron). Purple is due to manganese oxides, while the more common allochromic colours (from pale grey to black) are formed by the residue of organic matter.

At a distance some marble seems uniformly coloured (monochrome) even if, on close inspection, it is made of small diversely coloured but uniformly distributed minerals. If different areas of colour are visible even at a distance, marble is known as polychrome. The areas of colour are striped or mottled. The former are either straight, striped, ringed, linear, corrugated, snake-like or streaked, disjointed, fantastic or battlement shaped, concentric in zones or eye-shaped, or branched, veined, star or

flower-like, net-like or denticulate. Individual patches of colour are either clearly defined or fading: the first are caused by large amounts of one mineral (porphyric, goggle-shaped, corn shaped or graphic), angular (*brecciati*), rounded or lentiform (puddingstone, almond shaped), or to fossilised shells (snail shaped). The second are quite large and rounded (blotched, scraped, cloudy, lumpy), small (scraped, sprayed, dotted, cement-like), elongated (flame-shaped, variegated), or twisted (brocade, *broccatelli*, damasque and arabesque). When marble is cut or broken the colour appears less intense, since rough surfaces reflect light in all directions; wetting marble brings out the colour, as polish does, although some kinds of pigmentation alter with time: *limoniti*, for instance, become paler if continually exposed to bad weather, (from brown or orange they become yellowish). Carbon oxidises in the atmosphere and becomes paler too. These alterations are known as «*i colori del tempo*» (the colours of time, fading), and must not be confused with patine or crusts that are formed by particular chemico-physical processes in bad weather, and with efflorescences, whitish salts deposited in water and absorbed through the earth's capillaries.

Preservation of Antique Marble

Marble is part of the lithosphere and a large number of its componing minerals are not stable under chemical, physical and organic conditions different from those underground. As well as being consumed by abrasion, structural relaxation caused by static stress, dynamic stress and pollution (that in the last 50 years has increased tenfold in industrial countries), marble

57. Vertical model of the geologic evolution of the northen part of the Tyrrheanian sea. a) as it was about 50 milion years ago; b) as it was about 12 milion years ago (from M. Boccaletti, P. Elter, G. Guazzone).

58. Detail of the vertical model representing the evolution of the Apuan area; a) 50 milion years ago; b) 25 milion years ago; c) 12 milion years ago; d) as it is today (from F. Baldacci and others).

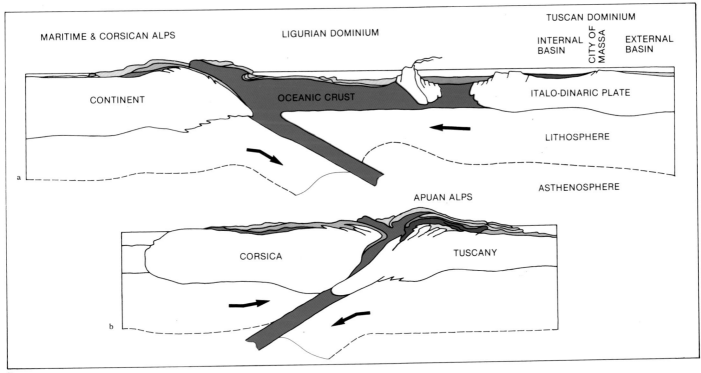

MARITIME & CORSICAN ALPS   LIGURIAN DOMINIUM   TUSCAN DOMINIUM

INTERNAL BASIN   CITY OF MASSA   EXTERNAL BASIN

CONTINENT   OCEANIC CRUST   ITALO-DINARIC PLATE

LITHOSPHERE

a

ASTHENOSPHERE

APUAN ALPS

CORSICA   TUSCANY

b

57

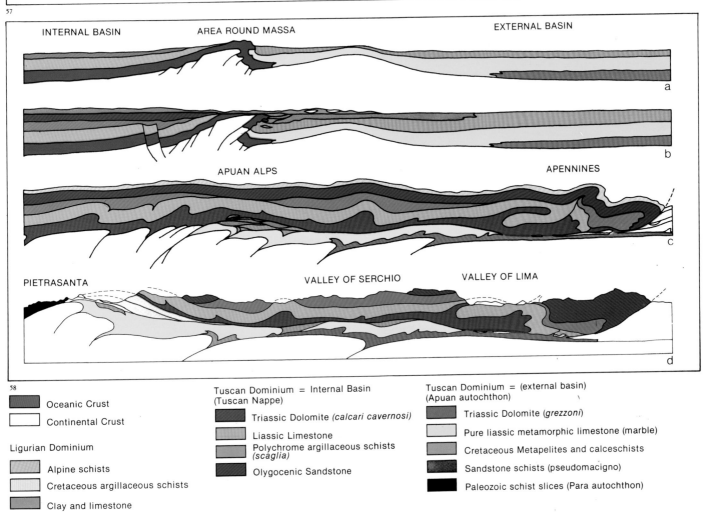

INTERNAL BASIN   AREA ROUND MASSA   EXTERNAL BASIN

a

b

APUAN ALPS   APENNINES

c

PIETRASANTA   VALLEY OF SERCHIO   VALLEY OF LIMA

d

58

Oceanic Crust

Continental Crust

Ligurian Dominium

Alpine schists

Cretaceous argillaceous schists

Clay and limestone

**Tuscan Dominium = Internal Basin
(Tuscan Nappe)**

Triassic Dolomite *(calcari cavernosi)*

Liassic Limestone

Polychrome argillaceous schists *(scaglia)*

Olygocenic Sandstone

**Tuscan Dominium = (external basin)
(Apuan autochthon)**

Triassic Dolomite *(grezzoni)*

Pure liassic metamorphic limestone (marble)

Cretaceous Metapelites and calceschists

Sandstone schists (pseudomacigno)

Paleozoic schist slices (Para autochthon)

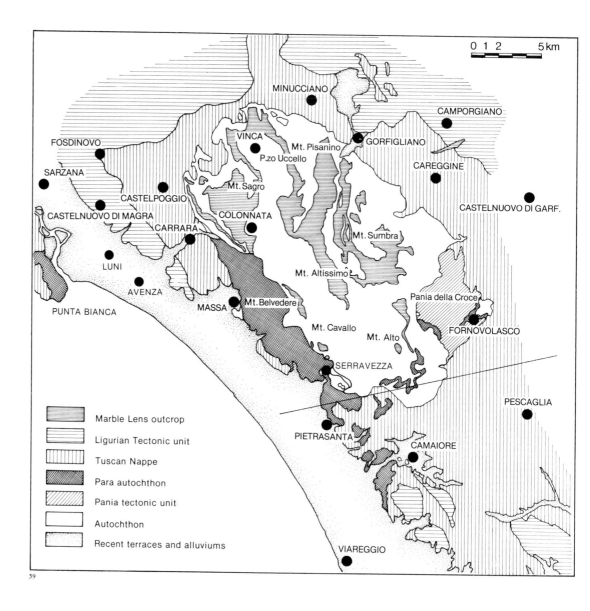

59. Geotectonic chart of the Apuan Alps (from the Guide of the XXIInd Congress of the Italian Mineralogical Society).

invariably deteriorates in subaereal enviroments. The causes vary according to whether marble is calcium carbonate or silicate based. Rain water slowly corrodes silicate based marble washing away the ions of sodium, potassium and calcium; consequently the quantity of silica, alluminium and iron increases, and together with the molecules of water, forms a new compound, that is more stable in the atmosphere, but not as stucturally coherent (argillaceous minerals): the rock becomes porous and capable of absorbing more water, and the marble disintegrates in depth as well as on the surface. Water containing large amounts of carbonic acid transforms carbonate into highly soluble bicarbonate, that is removable. Pure calcite is more resistant, and the water running down marble has not time to transform it chemically. The process is accelerated in porous and jointed limestone that has been corrupted by climatic changes. Atmospheric pollution increases the amount of carbon dioxide, sulfureous and sulfuric dioxide in the air; atmospheric sulfuric acid transforms calcite into calcium sulfate with water, chalk; the crystals of calcium sulfate

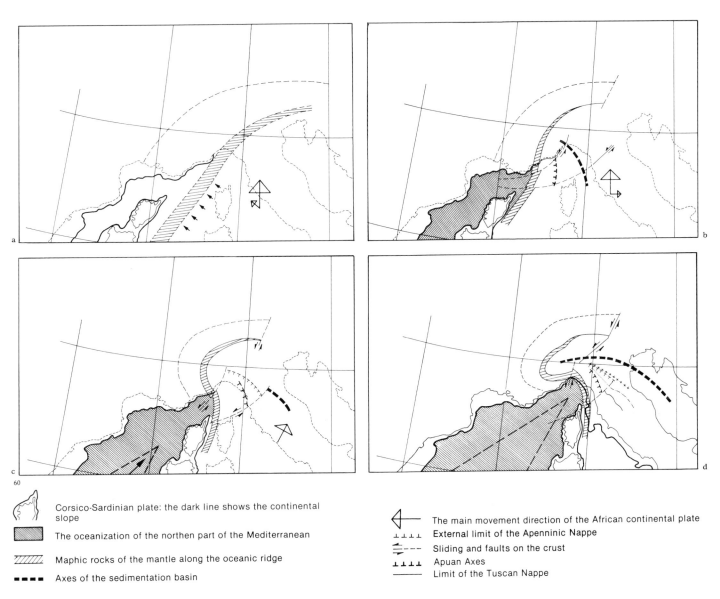

60

Corsico-Sardinian plate: the dark line shows the continental slope

The oceanization of the northen part of the Mediterranean

Maphic rocks of the mantle along the oceanic ridge

■■■■ Axes of the sedimentation basin

The main movement direction of the African continental plate

⊥⊥⊥⊥ External limit of the Apenninic Nappe

≡--- Sliding and faults on the crust

⊥⊥⊥⊥ Apuan Axes

——— Limit of the Tuscan Nappe

60. Paleographic evolution model of the Tyrrheanian area a) 60 milion years ago; b) 30 milion years ago; c) 12 milion years ago; d) 1 milion years ago (from M. Broccaletti and G. Guazzone).

form a spongy crust that absorbes large quantities of rain water polluted by black dust, and the process of disintegration is accelerated under the flimsy patina (see fig. 54). Because of this, many statues and monuments that have endured for centuries are now crumbling to pieces; mechanic scaling is the first vital step towards preservation, but it must be repeated periodically, since it does not stop sulfuration from re-occuring, unless the marble surface is soaked with resin that usually alters the original appearance (see fig. 55). Recent research work has delt in detail with

the problem of biological contamination, that is more complex than initially appears. Weeds infest monuments and archaeological sites and grow rapidly even in crevices that have been cleaned, and sometimes it would be better to re-bury archaeological remains in order to protect them adequately. Mechanic and chemical transformation of roots and trees, together with mechanic weeding have caused extensive and irreparable damage. On the whole chemical weed-killers are preferable, but they must be examined one by one depending on how, when and where

61

61. 63. *Westerly view of the
Apuan Alps with a
geotectonic model.*
62. 64. *View of the Apuan
Alps taken from North, with
a geotectonic model.*

62

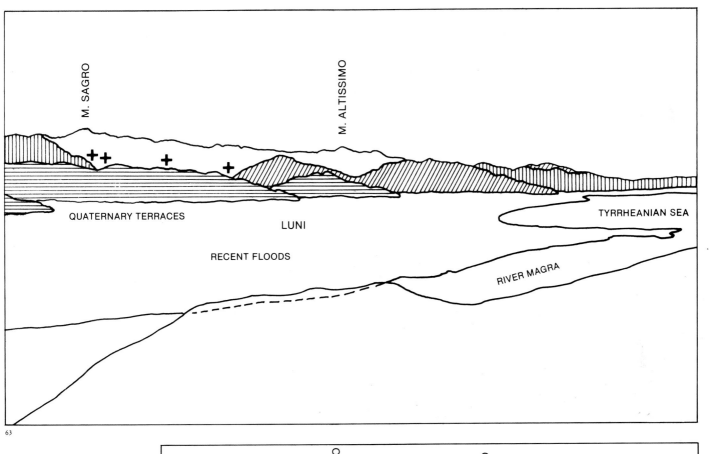

M. SAGRO

M. ALTISSIMO

QUATERNARY TERRACES

LUNI

TYRRHEANIAN SEA

RECENT FLOODS

RIVER MAGRA

63

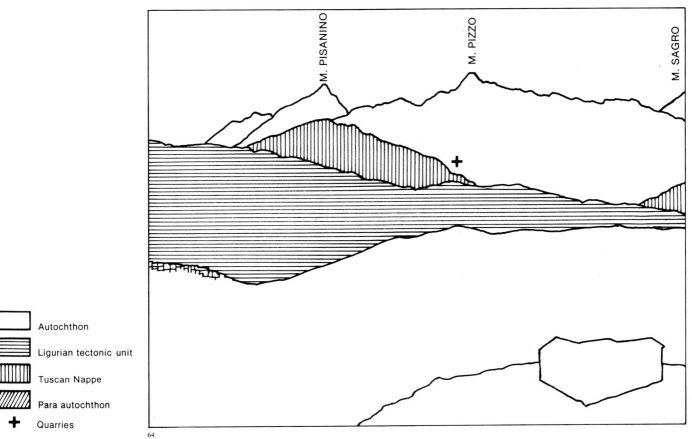

M. PISANINO

M. PIZZO

M. SAGRO

Autochthon

Ligurian tectonic unit

Tuscan Nappe

Para autochthon

+ Quarries

64

they are to be used; in Latium alone, over a hundred different varieties of weeds have been discovered. Lower forms of vegetable life such as moss, lychen and algae are also dangerous since they take root directly on the marble surface producing the typical alveolar-type corrosion; chemical weed-killers are again more effective and less harmful. Microbiological analyses have recently revealed that together with moss, lychen and algae there are colonies of unicellular algea and bacteria: they live also in the «patina of time» that covers the apparently undamaged surfaces of many monuments: cianoficee infest damp interiors, and sulfobacteria thrive in the patina of marble exposed to atmospheric pollution.

Marble Deposits and Geology: The Apuan Alps

The Apuan Alps are well known mainly for three reasons: firstly because of the extensive marble deposits that supplied raw material to the Roman Empire and Renaissance artists, secondly because of the beautiful landscape, and finally because they are excellent for mountineering: the chain of the northen Alps and Apennines and the Ligurian Apennines can be seen from their peaks. The geological structure is less well-known, and although connected with the Appennine corrugation, this small elliptical chain of mountains is geografically independent. The remains of three distinct stratografic layers, tectonically placed one above the other, are contained within a few dozen square kilometres: erosion has opened a window-like gap, and the geological history of the Apuan Alps can be traced as accurately as on tridimensional didiactic map. The super-

imposition of layers has, among other things, generated the huge marble basin, made up of a powerful continuous lens that in parts is more than 400 metres thick; it covers an area of about 200 square kilometres and outcrops on 1/4th of the total surface (see fig. 59). This unique deposit was formed by huge exceedingly pure calcareous rock deposits, squashed for a million years by layers of other material and by the sea. Under these conditions changes in pressure and temperature transformed the original limestone into saccharoidal marble. To better understand the process and outcome of this phenomena it is necessary to re-examine the model of the earth's tectonic crust in this area (see figg. 57, 60).
The history of the Apuan Alps starts at the end of the Primary Era, about two hundred and forty million years ago: before then, it was a large plane protruding from the Euroasiatic continent, still part of the Pangea of continents, over the Tetide, a vast gulf in the eastern part of the huge, single, primordial ocean. Clay sediment mixed with sandstone lens settled and was covered by magma formed by the fusion of the continental crust at great depth. Forty million years later, at the end of the first part of the Secondary or Mesozoic Era (Triassic), the foundation was covered by a shallow sea; new deposits of calcium carbonate, magnesium carbonate and organic matter were formed by chemical precipitation (grey dolomite). Meanwhile the Pangea had started to split into plates, and the Tetide was becoming smaller; one hundred and eighty million years ago, at the beginning of the Jurassic Period, the sea covering the future Apuan area was shallow, open and well-oxygenated, and in certain places the dead organic matter deposits,

contained in calcium carbonate had been completely destroyed. In other parts waves consumed small islands, and the clay cemented fragments collected on the sea bed to form todays breccia rock.

At the same time the Euroasiatic continent, no longer part of the Pangea, began to rotate anti-clockwise and the Tetide sea began to shrink in the East; a small plate broke away from the continent and formed the «Italo-Dinaric» plate on the site of the Apennines. The Apuan Zone was part of it (todays Tuscany), and comprised an area from 200 to 300 metres thick of pure calcareous rock, that in parts contained no organic matter whatsoever (Hettangia Plane). The «Italo-Dinaric» plate broke away because of a heat convection in the underlaying mantle, that was moving away in an opposite direction from the axis that coincides with todays pre-Alps (Insubric Line), forming a new crust and ridge on the sea-bed.

At the end of the Jurassic Period, one hundred and thirty million years ago, the oceans stopped expanding and a constriction process started: the «Italo-Dinaric» plate, pushed by the African continent, was constantly moving away from the American continent and getting closer to Eurasia. Along the Insubric Line the process of constriction caused one part of the oceanic crust to slide under another, while all the material on the surface was pushed upwards and formed the Alpine ridge. The sea in the Tuscan Dominium became deeper, and contained increasing quantities of organic limestone sediment, silica lens and even clay (marine): eventually silica and clay predominated (jasper, phtannite).

During the Cretaceous Period of the Mesozoic Era, layers of clay containing large quantities of calcium were continually being deposited.

The geography of this area was radically changed in this period: previously the Mediterranean was shut off towards the West and open to the East; the Eastern gap was gradually closing as the African continent moved north-east and Eurasia continued to rotate. Corsica and Sardinia were still part of the Eurasian continent and were placed at an angle of 90° regarding their present position in the Lion Gulf. The Alpine chain was not curved as it is today (geologically the Alps end near Genoa), but practically straight stretching from the Ligurian Alps to Corsica and Sardinia (in their original position) and to the Pyrenèes. The oceanic trough from which the Alps emerged continued south of Corsica (Ligurian Dominium).

At the beginning of the Third Era the Corsico-Sardinian plate broke away from the continent and began a slow rotating migration, compressing the Ligurian basin, towards East: the oceanic crust swelled upwards, and part of the compressed sedimentary material flowed over the Corsican Alpine corrugation and the Maritime Alps, irreversably bending the axis of the Alpine chain.

During the first part of the Third Era, from sixtyfive to twentyfive million years ago, a thick layer of sedimentary earth-like material collected on the Tuscan Dominium: with time it became more coarse (sandstone) and was finally covered with argillaceous limestone from the ever shrinking Ligurian basin (see fig. 58). The north-east thrust caused by Africa, Corsica and Sardinia produced the first symptons of tectonic disorder in the «Italo-Dinaric» plate. Along the Occidental edge of the Apuan zone (between Carrara and Seravezza) basement slice started to rise («para-autochthon») dividing the Tuscan basin into an external zone in the

East, and an internal zone in the West.

During the Miocene epoch (12 million years ago), the Ligurian oceanic bed was depleated, and Corsica collided with the Italo-Dinaric continental sole, pushing the entire sedimentary sequence, covered by Ligurian argillaceous limestone, on top of the external Tuscan zone (Tuscan nappe). The external zone did not shift (Apuan autochthon), but the pressure increased to about 1000 atmospheres and the temperature to 400°C circa; the entire autochthon sequence was transfromed by metamorphosis from limestone to white and *statuario* marble, that contains no organic carbon, veined or grey marble that contains a little; cipolines are metamorphic argillaceous limestone and arabesqued marble is a breccia rock.

From about ten to eight million years ago further thrusts lifted the Apuan autochthon causing the over-burden to slip towards the north-east, where it became part of the Tusco-Emilian Apennines. Later erosion completly demolished the central part of the Apuan ellipse revealing (in parts) the marble lens down to the basement of phyllade, gneiss and quartz that was formed by the metamorphosis of clay and sandstone at the end of the Primary Era (see figg. 61, 62).

The Apuan Alps ellipse is surrounded by the Tuscan nappe, a sedimentary sequence twin of the Autochthon tectonic unit, that has been transformed by metamorphosis, and shows what the Apuan Alps would have been like if covered by argillaceous limestone and common limestone. The Apuan Alps marble sequence is about 400 metres thick and is made up of three distinct geologic zones: a stratum 50 metres thick resting on dolomite (*grezzoni*), 99,9% composed of calcite crystals usually about 0,2 millimetres large, polygonal with regular or jagged surfaces; the only impurities are quartz crystals and white mica (muscovite) caused by small quantities of silica and argillaceous minerals deposited in the shallow, hot, shut-off sea together with calcium carbonate. A larger, equally pure strata comprising calcite crystals that measure about 1,8 millimetres; they are perfectly polygonal with a regular composition surface and were deposited in the open sea. The topmost stratum is of elongated calcite crystals (97% or 98%) that measure about 0,1 millimetres; they are interspaced with with quartz and large quantities of mica since, in the past, large amounts of clay was deposited in deep sea together with calcium carbonate, that later came in contact with calcareous flintstone. Small quantities of albite, pirite, clorite, sphalerite, tourmaline, epidote and hematite can be traced at certain levels and are interesting collectors items if the crystals are large.

See the Appendix for the list of commercial Apuan marbles.

Chapter Two
Marble Technology

Changes in Production Technique

The quantity and variety of marble products and technological know-how increased steadily over the centuries and was the result of changing techniques, the experience and skill of many different populations. Progress was not uniform since it depended on different factors: the development of applied sciences, relations between the lower and upper social classes and frequently no improvements were made for long periods. These transformations only affected certain production areas, and in some parts things did not alter for centuries. Occasionally, in very poor areas, primitive techniques survived notwithstanding the more recent technical innovations.

In Ancient times manual labour was done by slaves and prisoners who occasionally became expert artisans. Ever since the Middle Ages animals were used to transport marble over flat land, but, until the beginning of this century the blocks were still lowered to the bottom of the quarry by hand regardless of personal danger. Even after the Second World War when cableways and railroads had been revolutionised by more powerful machines with rubber tyres, cooperatives of «lizzatori» (stoneboat workers) in the Apuan Alps still lowered marble by hand; although sawmills were being converted from hydraulic motive power to electricity and steam, the blocks were cut using the same methods as the Romans, as shown in a number of photographs dating back to the beginning of this century: hydraulic motive power was used at mills and «folloni» (fulling machines) by the year 1000 A.D., but was not employed for cutting marble for the next five centuries.

On the whole the scientific discoveries of the 18th and 19th centuries in the Western World were not applied to the marble industry until much later, specially in countries that «imported» the new industrial discoveries. This was caused by the old-fashioned socio-economic structure and the technical difficulties to adapt mass production methods to marble: consistent improvements only date back to the beginning of this century.

Production Phases

The production cycle of marble, however modern the means and techniques, is divided into various phases; there are three initial phases: firstly marble is quarried in blocks the size of which depends on how they will be used; secondly the blocks of marble are turned into finished or semifinished products ready for future use (see fig. 65). The hard data of marble production is global, and includes every phase of production: if not, each individual finished or semifinished product is specified. The last phase concerns transport: special vehicles are used to move the marble to carving sites or distant construction sites and workshops (since blocks are exceedingly heavy and bulky). Each production phase follows a special technical procedure that varies according to the physical characteristics of marble, and has nothing to do with whether the work is organised singly or jointly; this creates a kind of bond between men working on different production phases: they understand their job from beginning to end, and are at home whatever task they undertake. Production techniques will be delt with later in a historical framework, from quarrying methods to transport and carving.

The illustrations are taken from pre-industrial archeological records in the traditionally most important production areas: the people of the Apuan Alps played a fundamental part

65

65. S. Salvioni, the Tarnone
quarry in the Carrara valley
(beginning of the 19th
century). A dislodged block
of marble split with wedges.

in the changes that have taken place in
the last hundred years. The technical
nomenclature, in brackets, also
originated in this area.

Research and Testing

In the past marble deposits were
revealed either by round stones in
streams that crossed the area, or by
landslides caused by erosion; very
often the rock was hidden by earth
and plants and its aesthetic qualities

were not immediatly apparent.
Traces left by skilled technicians
looking for metal deposits dating back
to the Bronze Age (5000 years ago),
have been found and it is possible that
the Mediterranean populations first
started to use marble for building in
consequence of these first empirical
geological discoveries; later
civilizations, Greece for instance, were
lucky to develop with marble on their
«doorstep». Later the Romans, helped
by the Imperial network of transport,

66

66. «Monticolo» drill in the Carrara quarries at the beginning of the 19th century.

looked for and exploited every kind of marble they could find within their dominions. Theophrast (371-287 B.C.) and Pliny (23-79 A.D.) left accurate descriptions of the marbles used in their times, how to distinguish the different varieties and how to work them out.

Unfortunaly it is sometimes difficult to interpret their work since many proper names have not survived the disintegration of the Ancient world, after which many precious materials were no longer used.

One thousand years later the old Roman quarries were re-opened, but the search for new marble quarries only started at the beginning of the Middle Ages (see Appendix), and only since last century has expanded out of Europe to other continents, on the wing of recent geologic discoveries and mining surveys.

Before opening new quarries even in areas known to hide huge quantities of marble, experts explore in depth with drills and test specimens to check the consistency and type of marble, and how it can best be worked out.

Colour, grain and flaws are examined as well as the banks that must not be fractured, and be sufficiently large and

67. The initial phase of exploiting a quarry after the «cappellaccio» (bad hat) has been removed along with the debris (beginning of the 20th century).

68

68. S. Salvioni: the floor of
the Polvaccio quarry in the
Carrara valley (beginning of
the 19th century). It was
first exploited by the
Romans and was practically
worked out by the 19th
century.

69. Preparation of the
«formelle», thin holes for
inserting wedges used to split
blocks of marble.

69

72

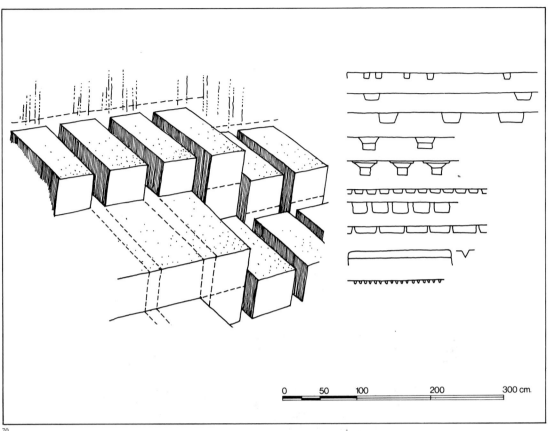

70

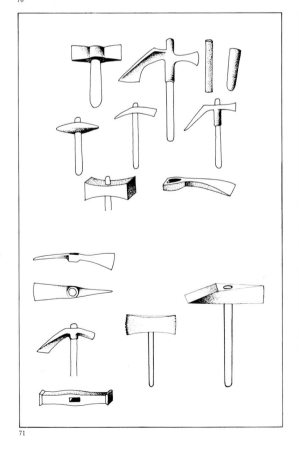

71

72

70. *Exploitation techniques in Egyptian quarries that later were adopted by the Greeks and Romans: vertical cuts were done by hand and the blocks were split horizontally with wedges. On the right there are different kinds of housing for wedges (from L.N. Bromehead).*

71. *Tools used by the Greeks and Romans for cutting (from J.B. Ward Perkins and R. Martin).*

72. *An ancient iron pick-axe found in an abandoned quarry near Carrara.*

follow the same direction as the lithoclastic metamorphic schistosity, «*peli*», the so-called hairs. Only then can the direction and quarrying site be decided upon.

All areas that are rich in marble show signs of testing: it is possible to distinguish the more recent tests of the past hundred years using small mines, rotating cutters and wire saws (see fig. 66) from those executed by hand - roughly cut small chippings - done before the Industrial Revolution.

Quarrying

Once a site has been chosen, all the covering material like earth and loose rock, known in the jargon as «*cappellaccio*» (bad hat) is removed revealing the deposit proper (see fig. 67). Marble is quarried parallelly to the lithoclastic natural cracks or «*peli*» giving birth to the quarry front and quarry floor called «*piazzale*». Only the means of extraction have altered with time, otherwise nothing has changed for centuries.

The blocks of marble are then quarried: this procedure is called «*abbattimento*» literally «pulling down», since the marble is lowered from the quarry face to the flat «quarry floor» below (see fig. 68). Special techniques are used to extract large and medium sized blocks — over a few square metres — while the small and consequently less valuable blocks are worked out with levers where the jointingnet is thickest.

There are two main techniques used to extract large blocks of marble: either cutting all round the chosen bank and letting it slip to the «*piazzale*» below, or producing a landslide hoping that some large blocks will remain intact. Obviously the first is more rational and less wasteful. In ancient times cutting was done painstakingly by hand, and last century such methods were revived with the help of more advanced machinery which is quicker and less tiring for the quarrymen.

Hand Cutting

The face and upper part of the selected bank are cleaned — the sides have already been defined by previous quarrying and coincide with «*peli*», or natural lithoclase — and then separated form the main bank by three cuts, one along the top and two along the sides: the height and width of the block depends on the depth and length of the cuts, and, since they are done by hand, on the tools. The block is then broken away from the base with gibs, and turned over with levers onto the «*piazzale*» that has been covered with debris and loose stones to break the fall. Iron gibs are inserted either in a thin canal, «*canale*», or in a series of holes, «*formelle*» (see fig. 69), so that greater part of force is concentrated on the sides; the gibs are inserted with a sledge-hammer and must all be at the same level (quarrymen can tell by the sound they make whether the gibs are level or not) so-called «*in tiro*», and the traction force overcomes the intercrystalline cohesion resistance and the rock breaks away evenly along the plane made by the line of gibs (see figg. 65, 75, 107, 108). Another way is to insert gibs of dry wood and then gradually soak them with water.

The oldest traces of hand cutting have been found in Egypt and date back to 2600 B.C. in soft rock quarries (used to build pyramids during the Ancient Kingdom) and to 2000 B.C. in granite quarries: monoliths weighing one thousand tons were quarried with these methods (see fig. 70).

Iron had not yet been discoverd, and bronze was too soft to work hard rock, so granite was cut by hammering with balls of an equally hard, but stronger rock, dolerithe. The rock was then broken away with bronze or wooden gibs fastened between two metal plates.

73. A typical quarry-front exploited with the old-fashioned method of cutting by hand. (Carrara valley).

75

74. *The disproportionate growth of quarry dumps at the beginning of the 19th century caused by the excessive use of explosives.*

75. *S. Salvioni: extraction methods used in Carrara at the beginning of the 19th century: at the top a block is being dislodged with the traditional wedges, at the bottom there is a «fornello» (a little oven) where a mine is being prepared.*

74

75

76. *A wire saw plant viewed from the power house.*

77. *Return pulleys belonging to various wire saw plants.*

Much less is known about extraction techniques in Greece, but most archeological sources seem to prove that they were imported from Egypt in the 7th century B.C.; Greek tools were better since iron had been discovered, and there are numerous pick-axes, axes, hammers, sledge hammers, chisels and even saws for very soft rock (see fig. 71), and a drill similar to that used in the Mount Pentelicus quarries. The marble in these quarries is metamorphic saccharoidal calcareous rock, and it is not possible to cut it in depth, only to break it away in blocks; this was done by drilling or boring holes through the block from top to bottom.

Greek slaves, *«technitēs»*, like their Egyptian counterparts, were experts in the matter of quarries, and it was mainly due to their skill and advanced techniques that the marble industry flourished during the Roman Empire.

78. *Dislodgeing marble with mines on a large quarry front.*

79. *The «filista» (the chain saw expert) explains how to set up a wire saw circuit to a young apprentice.*

80. *Large blocks being cut with a wire saw.*

80

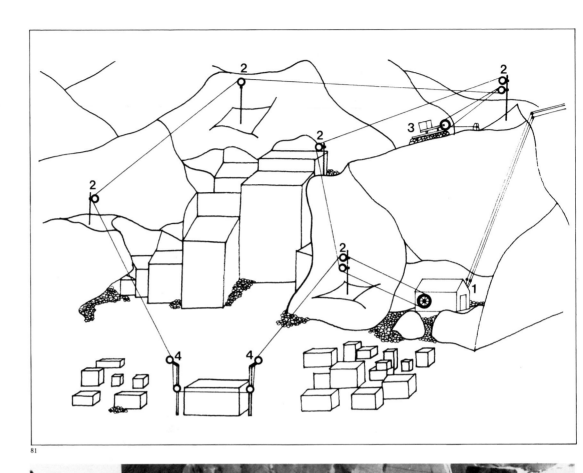

81

81. Model af a wire saw
circuit: 1) engine pulley; 2)
return pulleys; 3) pulley with
the counterweight trolley, 4)
pillars with cutting advance
pulleys.

82. Wire saw exploitation:
after the side cuts have been
executed the men are getting
ready to do the final cut; the
barrels contain a mixture of
quartzitic sand and water.

82

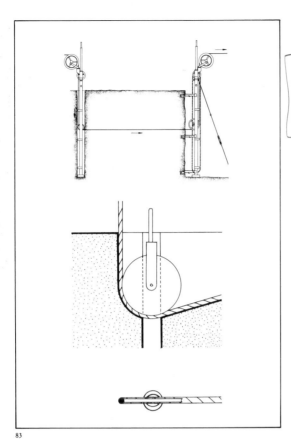

83

83. Model for wire saw
exploitation: a normal
external pillar and
penetrating «Monticolo»
tangent screw pulley. At the
bottom there is a detail of
the penetrating pulley.

They probably also opened new
quarries: the «Giallo Antico» (Antique
yellow) in pre-consular Tunisia and
the Lunensi quarries in Italy at
Carrara. The Luni quarries were the
most important suppliers of white
marble in the Western part of the
Empire.
Unfortunatly no proper archeological
research took place during last
century's production boom, although
many Roman remains were
discovered: initialled blocks, inscribed
sacred aediculas, (one in particular
done by a team of quarrymen was
carved directly inside the quarry),
pieces of sculpture and tools (pick-
axes, gibs and other metal
implements) coins, masonry and hand
chippings (see fig. 72), (see Ch. V and
Appendix). Ancient working out
techniques have been revived with the
additional advantage of modern
scientific equipment.

Dislodging Slabs («Varata»)

The first alternative source of energy
to man-power used in quarries were
explosives; there are two main kinds:
quick combustion (fragmentation) and
slow combustion (deflagration)
explosives.
The first reduces the rock to fragments
with shock waves before demolishing
it, and is no good in the case of large
blocks; the second can tear even large
blocks away without breaking them.
«Polvere nera» — (black powder) —
belongs to this variety: it is composed
of carbon sulphur and salpeter earth.
Although it had been discovered by
the Middle Ages it was not used for
quarrying until the 18th century after
the invention of the slow match, that
was universally used to light charges
after 1831. It was a quicker method
and many enthusiasts thought it would
give quarrying a new lease of life: but
on the contrary, it was to be its death
warrant: soon quarrymen began to
realise that the greater part of
dislodged rock was useless because the
pieces were either too small or
cracked. To avoid this and to obtain
large blocks, the dislodging volume
was increased and slabs of marble
large enough to provide material for
many years of work were brought
down to the «piazzale» of the quarry.
But even by the end of the century
quarrymen began to protest against
this method that in a short time
threatened to smother the quarries
with mountains of debris (see fig. 74).
The word «varata» was used every
time a landslide was produced either
manually or mechanically. Initially
black powder was placed within
natural cracks in the rock above the
block that was going to be dislodged.
Mines were placed in long holes
carved with chisels in the bank that
were transformed into proper
combustion chambers: hydrochloric
acid was used for calcareous marble;

81

84

85

for all other types of marble, and for large charges proper combustion chambers were carved out by hand (french mines) (see fig. 78). The meaning of the word *«mine»* comes from the french *«mine»*, the lead needed to produce the explosion. After the period of the great *«varate»* (dislodgements) small deflagration charges were used to reclaim unsafe quarries, to remove covering material before a new quarry was opened, and for blocks cut entirely, or in parts, with wire saws. Today this method has been substituted by mechanical dislodging, since explosives invariably damage parts of serviceable blocks.

Wire Sawing

The necessity to find other ways to extract marble than by man-power and explosives was urgent especially in small quarries. A Belgium patent put

foward a solution in 1854: it was perfected in 1880 and presented at the International Exhibition of Paris in 1889. The new method was based on the non-violent separation of the serviceable blocks from the bank: gibs were substituted with the abrasive action of a wire saw drawn across the marble, and powered by a steam engine. This was a continuation of the methods used in ancient times to saw blocks into slabs, but substituted rigid blades with wire that could penetrate deep into the rock.
It was successful, and by the end of the century was widely used even in countries that were industrially behind times; it was first used at Carrara in 1895, and within less than thirty years the physical and human conditions of quarries were radically changed, and, above all, the problem of increasing waste had been drastically reduced. The diametre of the wire was of about four or six millimetres, and was made

84. *Electric drill called «macchinetta» that prepares holes for the penetrating pulley.*

85. *Winded old wire (originally from wire saws) used for hoisting, and as braces.*

86. A quarry front prepared
for exploitation with a
pneumatic drill. The debris
is removed with a mechanic
shovel.

86

of three twisted steel wires producing a helicoidal movement that dragged a mixture of sand and water (90% one millimetre sized grains of quartz) across the surface. Water cooled the wire heated by friction, and as much as 50% of the sand that came out of the block together with the marble flour could be re-used. Since continuous movement was essential, the closed circuits must be from one thousand to two thousand metres long so the wire had time to cool off and did not wear out too quickly.

A quarryman discovered the best way to join the ends of the wire without lumps: the ends were unravelled and each piece of wire was cut at a different length: the wire was twisted again, and the three joins were placed a few metres one from the other. The drive circuit was wrapped round a pulley connected to the engine by means of a clutch: initially the engines were powered by steam, then by internal combustion and finally by electricity at speed of five or six metres a second (see fig. 76).

The necessary return parts of the circuit were worked by free revolving pulleys pivoted on rods fixed into the rock (called *poteaux*) (see figg. 77, 79). One pulley was attached to a trolley that moved along an inclined plane so the weight of the trolley itself regulated the tension of the circuit. The length of the wire used for cutting, called «*tesa*» (stretch out), was more than 30 metres long: there were two return pulleys at each end connected to two pillars that could be lowered to about ten metres, the so-called «*cala*», and keep the cutting force of the wire, fed with sand and water, constant (see fig. 80); this machine could cut saccharoidal calcareous rock at a speed of 10 cm. an hour (see figg. 81, 82).

To extract marble from a hand-cut terraced bank it is necessary to cut the sides, base and top. Wire saws can only cut one single straight line at a time, and two holes must be carved out above the block to fix the «*cala*» pulley pillars. At Carrara in 1897, two years after the introduction of the wire saw, the *puleggia penetrante Monticolo* (Monticolo penetrating pulley) was patented. It was powered by the wire saw itself and worked with a rotating diamond crown and produced holes with a diametre of 10 centimetres, in any direction. Later the crown was substituted by a special pulley that giuded the wire into the hole itself. The more recent cutters, «*macchinette*» (little machines), are electrical (see fig. 84).

To extract large blocks it is occasionally necessary to make an opencut on the side of the mountain with mines and wire saws and exploit the natural jointings. One open-cut is imperative for feeding the wire with water and sand. The base of the block can be cut obliquely towards the outside to facilitate its removal from the bank: it is then dislodged with levers, railroad jacks, hydraulic jacks or small charges of black powder. Another way is to make two small tunnels at the side of the block, after having taken away a wedge-shaped piece of marble from its base («*cala*» floor cut): as soon as the marble breaks away from the bank it capsizes onto a prepared bed of rubble on the «*piazzale*» of the quarry.

The large quantities of wire that have become cylindrical with wear and tear are used to wrap and hoist marble and as anchor slings (see fig. 85).

Wire is also used to tie-up vines and hedges, and wire-decorated landscapes are typical of marble producing areas.

Pneumatic Drilling

For the past sixty years magmatic and metamorphic ornamental rocks, have been cut by making a series of holes

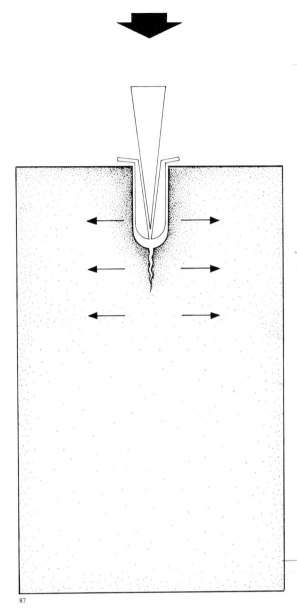

close together in the sides of the block, from top to bottom, using a pneumatic drill (see fig. 86). If the structure of the rock is homogeneous it is easily separated either with thin wedges, *«puntazze»*, that are fitted into the holes with two upside down wedges, *«formelle»* (see fig. 87), or with black powder connected with instantaneous fuses that all explode at the same time.

Pneumatic drills have substituted manual perforation executed with long chisels and hammers that were used for mining up until last century: pneumatic drills worked on a mixed system of percussion and penetration by rotation and air insufflation to remove the dust. The perforating end of the drill is of special steel, that has been tempered, not forged, and lasts much longer than the old-fashioned chisel that had to be continually re-sharpened. The diameter of the headstock is a few centimetres wide and varies according to how hard and tough the rock is, since perforation speed depends on these factors. The holes are up to 15 metres are long if an extention rod is used. Today sets of simultaneous drills, that produce a series of parallel holes are available on the market.

87

87. Model of how rock splits using wedges with iron fins that are placed in holes produced with pneumatic drilling.

88. Geologic section that shows underground quarrying in the Roman quarry of Aurisina in Istria (from C. d'Ambrosi).

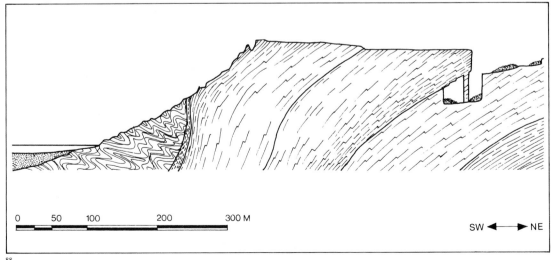

0   50   100   200   300 M

SW ◄——► NE

88

Exploitation Methods

The most conventional kind of quarry, mentioned in the chapter 'Dislodging Slabs' («Varate») are those opened on mountain-sides and developed in a series of terraces with the «piazzale» at the bottom, and the quarry face at the top (see fig. 89). It is necessary to continually shift the quarry face further up the mountain side to exploit it longer.

This is possible only if the marble deposit is very large, otherwise the quarry works out quickly and only the «piazzale» is left at the foot of a huge vertical wall.

Terrace-like exploitation from 6 to 18 metres high is still visible today in some Egyptian quarries; the most ancient geo-mining map known, the Papyrus of Turin (see fig. 90), dates back to about 1500 B.C., during the 18th Dynasty. It proves that there were already skilled geo-mining surveyors who had mapped out the production areas, communication routes, different varieties of rock and soil, the location of mines and quarries and even the quarrymen's settlements. The area mapped out in the Papyrus of Turin is that of Mount Basanite — Waradi Hammanat in the Oriental desert — where Beken was extracted. Beken, known incorrectly as Basalt, is a dark green compact metamorphic sandstone used for sculpture (grovacca).

There is also evidence of terrace-like exploitation in quarries of Ancient Greece: from top to bottom in the quarries of Naxos, Thaxos, and Karystos, or from the bottom using the undercutting method where the blocks turn over by force of gravity in the quarries of Thaxos, Skyros, Pentelicus: slabs twenty metres high were detatched in this quarry.

Underground Quarrying

When it is no longer viable to exploit banks of marble with the more conventional terrace-like system, other methods are employed: the oldest is that of underground quarrying which dates back to the Bronze Age, and no doubt was suggested by mining techniques; in some Egyptian quarries there are tunnels up to six metres high carved in the face of the rock: they slope gently towards the outside to facilitate drainage and transport. First a horizontal opencut is made in the roof, called «a tetto», with a hammer and chisel, then, from the inside, quarrymen cut the marble as in an open-air quarry.

In the quarries of Ancient Greece only statuario marble of Paros was worked-out in tunnels: statuario is a saccharoidal marble generated by contact metamorphosis, and the serviceable banks were only a few metres thick. Pliny records how in Paros the marble was extracted using oil lamps. The Roman quarry Aurisina in Istria was also developed underground, and during the Western Roman Empire and the barbaric dominations it supplied all the cities of Northen Adriatic coast with marble (Theodoric's Mausoleum in Ravenna). The only serviceable bank was fortyfive metres wide and went deep into the mountain: the marble was worked out in terraces from top to bottom (from «tetto» to «letto»). Columns of marble were left to strengthen the roof (see fig. 88) since the underground chamber was forty metres wide at the entrance, and sixty metres high. The same method had already been tried out in the silver mines of Laurion near Athens in the 6th century B.C.; the seams of silver were placed horizontally, and in 339 B.C. a law was issued that severely punished those who stole silver form the columns endangering the stability of the mine. Only fifty years ago quarrymen were considering underground quarrying in the Apuan Alps to extract statuario marble and these methods are still used today.

89. *Open-air quarries in the Carrara valley: step-like exploitation executed with wire saws.*

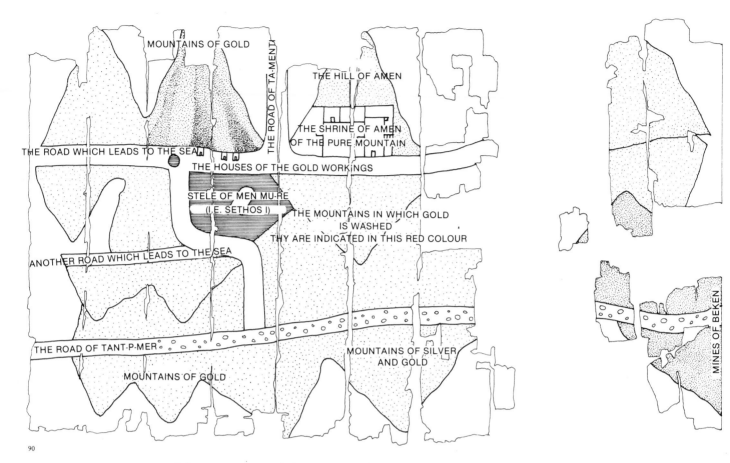

MOUNTAINS OF GOLD

THE HILL OF AMEN

THE ROAD OF TA·MENTI

THE SHRINE OF AMEN
OF THE PURE MOUNTAIN

THE ROAD WHICH LEADS TO THE SEA

THE HOUSES OF THE GOLD WORKINGS

STELE OF MEN MU·RE
(I.E. SETHOS I)

THE MOUNTAINS IN WHICH GOLD
IS WASHED
THY ARE INDICATED IN THIS RED COLOUR

ANOTHER ROAD WHICH LEADS TO THE SEA

THE ROAD OF TANT·P·MER

MOUNTAINS OF SILVER
AND GOLD

MOUNTAINS OF GOLD

MINES OF BEKEN

90

90. Transcription of the «Papyrus of Turin» (15th century B.C.). It is the oldest existing geo-minerary chart, now preserved in the Egyptian Museum of Turin (from R. Forbes).

The vast size of the Apuan deposits was caused by uniform regional metamorphosis, and the best marble for sculpting was in banks a few metres thick near the base of the stratigraphic series, where, due to metamorphosis recrystallization of the primigenial calcareous rock, the grain is homogeneous. Modern underground quarrying techniques do not differ much from those described above; internal columns, protected by Mining Police Regulations, and a sufficiently large clear «roof» to allow vertical cutting (see figg. 93, 94, 96); however this entails wasting large quantities of the adjoining less valuable material that can be in part avoided if the banks are cut vertically, and the open cuts are done on one side.

The main differences between present day quarrymen and their forefathers are firstly the altered socio-economic relations within the productive structure, and secondly the use of mechanic means and external sources of energy: but the experience and wisdom acquired over the centuries is still priceless. The mechanical means most frequently used to dislodge and drive blocks are wire saws, penetrating pulley cutters and removal jacks; pneumatic drills and small charges of black powder for open-cuts; more recently, belt cutters for frontal cutting that substitute leads and holes; they are made with special steel chains from two to four centimetres thick with arms that can penetrate up to three metres powered by electric or compressed air engines (see fig. 95).

Wall Exploitation

In Apuan dialect a «tecchia» is a natural rock wall, but over the centuries it has also come to mean the man-made face of a quarry. Under-«tecchia» exploitation means working

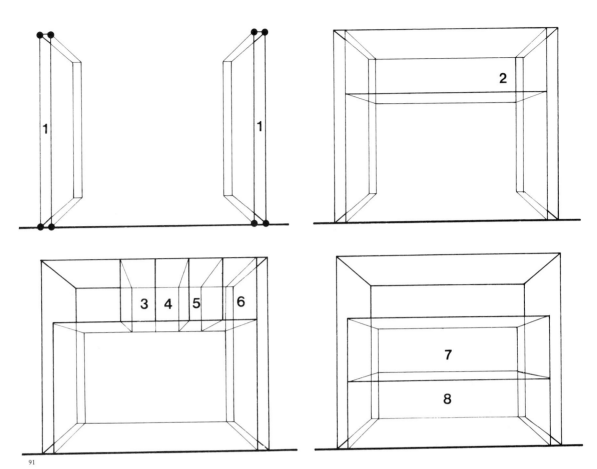

91

out marble from under the perpendicular quarry face. Unlike underground quarrying where an entrance tunnel and a huge inner chamber (sometimes a dozen metres high and wide) have been carved out in the deposit itself, «under-*tecchia*» exploitation is always open-air. When working on the quarry face it is always necessary to remove overhanging rocks, a process called «scaling». This is done by skilled quarrymen called «*tecchiaioli*» («*tecchia*» workers) who let themselves down from the top of the quarry with ropes and dislodge the rock using levers, sledge hammers, jacks and more recently pneumatic chisels and small mines. Chain saws are used to extract blocks, but since only one side of the bank is accessible, two perpendicular tunnels, called manholes, are carved out at the sides (about 180 centimetres by 120 centimetres large) and as deep as the

block itself. Then using penetrating pulleys and chain saws the base of the block and the sides are cut away from top to bottom; then the marble is lowered on to the quarry floor.

Open-Pit Quarrying

Even after the terraced part of the quarry has been worked out there is still marble left under the quarry floor that can be worked out vertically; if the deposits are in flat areas this problem crops up from the beginning. Until fifty years ago machinery capable of hoisting large blocks of marble on to the quarry floor did not exist (see figg. 98, 100); nowadays there are bridge-cranes that can reach every part of the quarry, and chain saws are used for working the marble out. The first bank is made by cutting a vertical open-cut, «*sbasso*», at the foot of the quarry face to remove the

91. Model of how wall exploitation progresses using wire saws.

92. Underground exploitation of statuario marble of Carrara.

93. Modern «roof» exploitation in an abandoned tunnel of the old marble railway near Carrara.

94

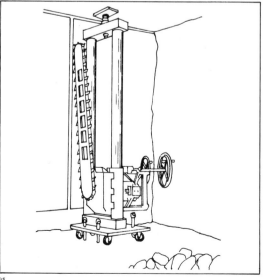

95

96

94. *Underground exploitation of white streaked marble using wire saws.*

95. *Drawing of how a chain saw is used for underground exploitation.*

96. *Model of how blocks are dislodged in tunnels with the «undercutting» method.*

97. *Wall exploitation method known as «undertecchia». A small tunnel is visible at the top, called «passo d'uomo», and made for the wire saw advance pulley.*

98

first layer of blocks; a second bank is then cut leaving a security offset. The quarry grows narrower the deeper it is worked (see fig. 99). The cuts are never longer than eight metres, and the bridge cranes lower all the necessary equipment into the open-pit as well as removing the debris.

Site Organization

The site called «piazzale» has only been mentioned in relation to the different extraction methods and a dumping ground for marble, which is,

98. A quarry that has been exploited in depth (pit exploitation) after the marble has been worked out from the walls.

99. Model of pit exploitation progression.

100. Pit exploitation with a wire saw. The steps are clearly visible together with the powerful equipment required for hoisting.

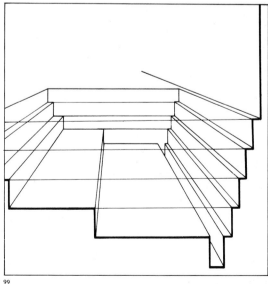

99

101

102

103

101. Quarryman at work
squaring a block of marble
on the quarry floor,
beginning of the 20th
century.

102. 103. Quarrymen in
charge of removing the
debris from the quarry front.

104

104. The hand cart, called «galeotta» (slave galley) in the quarries of Carrara. In ancient times in was used to transport debris and is still used today for light weights.
105. At the beginning of the 20th century the decauville trolleys were used to take debris away from the quarry floor.

105

107

108

109

106. Nowadays, since roads reach the quarry floor, debris is loaded on to self-tipping lorries with mechanic shovels.

107. 108. Blocks of marble have to be prepared for the market, and all the sticking out edges must be knocked off. If mechanic tools are not available workmen still square blocks with old fashioned wedges and chisels.

109. Holes made with a pneumatic drill in order to split marble with wedges. (See fig. 87).

to say the least, a very inaccurate description; the «piazzale» is an open air opificium, and good organization is vital (see figg. 101, 111): a foreman's ability is judged on how he runs the «piazzale», whether infact the quarry is a going concern or not.

All the work is sorted out on the «piazzale»: the blocks of marble are made ready, the debris is collected before being disposed of, and new equipment is stored in out-houses made of marble waste. Last century what were thought to have been Roman buildings were found in the Lunensi quarries, and they are

practically identical to those built today.

After the introduction of black powder new storage sheds had to be built as well as strong shelters for the men during explosions, which were heralded by horns or old-fashioned bugles; today all machinery is roofed-over, chain saws, engines, air compression stations and attachments. The «piazzale» is like a stage for quarrymen; the foreman, who is responsable for the technical organization, decides where to cut the marble bank and singles out the individual blocks like his forefathers the technitēs (see fig. 126). The chain saw expert is in charge of cutting; the «rock man» is in charge both of the removal, the shifting and falling of blocks; the «*tecchiaiolo*» (*tecchia* worker) is in charge of breaking operations the quarry hands cooperate with the skilled and unskilled workers to clear the road to the working sites using two-wheel carts appropriatly called «*galeotte*» (galley slaves) (see fig. 104) or the more recent decauville railvans, they take rubble to the mine dump (see fig. 105), and generally keep the «*piazzale*» tidy. The «*piazzale*» is covered with a layer of «*calpestio*» compact crushed marble that is fairly elastic and does not damage or chip the blocks of marble while they are being shifted. Nowadays roads reach most quarries and the clearing is done with mechanical shovels (fig. 106).

The division of labour and responsability is still the same as in pre-industrial times: all hands start from the bottom of the ladder and gradually work their way up to the more responsable positions that can be achieved only after all the different quarrying skills have been successfully mastered.

Not much is known about quarrying in Roman times; skilled marble workers were called *marmorarii* (including stone cutters, masons and sculptors and epigraphic engravers) and marble merchants *negotiator marmorarius*. Marble workers belonged to the most prestigious class of artisans and were organised in *collegia* (guilds) even though there were many slaves, freedmen, foreigners as well as free born men among them. This meant that the manual labour was done by slaves, as in Greece, supervised by skilled hands, and occasionally even soldiers. At the beginning of the Roman Empire when marble was much in demand it was not difficult for a slave to improve his position and train as a skilled worker,

110. Squaring a block of marble with a pneumatic drill and wedges called «puntazze».

thereby bettering himself both socially and economically.

Preparing the Blocks of Marble

As they are, the freshly cut blocks have no immediate commercial value: they are usually too large, flawed, oddly shaped or have been damaged in the quarry, and must be prepared for the market. This process is preliminary to the final stage, but from the point of view of organization it is still part of the initial working phase. The size and quality must be checked and then each block is initialled by the foreman who must also supervise loading operations, exactly the same as two thousand years ago. Blocks that have been numbered, dated and initialled by the foreman and an inspector, and bearing the name of the quarry from which they came from, have been found at Synnada in Asia Minor. The Roman period provides yet more archeological evidence: initialled blocks have been found in various quarries, in ships that have been wrecked on known commercial routes, in Rome along the banks of the Tiber, both near the harbour and at the Marmorata near Campus Martius.

Blocks of marble were sent to Rome from every corner of the Empire where they were checked and initialled again. In 132 A.D. an inventory was made of a marble store-house, and according to this source, a North-African block of yellow marble was used in Ostia near Rome three hundred years after it had been extracted. In Roman times marble was not extracted in roughly standard sized blocks, on the contrary the *marmorarii quadratarii* who prepared the blocks in the quarry cut the marble to fit the buyers' demands (mainly sarcophagi, architraves and capitals). From the Middle Ages until last century the blocks of marble

111

112

113

114

were individually prepared to meet all requests, but when the market began to expand internationally in the 19th century, blocks were cut and classified according to set standards (slab cutting yielding percentage), and on the whole, cutting techniques did not differ much from those used to extract marble. The oldest method is wedging, (wedges were called «*punciotti*») that is still used for small divisions when mechanic means are superfluous. A V-shaped groove is cut with a mallet and chisel, and then the wedges are inserted; they are placed between iron bands that ensure an equal distribution of pressure (see figg.

65, 107, 108). The block is then split along the line of wedges. If compressed air drills are used a series of holes are made instead of the V-shaped groove, and «*puntazze*» (up side down wedges) are inserted (see figg. 109, 110).

In some quarries the total span of a chain saw called «*tesa*», can reach the quarry floor and the marble is placed on a bed of debris between two pillars with tangent screw pulleys, and then cut (see fig. 111).

Another method that dates back to Roman times is a manual steel saw attached to a wooden trestle: while the marble is being cut a mixture of

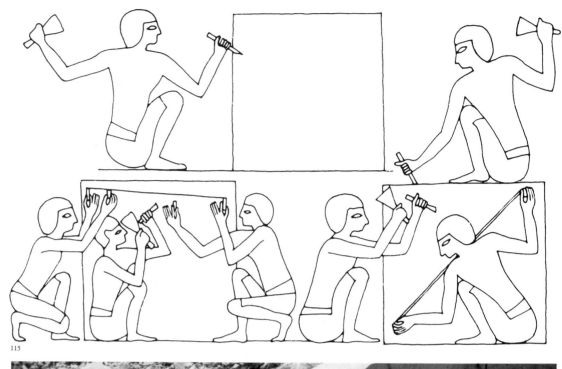

115

115. *Fifthteenth century B.C. Egyptian representation of the techniques and tools used to square blocks of marble. (See fig. 167).*

116. *Preliminary preparation of a large block that has been dislodged with explosives after it has been cut with a wire saw: the flawed parts are removed with mallets (beginning of the 20th century).*

117. *Extraction of large blocks after having made an oblique cut at the base of the block.*

116

J.F. KENNEDY CENTE

118

119

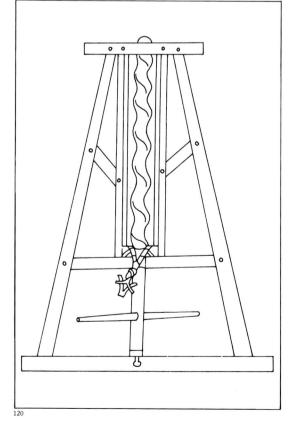

120

118. *A chisel and mallet are used for the final squaring.*

119. *Separation with the help of the lever from a block that has already been sawn.*

120. *Drawing of a screwjack by Villard de Honnecourt (13th century) (from B. Gille, Machines, in «A History of Technology», Oxford 1954).*

121

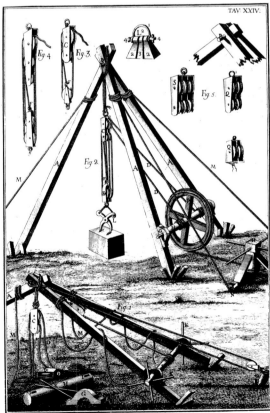

122

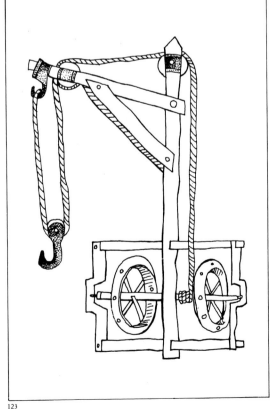

123

121. Hoisting a block with a rack jack called «binda».

122. Various machines, described by Vitruvius, used for hoisting blocks (B. Galliani Editions 1970).

123. Representation of a crane in a manuscript of 1430. (from B. Gille).

quartz, sand and water is used for feeding (see figg. 112, 113); it was frequently used to reduce the size of blocks up until the beginning of this century and will be delt with in greater detail in the next chapter. Two more recent methods for reducing the size of blocks are the electric diamond saw and the fixed rapid wire saw (see fig. 114): this saw has two ends and is fed with water and carborundum an extremely hard abrasive, and progresses at the speed of fifty centimetres an hour. The most recent method, the diamond wire saw, is faster than the two mentioned above.

Preparing a block of marble entails cutting and reducing its size, eliminating all the flawed areas, micro-fractures and natural cavities called «peli furbi», sly hairs, or «tarli», macro-crystal patches and veins called «lucciche», (shiners), and finally coping; the coping technitian checks a block of marble for any flaws that have been overlooked, and outlines the final shape and cutting planes with a ruler and set square; good technical, aesthetical and commercial exploitation of the block depend on his skill. In the quarries of ancient Rome, Greece and Egypt there was always a skilled worker with a similar job called quadratarius (see fig. 115); this explains why roughly hewn decorative motifs, the so-called «pre-fabbricati» pre-fabricated pieces, were made in old quarries.

Hand coping is done with a sledge hammer to remove flawed parts and knock off the rough edges, while a chisel and hammer are used for finishing off (see figg. 116, 118). Starting from the corners, every side of the block is levelled and made ready for the final smoothing down. Nowadays coping is done with electric diamond saws and rapid wire saws to reduce the sizes and finish off large blocks.

124. A crane hoisting a ten ton block of marble on to a cableway on Mt. Sagro in the Apuan Alps (beginning of the 20th century).

Transport

Transporting blocks from a quarry to their destination, occasionally over bad roads, is an exacting job because of the weight and size of marble, and requires a great amount of power and technical know-how, and involves lifting and moving the blocks to the foot of the quarry, transporting them to the bottom of the valley and then over flat land or water. Fortunatly the technical innovations of the 19th century have reduced the cost of transport, that however has always been high (see Ch. 4 & 5). Once the blocks have been cut away from the quarry face they are taken to the quarry floor; the most common method is to dislodge, turn over and slide the block downwards with the help of levers, jacks and black powder (see fig. 117); blocks are only hoisted in open-pit quarrying. The blocks are hoisted and and turned over during cutting and coping operations and transport.

Hoisting

Levers are the oldest and most simple hoisting machines, and have been used for quarrying ever since the Bronze Age (see figg. 119, 130); they are worked from the bottom upwards and can move a block a few centimetres at a time, and an improved version, the jack-lever, can move a block by a few decimetres. By the end of the Middle Ages crank operated jack-screws and racks (see fig. 120) were used for quarrying, and a modern version, railroad jacks, are able to hoist up to ten tons at a time (see fig. 121). But now they have been sustituted by the more efficient hydraulic-jack. Another simple hoisting machine operated from the bottom is a lever and an inclined plane: this also dates back to the Bronze Age. When it was not possible to load directly from a higher level (the so called poggio di carico,

125. *A modern trestle crane.*

125

110

loading point) inclined planes were used to hoist the blocks on to the means of transport, as in the Roman quarries in North Africa.

The first hoisting machines operating from above were used for building and date back to Ancient Greece; traces have been found (building joints) in many classical temples. There is also an accurate description in the Tenth book of Vitruvius: wooden trestles with either two mobile angle posts and stays, or three mullions supporting burtons and systems of ropes and pulleys, worked by monkey winches (see fig. 122). A similar collection including a jackscrew is housed in the Museo dell'Opera del Duomo in Florence, and was used to build the Church of Santa Maria del Fiore. Hoisting machines were used in construction sites for loading and unloading marble, and what was lost in speed was gained in power. Loads could not be moved horizontally unless by swinging, and although rotary cranes were shown in 15th century illustrations, it is doubtful whether they could lift heavy loads (see fig. 123), since iron cranes were not made until the middle of the 19th century. At the same time the marble industry was revolutionised by machinery: iron gibs and pillar cranes fixed on to masonry bases were installed in key positions at loading and unloading posts (near saw-mills, railways, cableways and landing stages) (see figg. 124, 150); at first cranes were worked by gipsy winches, that were gradually substituted by steam engines: oddly enough loads were still jacked up by hand in the quarries themselves.

Only in the past thirty years with the second Industrial Revolution have cranes become an essential feature of the quarry floor, and are built with iron lattice gibs attached to cement bases and lined up with adjustable steel rods supporting burtons powered by electric winches (see fig. 125);

bridge cranes were used in open-pit quarries and occasionally in underground quarries too, and above all in large storage areas (see fig. 172); self propelled cranes are easily movable within the quarry (see fig. 152), but could not be used until access roads had been built up the mountain-side.

Marble Skids

The most simple way to move blocks from the quarry front to the quarry floor is sliding them down the mountain side, rather, down gorges that have been filled with debris and rubble, called *ravaneti* (ravines) (see fig. 126); but the marble is easily chipped and occasionally badly smashed.

Over 3500 years ago the Egyptians found a way of transporting marble statues weighing dozens of tons by binding them to wooden skids, dragged along, or held back with ropes as shown in some surviving illustrations (see fig. 127). In Greece the remains of carefully paved inclined planes with holes for clutch poles are still visible in the white marble quarry of Mount Pentelicus (see fig. 128), that was used to build the Acropolis in Athens, and that of Mount Porfirite in the Oriental desert of Egypt that was exploited by the Romans. The Romans transported monolithic columns weighing two hundred tons for the Pronaos of the Pantheon over nearly two hundred kilometres km. from the granite quarries of Mount Claudianus, that had been named in honour of the Emperor Claudius, to the Nile.

Skids are still used today in steep parts, or to recover blocks of marble from abandoned quarries that are not equipped with modern machinery. It is not possible to say for how long they were used on flat ground where the loads had to be pulled by hand; down the mountain-side the marble had merely to be kept in check.

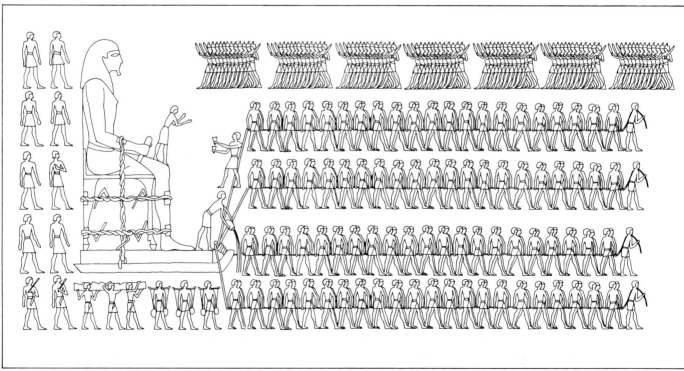

126. *A large block of marble being prepared in a mine dump at the beginning of the 20th century. After it was initialled, the quarrymen eliminated the flaws supervised by the foreman.*

127. *The colossal statue of a Pharo being dragged on a sledge (from an illustration of El-Berscheh, about 2000 B.C.).*

128. *Reproduction of the ancient «lizzature» (stoneboats) used by the Greeks in the quarries of Mt. Pentelycus (from R. Martin).*

129. *S. Salvioni: transportation using sledges in the quarries of Carrara at the beginning of the 19th century.*

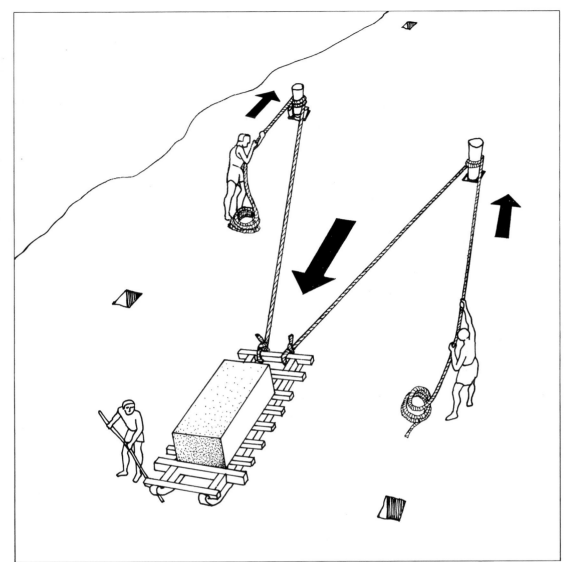

128

129

130

130. *Starting the stoneboat off from the quarry floor, called «piazzale».*

131. *«Lizzatura» along a slope covered with debris; the stoneboat is held back with ropes made of hemp and runs on crosspieces of wood (beginning of the 20th century).*

132. *Artificial stoneboat run with fixed crosspieces of wood.*

131

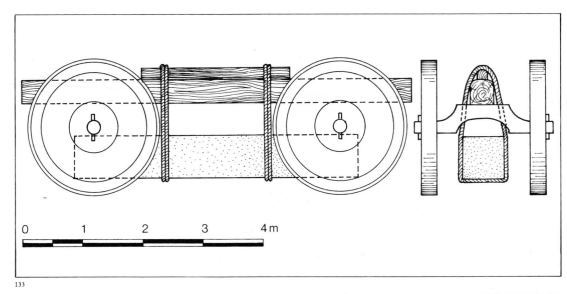

133

134

133. *Reproduction of a cart used to transport marble by the ancient Greek (from R. Martin).*

134. *A typical marble cart used in the valleys of Carrara; the illustration dates back to the beginning of the 19th century.*

A print of a Carrara quarry of the year 1800 shows a block of marble on a sledge pulled by oxen, at the end of a steep slope (called *lizza*) near the loading post (the *poggio di carico*) (see fig. 129).

The original Apuan *lizza*, (stoneboat), is probably the only kind of sledge that has not been altered over the centuries: one or more blocks of marble — weighing up to 25 tons — were hoisted with jacks on to skids of oak, holm-oak or beech six to twelve metres long; the skids rested on greased or soaped wooden crosspieces called *parati*, and the load was fixed on with cables called *canapi* made of hemp; three of these were used to hold it back during the descent. The *lizza* slid down a special gorge a few metres wide with a gradient that was sometimes over 100%; every ten metres or at corners short poles made of hard wood (known as *piri*) were

135

135. A two wheeled marble cart for small loads.

fixed into the ground and the cables were wound round them; with the help of levers the stoneboat started its downward journey and the stoneboat workers, (see fig. 130) who prepared the run called *carica* with the help of unskilled workers, took the cross-pieces from behind and put them in front of the *lizza*, and eased the sledge gently round the corners (see fig. 131); meanwhile the head of the team called *capo lizza*, who supervised the whole operation, shouted the conventional orders to the *mollatori*, the cable workers, who eased the cables round the wooden poles and controlled the speed from one pole to the next. If the team was expert large blocks of marble could be lowered at a regular pace, and although the creaking and shouting sounded omnious and echoed throughout the valley, the marble usually reached the bottom intact;

117

136

136. A two wheeled cart
called «mambruca» used on
roads to transport slabs of
marble.

137. A large cart pulled by a
team of thirtyfour oxen; it
dates back to the beginning
of the 20th century.

137

unfortunatly sometimes the *lizzatori* themselves were not so lucky. The descent (see fig. 132) ended slightly above the road so the blocks could be loaded easily on to the means of transport.

In other regions, Veneto and Lombardy for instance, where the slopes were not so steep different methods were used; long poles were fixed under the sides of the runners, instead of crosspieces, to work the stone-boat along; or the stoneboat was controlled by one central fixed runner. During the Renaissance the Apuan method was used in Istria.

Marble Trucks

Juvenal, in the Third satira, explains that he is afraid of what might happen if the axel of a loaded Ligurian marble truck gave way in the crowded streets of Rome; Juvenal is a very realistic writer and it is interesting to speculate whether he was describing something that had actually happened or if he merely imagined the disaster; however Juvenile's is not the oldest existing record about the trucks used to transport marble over flat ground. An inscription of 332 B.C. listing the expenses incurred for the construction of the Eleusis temple in Greece described a cart drawn by oxen used to transport blocks of marble weighing about five tons, from the quarries of Mount Pentelicus to the construction site about 40 km away. The description corresponds exactly to the small terracotta models found in archeological sites at the beginning of this century in marble production areas (see fig. 133).

From another written source, a commercial contract, much information has been gleaned about the carts used in Carrara at the end of the Middle Ages, when the quarries started to function again. A so called *carrus* was used for normal loads: it had four joined together by a strong axel called *antenna*. *Carrettas* were used for heavy loads, but little is known about them. The former are similar to the Apuan carts used throughout the 19th and 20th centuries to transport marble from the loading posts at the bottom of the *lizza* to saw-mills, workshops and harbours, and some invaluable descriptions and iconographic documentation on shipping methods have survived (see fig. 134); the *carrettas* of this period have only two wheels and were used for smaller loads (see fig. 135), while a cart with two large wheels (called *mambruca*) was used to transport slabs of marble (see fig. 136). According to how much the block weighed to one or more teams of oxen were harnessed to the vehicle (see fig. 137); during the Middle Ages one team of oxen was thought to be able to pull about 800 kg, excluding the cart, over flat ground. This came to be accepted as the conventional unit of measurement for commerce and custom duties; it varied only in the 15th and 17th centuries when the Genoese method called *carrata* (truck-load), based on the volume rather than the weight, was adopted instead: a load varied from twentyfive to thirty square spans, about 3/4 of a ton. The Genoese span is still used in the quarries of Carrara today.

It is difficult to say whether the illustrations of *De Architectura* by Vitruvius published throughout the 16th, 17th and 18th centuries showing huge blocks of marble packed into moveable open crates used, according to the author, to transport the enormous architrave of the temple of Arthemisia at Ephesus, and also during the construction of the Greek temples in Sicily, influenced contemporary methods of transport over flat land or not: if so, no trace has remained in the marble producing areas, and probably any interest is academic rather than practical.

138. A mechanic stoneboat run along an «inclined plane» or «funicular».

138

120

139

139. Whenever a mechanic run is not straight, it is important that the steel cables do not come off the guiding pulley.

140. A small cableway to supply high up quarries.

140

The Mechanization of Over-Land Transport

The boom of new means of transport, capable of standing up to the most testing enviroment, exploded during the 19th century, but new equipment and machinery was not introduced into the marble industry until the beginning of the 20th century.
The first innovations were funicular and cable railways used to move blocks of marble from the quarry floor to the bottom of the quarry; steam tractors and special marble railroads were used to transport marble to the bottom of the valley or across the country-side; lastly decauville-type self-tipping trolleys (see fig. 105), initially worked by hand and later powered by an engine, winches and cables, were used to move debris and rubble from the quarry to the mine dump.
Although the equipment and means of transport were mechanised the technique did not change: the empirical but extremely practical system based on the division of labour dated back to ancient times.
The most radical transformation in the history of marble took place only twenty years ago when roads were built leading directly to the *piazzale*, rather than to the foot of the quarry, thus cutting the loading, unloading and transport operations by half.

Funicular and cable railways

Steel cables are essential for transporting marble by funicular or cable railways, and have also become vital in other sectors since the 19th century, for fixing loads, securing blocks ready for hoisting, and for dislodging blocks with winches. They are mainly used to transport blocks over steep slopes, and were initially used instead of *canapi*, (ropes made of

141

142

hemp), that were not hard wearing and occasionally broke during the *lizzatura* with disastrous consequences; subsequently they were used for cable and funicular railways and have a tensile strength of sixty tons.
Funiculars (also called «inclined planes») are operated over steep slopes by means of two trolleys connected by steel cables that run up and down a central track; at the top there is a tension pulley and, as the loaded trolley travels downhill, it pulls up the empty one; at the point were they cross half way down the slope, the haulageway is divided into two tracks by switches (see fig. 138). The

haulageway is usually very tortuous since it depends on the layout of the land, and the connecting cables follow the track by means of tailshaves (see fig. 139).

Ever since the beginning of the century funiculars have been were installed in preference to cableways since the chances of a cable slipping off a pulley under stress are much less. However cableways were easier to install over rough ground, and the trolleys were attached to straight aereal tramways. Initially the main difficulty was caused by large blocks of marble that could overstrain the tramway, (there were no problems as far as light loads were

concerned — i.e. small blocks and supplies —) (see fig. 140).

Cableways capable of carrying heavy loads were built only in a few quarries; today all the technical difficulties have been overcome, but it is no longer financially viable to use cableways instead of roads.

The most spectacular cableway ever built known as *Balzone* (Great Leap) was erected in 1907 on the north face of Mount Sagro in the Apuan Alps; unfortunatly it has been recently dismantled to recover the metal. It was built to replace the old and extramely dangerous *lizza* carved out of sheer rock, and practically

145

144. The marble railway of Carrara.
145. Marble carts pulled by steam tractors at the beginning of the 20th century.

vertical in some places; the *Balzone* spanned a chasm 650 metres long in one single leap; it was restored in 1930 and the difference in level form top to bottom was 700 metres; there were two tramways for trolleys carrying loads up to twenty tons — they had been tested for sixty tons gross-weight — and a third tramway for loads up to ten tons (see figs. 141, 142, 143). All that is left now is the hoisting counterweight shaft, fifteen metres deep, carved out of sheer rock.

The upkeep of cableways was extremely expensive, as the cables had to be replaced periodically, and this is the reason why the cheaper method of *lizzatura* was still used up until after the Second World War.

Tractors, Standard and Narrow Gauge Railroads

The *lizzatura* slopes were by no means easy, but transporting the marble down to the foot of a quarry did not require a lot of energy since the blocks slid by themselves. The opposite is true for journeys across country, roads are smooth but a considerable amount of energy is required, and is detrimental to the

146

146. Marble carts pulled by diesel tractors during the first half of the 20th century.

147. A modern self loading lorry.

148. Modern roads can reach even the most isolated and high up quarries, and with a single means of transport marble is taken directly from the quarry to the workshops.

147

126

means of transport. In the past long lines of oxen were used, and breeding costs had to be budgeted for. As soon as possible transport was converted to the more economical steam engines. After the railroad boom in the second half of the 19th century there were two alternative solutions: railroads or tractors. Plans were made to build narrow gauge and normal gauge branch lines, along with saw mills, workshops and loading posts at the feet of quarries in marble areas. One of the most impressive was the normal gauge railroad built in the valleys of Carrara between 1876 and 1890. Not counting the branch lines, the main line alone was 20 km. long; it went up to 450 mts. above sea level (see fig. 144) winding its way round numerous hair-pin bends, over sixteen bridges and through fifteen tunnels. Today, like many constructions that date back to the first part of the Industrial Revolution, it is outdated and parts have been dismantled and converted into a road; the more imposing structures have become part of the 20th century quarry landscape.

The other solution was to continue using the old tracks, but replace the teams of oxen with steam tractors. These steel giants were nearly 4 mt. tall, with huge wheels equipped with transversal bars to prevent them from slipping.

In the Apuan Alps they were used for a long time and at the beginning of the century they were known as *ciabattone* (big slippers) (see fig. 145) because they moved so slowly; the *ciabattone* were capable of pulling a line of loaded wagons attached together like a train; the wagons were traditionally made in wood and the wheels were usually iron.

Ciabattone were mostly used when roads did not reach the foot of the quarry: soon after the first diesel engines appeared and further revolutionised marble transportation (see fig. 146).

149. *A Flemish painting of the 18th century, illustrating how ships were loaded with marble at Marina dell'Avenza near Carrara.*

150. *Marble being loaded on board sailing ships moored to a landing-stage that was linked to the railway network of Carrara (end of the 19th century).*

151. *Marina of Carrara at the beginning of the 20th century: the marble railway and wooden bridge with grinders to load ships.*

Lorries and Quarry Roads

Quarries were equipped with machinary by the beginning of the 20th century, but the pre-industrial division of transport for steep slopes and gentle slopes did not change.

The technical inventions of the Industrial Revolution were fully exploited and colossal machines built with steel cables and powered by steam engines replaced the traditional means of transport. These giants only lasted seventy years, and compared with the new, technologically advanced machinery of the past twenty years, (that unified the two stages), they soon became obselete and too expensive to run.

Lorries and bulldozers were equipped with immensely powerful diesel engines, and the full potential of air compressors and engines was exploited; lorries could move more quickly up and down the old windy roads that linked the quarries to the bottom of the valleys, and bulldozers could climb even the steepest slopes over rubble and debris and carry down blocks of marble weighing ten or twenty tons, and, in a single journey, take them to the open saw-mills at the bottom of the valleys (see fig. 89). Some lorries were self-loading with incorporated hoisting machines to load blocks on at the back (see fig. 147).

The existance of a road meant that rotary cranes could be used to hoist blocks of marble, mechanical shovels to remove the debris to the mine dumps, and it was easier to deliver large and bulky pieces of equipment; new machinery reduced risks both for quarrymen and the blocks of marble, but, even at the best of times, quarrying still was a hard and dangerous job.

The landscape of today has been further modified by sharply winding roads carved out of rock that slowly

151

snake their way up mountains to considerable heights.

Marble Ships and Boats

In *Naturalis Historia* Pliny explaines how Ptolomy Philadelpus in the third century B.C. had an obelisque thirtyfive metres high shipped along the Nile and erected in Alexandria. According to Pliny this was more difficult than cutting and carving the monolith of red granite in the quarries of Assuan by order of King Necthebis. To transport the obelisque Ptolemy's architects dug a canal from the Nile to the obelisque that was lying horizontally on the ground, so its sides were resting on the two banks. Then two wide boats were loaded with granite twice the weight of the obelisque itself. As soon as the boats were under the obelisque the blocks of granite were thrown overboard.

Pliny also mentions some special ships commissioned by Augustus to transport a number of obelisques from Egypt to Rome. From a technical point of view this was an extraordinary achievement, but the number of monolithic columns and other smaller blocks coming from Egyptian, North African and Asian quarries in Rome today, show that marble was frequently shipped from one country to another in Roman times.

It was more difficult to travel overland than by sea, and even the blocks from the relatively near Lunensi quarries in Liguria were shipped to the harbour Emporium and the Marmorate on the river Tiber near Rome; the same thing happened in all the marble importing cities in the Roman Empire.

Not much is known about loading and unloading techniques, but submarine archeologists have discovered a number of wrecks dating from the 1st century B.C. to the 7th century A.D.

carrying loads of 100 or 200 tons of marble. It has not yet been established if the ships were specially designed, or merely ordinary boats hired for the journey. After the fall of the Roman Empire in the West an exceptional cargo was shipped from the quarries of Istria to Ravenna: the monolithic cupola of Theodoric's mausoleum (see fig. 191).

Scraps of news concerning shipments of marble and shipwrecks date back to the Crusades when it was customary for knights to vandalise monuments and send the most beautiful pieces home.

The oldest information on ships made specially to transport marble, dates back to the 14th and 15th centuries, respectively for the *Opere del Duomo* of Florence and Milan. Traditionally the origin of the words *a Ufo* — free of charge — is a corruption of the initials A.U.F. — ad usum fabricae (for factory use) — that marked all tax-exempt blocks of marble.

Fifteenth and 17th century notarial deeds of Carrara provide useful information about ships and their cargo: flat-bottomed boats were used to sail up the Arno; *leuti, saette* (arrows) and *naviglioni* (big boats) that could transport from a minimum of 8 to a maximum of 100 tons and were used for coastal traffic; the purchaser usually supplied the equipment necessary for unloading the marble at its destination.

Throughout the 15th, 16th and 17th centuries Genoa was considered one of the most important marble commercial centres in the Mediterranean; recent archeological excavations round the loading/landing stage in the medieval port have revealed a solid stone quay built on a foundation of wooden piles.

The first complete picture of how marble was loaded and shipped in marble producing areas is quite recent: it was drawn by an 18th century traveller from Saxony, who, during a visit to Carrara was struck by the fact

152. Loading operations in the modern port of Carrara.

133

that all marble was quarried and transported to the foot of the quarry by hand; he went on to say how a small ship called *navicello* was dragged up on to the beach, then practically buried with sand. The block of marble was then heaved on board, and the workmen, after having removed most of the sand, dug a canal to the sea. An 18th century illustration depicts a similar operation where a boat is dragged beneath a wooden gin that was used to hoist the marble on board (see fig. 149).

Written sources mention gins having been used as early as the 16th century to load and unload marble at Avenza near Carrara, and in Rome. In 1851 a wooden whraft with an iron crane was built at Carrara for loading and unloading the ships at anchor (see figg. 150, 151). A proper harbour was only built between 1920 and 1930, but even then special wooden marble boats continued to be used, and are occasionally still used today (see fig. 152).

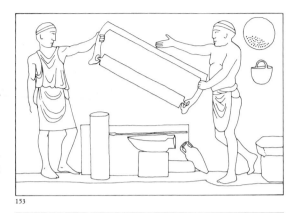

153

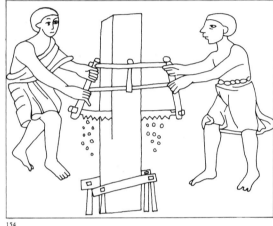

154

Working Techniques

It is not necessary to follow a fixed pattern to work marble: it can be done at any time, place and in any way, and the end products differ radically from one another in shape, size, working technique, use and treatment. In the past, before the Industrial Revolution over-size or oddly shaped blocks were worked directly on the quarry floor or at the loading posts at the foot of the quarry in order to reduce bulk, weight and travelling expenses. Pre-industrial means of transport by land and sea were very rough and the marble was easily damaged, so the next stage was done directly at the destination or on the construction sites (sculpture and decorative pieces), and many classical statues and capitals have been

damaged by travel during the Renaissance.

Marble was easily available in small towns near quarries, especially in small pieces that had practically no commercial value whatsoever, and the local people began to produce large quantities of small articles like tiles and mortars, that date back to the Middle Ages. Semi-finished slabs of marble were sold for the buyer to shape and polish, and the local artisans produced pieces of sculpture inspired by local culture and tradition, that were sold on regional markets (see figg. 21, 239).

Extracting and working marble were two separate industries, but there have been some exceptions; in ancient times when quarries were either public property or part of the Imperial revneue, and large amounts of roughly hewn blocks were ordered for public buildings; in the Middle Ages when the religious orders bought or gained

155

153. Sawing slabs of marble
in the workshop of a
«marmorarius» in Roman
times (from the archeological
digs at Ostia, J.B. Ward
Perkins).

154. Sawing marble into
slabs as described in an 11th
century Italian manuscript
(R.H.G. Thomson, Medieval
craftsmanship, «A History of
Technology», Oxford 1954).

155. Sawing marble into
slabs with a multiple blade
frame suspended from a
mobile girder (beginning of
the 20th century).

156. An old fashioned single
blade marble saw powered
by a diesel engine dating
back to the beginning of the
20th century.

156

the right to exploit a quarry *ad usum fabricae*; in the Indusrial Age when the owner, capitalist, or concessionary agent wanted to carry out «in loco» the complete productive cycle and set up a saw mill and workshop near the quarry.

Saw Mills

Four thousand fivehundred years ago during the Ancient Kingdom in Egypt before marble was used for sculpture small slabs of basalt that had been split and polished, were used as floor and wall tiles. It was a long and difficult task and was never fully developed.

Soft rock that had been cut, not split, was first used for building during the Mycenae period in Crete. A copper saw with emery teeth and $1^1/_2$ metres long has been found in the archaeological site at Tirynthos. Also the Greeks used metal saws for cutting soft rock; Theophrast mentions them in his book on rocks, and traces of sawing are still discernible on the masonry of some classical temples. Saws were not used to cut marble into slabs, and Greek buildings were mainly made of carved and polished blocks.

The Romans at first only used marble for important public buildings, but, by the end of the Republic, private families began to embellish their houses with coloured marbles as a sign of power and wealth. By the beginning of the Empire it was the height of fashion to cover the walls of ones home with *crustae* (layers or crusts) of precious marble, and the philosopher Seneca complained that wealthy Romans wasted huge sums of money on redecorating and refurbishing. But the costs of production were reduced and the trend spread to the less wealthy classes, and demand increased: over fifty square metres of slabs could be

157. Modern automatic frame with seventy blades used to cut marble into slabs.

produced from 1 cubic metre of marble.

Pliny records that king Mausolus of Karya in Asia Minor was the first to decorate his palace with slabs of marble, and that Mamurra, Caesar's prefect in Gaul, first used them for his house at the Celio in Rome.

Pliny confirms that the roots of this sudden fashion were social and economic, and severly admonishes the man who invented marble saws, thereby multiplying superfluous luxury. He goes on to say that marble saws cut by dragging sand over the blocks and explains at great lenght which sands are most suitable.

Traces of sawing have been found in the «antique yellow» (Giallo Antico) quarries in Tunisia, and an iron blade four metres long and four millimetres thick was found near the German *limes*, defensive work along the Imperial boarder, in the granite quarry of Olden-Wald.

A bas-relief at Ostia shows a marble cutter (*marmorarius subaedanus*) and his assistant at work, surrounded by all the necessary equipment: a saw with a wooden frame about $1^1/_2$ metres long, a sift and bucket for sand, an anphora for water, another anphora cut in half lengthwise to pour the mixture of sand and water and a piece of string to mark the marble (see fig. 153). The similarity between these tools and those used at Carrara up until the beginning of this century is striking (see figg. 113, 156).

This process was used until frames with several blades powered by water were introduced a few centuries ago (see figg. 112, 154); the only important post-Roman technical innovation was a wooden trestle from which the saw was suspended with ropes, so the blades could be lowered gradually at a constant speed, and did not have to be adjusted by hand. It is difficult to say whether this machine was invented during the Middle Ages

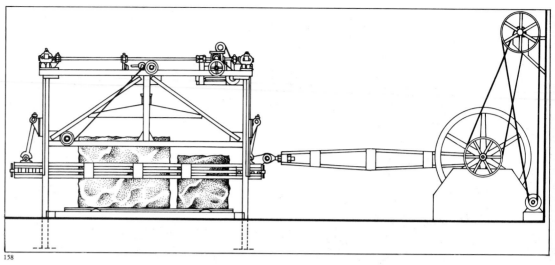

158

(copied from frame saws for wood) or if it was a further adaptation of Roman technique; however this would not have been possible in the Apuan Alps where the production *iatus* is centuries old, so the technique must have been imported from another marble centre.

In the 4th century A.D. Ausonius talks about the unmistakable sound of the marble saw mill powered by the river Mosella; experts doubt the authenticity of this passage, and, since it is an isolated example, do not think it to be of great value. Other written sources testify to the existence of multiple blade saw frames near Milan in the 15th century and near Carrara in the 17th century. Water powered saw mills for wood had been built near Pistoia about two centuries earlier.

In 1588 Agostino Ramelli published a plan for a marble water saw mill using frames with multiple parallel blades that all cut simultaneously, but the drawings were so complex that Ramelli's contemporaries probably took them for a piece of academic virtuosity rather than a practical labour saving device. In the Apuan Alps up until the 18th century all water powered saws had only one blade fixed in a wooden frame like hand saws, hung from moveable girders (called *ugnero* saws); first

one half of the block was sawn, then it was turned over and the other side was done. A spindle shaped mark was left in the middle that is still visible on some Roman blocks that have not been polished.

Technical innovations for marble saws only reached the Apuan Alps after the beginning of the 19th century; tradition has it that a local workman first thought of the multiple blade frame, and the owner of an Apuan quarry was the first to replace the mobile girder with a mobile arm powered by a crank and connecting rod (see fig. 155). Eventually, following the advice of French and English engineers, iron crossheads with cast iron columns were installed. The slow vertical driving wheels (copied from water-mills) were replaced by fast moving horizontal paddle wheels powered by penstocks (called *trombini*) that increased sawing speed.

Some frames were over five metres long and had about forty baldes and could cut regular shaped blocks; a slab one centimetre thick was awarded a prize at the Paris Exhibition in 1866. The saw was gradually perfected over the years and the most important innovation was the *cala automatica*, an automatic lowering device; diesel and electric engines replaced water powered machinery, but, even so, in

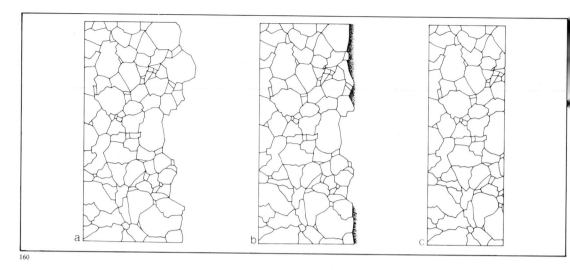

160

one hundred years the speed had only
increased from 1 centimetre to 2
centimetres an hour: it took
two or three weeks to cut a
2 by 4 metre block into slabs
(see figg. 157, 158).
In 1869 diamond saws similar to the
Mycenae copper and emery saw found
in Tirynthos were experimented with,
and although they were quicker
(which is important for cutting hard
marble) they were more fragile and
could not cut very thin slabs.
The method was abandoned after the
invention of industrial diamonds
embedded in a copper alloy, that
gradually wore away revealing the
diamonds. The edges of thin metal
disks with diametres varying from 20
centimetres to 2 metres were covered
with the copper alloy; the disks were
powered by electric motors and cooled
off with jets of water (see fig. 159).
Small diametre disks were used either
to sharpen the edges of the slabs, or to
cut them into small size tiles; large
diametre disks were used to cut small
blocks or rejects for paving, and while
disk saws were faster than multiple
blade frames they could only make
one cut at a time. Alternate linear
diamond blades are used to cut large
blocks and are ten times faster than
iron blades and fed with sand or iron
or cast iron powder for the harder
varieties of marble.

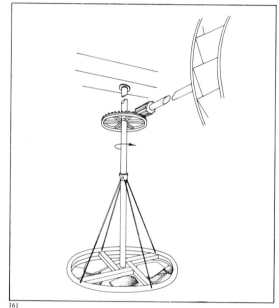

161

Smoothing and Polishing

Before polishing marble it is
necessary to make sure the surface is
perfectly smooth with no lines or
scratches; smoothing is done by
sanding. To save time and labour
this process can be simplified by
chiselling away all bumps and notches;
large grain abrasives are used first
and then finer and finer ones until
all traces of scouring have
disappeared.
Crystals can be cut to the same
level only by smoothing: percussion,
splitting and cutting either seperates
the single crystals or crushes them to

162

160. The section of calcitic marble enlarged 10 times: a) on the right, the surface after it has been split; b) after percussion working; c) after it has been smoothed and polished.

161. The model of a smoothing machine called «frullone» powered by running water (G. Bottiglioni).

162. A modern workshop for squaring, smoothing and polishing.

powder, and in both cases the surface feels rough and granular.

In the case of soft marble, like saccharoidal calcareous marble, different size quartz sand and rottenstone are sufficient; for hard marble, emery that contains corundum, or the more recent hard artificial abrasives (carbonundum) are used. Pliny mentions stones from the island of Naxos and from Armenia.

In the 18th century in the Apuan area *marmette* — floor tiles — were produced; pieces of marble were split into small slabs and the surfaces were smoothed with *dente di cane* (dogs' tooth) or *gradino* (step) chisels; the slabs were polished by rubbing one against the other with water and sifted river sand.

At the same period the larger slabs that had been cut with iron blades were smoothed by water powerd machines called *frulloni* (big blenders). A disk with dented spokes rotated round a vertical axle and the slabs of marble were wetted with sand and water and dragged one over the other (see fig. 161).

An improved version of the *frullone*, used up to the 20th century, was powered by an electric motor and worked with a pivoted arm. Different sized abrasives and felt were fixed on

141

163

the horizontal rotating disk; marble slabs that have been cut, not split, do not require hard abrasives.

In the past twenty years automatic conveyer belts have been introduced in this sector; slabs pass under rotating disks covered with finer and finer abrasives, and once smooth they are polished with felt (see fig. 162).

A smooth surface is invariably opaque (*matta*) and does not reflect the light since there are still microscopic scratches left by the action of the abrasives: light is diffused, not reflected. Colours become brilliant and the texture shiny when marble is polished, and in comparison the surface of opaque marble looks dead and whitish. Achromic crystals become transparent when polished, and the marble surface gives the impression of depth, one of its most beautiful qualities.

Mirror-like surfaces are produced by rubbing marble with a wet cloth together with substances like sulphur, ground metal oxides, rottenstone and oxalic acid: the reason why this happens is not known. Such methods date back to the end of the Renaissance when they were first used for polishing white marble. Previously marble was only smoothed and colours were applied on a thin layer of

164

plaster. After the 4th century B.C. the parts that had not been coloured were covered with oil or wax.

Workshops

Except for cutting, marble is entirely worked in workshops. The history of each different technical process, rather than the different categories of material and destination have caused this division.

Workshops were set up near quarries even in the most ancient settlements for rough-shaping

163. Egyptian illustrations of how marble statues were worked and polished (Thebes 16th century B.C.) (S. Lloyd).

164. A wooden mallet and bronze chisel from an Egyptian tomb of the 15th century B.C. (Archeological Museum of Turin). (See fig. 115).

columns, sarcophagi, basins and
occasionally architectural pieces;
marble workers built workshops on
construction sites to carve and finish
off pieces of masonry, and craftsmen
carved and sculptured on commission.
Saw mills were first built on the
construction sites or by merchants
next door to their workshops and
were worked by hand; later, during
the Middle Ages, they were moved
near rivers to exploit the driving
energy of water, and became
independent concerns.

Marble, like all other varieties of stone
and rock is shaped by cutting and
hewing pieces away, and one false
blow is enough to ruin the whole
block; the sources of energy and
equipment vary, but working
techniques are usually the same: it is
difficult to work without a model and
once a piece has been cut away it
cannot be put back.

*165. A representation Leon
Battista Alberti's method
used to transfer
measurements from a clay
statue to a block of marble
(G. Giubbini).*

*166. Piece of sculpture in
marble copied from the
chalk original (beginning of
the 20th century).*

*167. The colossal statue of
Apollo that lies unfinished in
the quarries of Naxos in the
Aegean.*

143

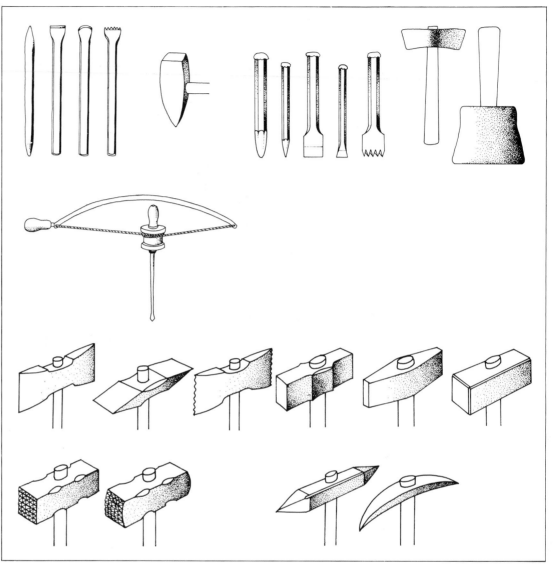

168

Good quality marble must have a homogeneous structure, no flaws or fractures (natural or caused by transport), that could mar the finished product. Marble must be worked along the cleavage planes, especially in the case of pieces used for static architecture and sculpture.

Marble shaping techniques have not changed for centuries: the block is rough-hewn with a hammer and chisel to remove all the sticking out pieces, then it is boasted with finer tools; it is finally buffed with abrasives and files, and then polished.

In ancient Egypt when tempered iron and steel were still unknown, balls of dolerite, a very hard variety of granite, were used to rough shape marble by beating the pieces that stuck out into powder as explained previously. Then it was boasted and finished off with pointed bronze tools or chisels and wooden hammers; harder stones were used for buffing.

Contemporary iconography (see fig. 163) illustrates the different stages, and interesting archeological remains have been found: rounded pieces of sculpture worked in shallow detail, unfinished pieces of equipment and tools; the most famous is a wooden mallet of the 15th century B.C. housed in the Egyptian Museum in

168. Antique and modern tools for working marble (R. Martin, H. Hodges and G. Tortora).

144

Turin; similar mallets are still used today (see figg. 115, 164).

Carbide and tempered iron tools were used after the 10th and 12th centuries B.C., and in ancient Greece traces of metal tools have been found on the remains of huge saccharoidal limestone statues that were never finished because the marble was flawed. A huge statue of Taxos in the Acropolis was carved on the Acropolis construction site near the quarry, while the Apollo of Naxos, 11 metres tall and weighing about 150 tons, was sculpted directly in the quarry on the island where the marble was extracted.

The statues were rough-shaped, layer by layer with quarry mallets — one side of the hammer was used for cutting, the other was flat — and pointed metal, worked obliquely to chip the pieces away more easily and the boasted surface was made ready for the plaster and colours. Statues were probably carved from three — dimensional drawings since all 4 sides were executed at the same time. The Egyptians in Mesopotamia were the first to use this technique, and the Greeks learnt it from them. One single drawing was used for bas-relief sculpture and statues in full relief (*tutto tondo*) were shown from four points of view. The surfaces that were going to be plastered were buffed with rottenstone, the diffcult corners were done with a chisel, and a drill was used for working in depth; files were used for buffing only after the 5th century B.C.

Clay models were the greatest innovation of the classical period, and are illustrated on some contemporary vase paintings. One could view a clay model from every angle and make alterations if necessary; a plumb line was used to measure the concave and convex spaces, so they could be more accuratly reproduced in marble.

Apart from rough-shaping the block, Greek sculptors executed the originals without the help of assistants, and by the Hellenistic Age the same technique was used for making copies of classical originals.

In Rome, after the fall of the Republic, both public and private demand for carved marble increased tenfold, and the *marmorarii* started to mass produce the same objects employing armies of workers, who carved either whole statues or parts of architectural elements that were assembled later (see fig. 222).

During the Roman Age, and specially after the 2nd century A.D. drilling became essential for mass-production and also started a trend for chiaro-scuro effects.

Although the basic sculpting tools have not changed much since Roman times, the importance of marble has altered over the centuries mirroring all new economic and cultural developments of the Mediterranean culture.

Clay models were used during the Renaissance, but throughout the Middle Ages artisans had gone back to carving from drawings like the archaic Greek craftsmen as shown in the marble bas-relief by Andrea Pisano *La Scultura* in Giotto's Campanile (Florence).

New, more accurate methods for copying clay models were invented: Leon Battista Alberti explained the «Definitor» method in his treatise *De Statua*; impossible mazes of co-ordinates and complicated systems using set-squares were devised (see fig. 165). A fairly simple method called *macchinetta* or *crocetta* (little machine or cross) was invented last century and enabled an artist to work out the exact position of any point within a given area defined by three principal points, using a slide-rule.

In the 19th century the traditional craftsman's workshop called *bottega* was split into two establishments: the workshop where the blocks were

169

169. *Architectural moulding workshop with large lathes used to make columns (during the Thirties).*

prepared and the artists' studio. Clay models were replaced by small plaster casts of the orginal (see fig. 166). Nowadays in sophisticated studios light and easily portable plaster casts are reproduced perfectly in marble using pantographs, and only occasionally is the artist required to give the finishing touches. The traditional iron and wooden hammers, sledge hammers, flat or boasting chisels, drills, files and abrasives that were used for centuries, have been replaced in the last fifty years by compressed air and electric equipment: sculpting is no longer hard work, and the tools are fixed on the end of flexible shafts, pneumatic microhammers and electromagnetic shakers which shape the marble as easily as if it were clay (see fig. 170).

170. A sculpture workshop (of the Thirties).

170

147

171

171. Saw mills, workshops and marble depots dating back to the end of the 19th century.

172. Modern marble depots equipped with bridge cranes.

172

148

Industrialised workshops produce building materials as well as statues and decorative elements. The Greeks and Romans quarried columns of the required shape and size: a four-sided prism shaped block was extracted and the corners were chiselled away so the sides increased to 8, 16, 32 etc. until the block was cylinder shaped. From the beginning of this century marble columns were first rough-hewn and then finished on a lathe (see fig. 169); previously linear mouldings like fillets, ovules and snake-like designs were rough-shaped by hand with metal points and finished off with chisels; today they are shaped with circular saws and milling cutters.

In pre-mechanization days flat surfaces were cut by hand; the corners were outlined with a set square and ruler and then a strip of marble was cut away from round the edges with a chisel and mallet. The central part was then levelled off and smoothed with a dented chisel and with abrasives. Most rock used for masonry was treated in the same way, but unlike marble, it required less preparation.

Special methods are used to obtain special effects: floors, walls and even furniture can be decorated with inlays of coloured marble placed side by side to form geometric figures or patterns (Roman *opus sectile*) (see fig. 188); mosaics are made using different techniques, small cubes of coloured stone set side by side (*tasselatum*). Another technique used by the Romans and Sumerians called *opus interassile* consisted in setting thin slabs of marble cut in different shapes (figures or geometric patterns) into holes made to measure, where they were fastened with mastice. To increase the colour range «tesseras» made of vitrus paste were first used in Egypt at the end of the Empire (*opus alessandrinum*). Later this technique was used by Byzantine and Islamic craftsmen, and later for decorating Romanesque churches in Rome and in Campanium; the «tesseras» not made of vitreous paste were made with waste Roman materials and the decorations were called *cosmatesche*, from Cosma (see fig. 189). The art of decorating with graffiti coupled with inlay was revived during the Renaissance.

Another technique consisted in cutting polychrome figures out of thin slabs of marble with fret-saws or emery grit, and then fixing them on to pieces of slate; good examples are housed in the Carthusian Monastry of Pavia and in Florence in the Opificio delle Pietre Dure together with 18th and 19th century work-tables and tools (see fig. 27).

Organization

Unlike quarrying which is done in the open, saw mills and workshops have always been built and run like factories; even the oldest works were roofed over, and following an ancient tradition marble workshops (called *marmisti*) were still built in towns. Last century however, the first industrialised workshops were built in marble producing areas partly because transport had improved and marble could travel safely, and partly because of the new capitalistic management (see fig. 171). The quarry, saw mills, storage depots, workshops and administration offices (see fig. 172) became proper industrial units (and very profitable investements).

As we have seen it is difficult to mass-produce marble since so much depends on the skill and experience of the quarrymen and artisans; the division of labour is hierarchical: the sawer at the saw mill decided how to cut the marble, and the timbering sawer did the cutting. The polisher polished the finished marble surfaces that had been cut and squared by another workman called *scapezzatore*. An overseer checked the *scapezzatore's* work, and, if the marble was going to be used for building it was rough-shaped by the stone-dresser who also made the plate models from the chosen drawings. The milling machine and the lathe hand did the mechnical work, and the decorator finished off and decorated the marble. If the block was going to be sculpted the pattern maker rough-shaped the model and the sculptor executed it.

Working conditions were (and still) are not easy: marble dust can cause serious lung damage and the atmosphere is invariably damp because of the water used to feed and cool off the sawing machines.

There are two types of marble production centres: old centres that have been given a new lease of life by the recent industrial developments and increasing commercial demand, and are equipped to produce every kind of marble article; and centres that have never recovered after the decline of the Roman civilization, or if they have, are run with primitive means, and like most family concerns are based on rural economy, and produce a limited range of simple everyday articles.

Conclusion

In conclusion the saw mills and workshops were technically revolutionised sixty years before quarry infrastructures. However, compared to other industrial activities the whole organization is between fifty and one hundred years behind the times. Notwithstanding, there have been many important technical innovations throughout the pre-Industrial period right back to the Bronze Age. New techniques were developed, specially during the Roman Empire and from the end of the Middle Ages to the beginning of the 19th century, in great part due to the revenue authoroties and merchants.

It is important to understand and appreciate the means and conditions under which marble has been extracted and worked, that have lasted for a few thousand years, undeniable proof of the high cultural level of the Mediterranean people and the power and prestige of patrons.

There is still much research to be done in this field ; old iron machinery, industrial and pre-industrial equipment and buildings should be rescued and archeological museums set up in marble producing areas. Fortunately a complete catalogue of the Apuan area was compiled by Gino Bottiglioni (an etnolinguist) in 1914, but it has never been translated from German (it was first published in a German review) into Italian. A Lunensi marble Museum has recently been opened in Carrara, and although only Roman quarrying techniques and remains are fully documented, it is to be hoped that soon the Middle Ages, Modern and Contemporary periods will be included.

Chapter Three

The Different Uses of Marble

The Consumer Side

Up until now only the production side of the marble industry has been examined.

Marble is not a precious material in its natural state, merely a shapeless mass buried deep inside the earth; it is extracted with much labour, cut into blocks and slabs, and the chosen pieces are transported to destination after having passed through many pairs of expert hands: and all this is merely preparation, not the end product.

The marble industry has been organised in different ways throughout history; quarries were either selected and organised to meet specific demands or were developed commercially at a later stage to cater for new markets. In the first case a proper dividing line between production and use did not exist; quarries were opened in areas that were easily accessible, both for transport and working.

The easiest way to transport marble was by water and soon it became financially viable to import different varieties of marble from distant countries. Transport has always been more expensive than quarrying and carving, so as demand increased proper commercial organizations run either by merchants or directly by the producers were set up, and skilled quarrymen would gravitate round newly opened quarries as the financial potential increased and the market expanded.

Marble has always been comparatively inexpensive, specially before production was partly industrialised and transport mechanised.

Although marble is not essential to every day life it is still used to mass produce a number of useful household articles in preference to other materials. However, throughout the centuries it has been a symbol of luxury and wealth and rich, priviledged families used it to embellish public, private and sacred buildings. It would be interesting to examine the different uses of marble in a historical context, but it is too long an undetaking for the purpose of this book.

Marble can be divided into various groups: functional and decorative marble used for building and furniture; marble used for sacred, didactic and commemorative representations, and finally marble used for all other practical purposes not included in the two above groups.

As La Fontaine said in his fairy-tale «The statue of Jove and the sculptor»: — «An artist bought a block of marble because it was beautiful. But what should his chisel shape? A god, a table, or a bowl?» —. Marble is both useful and beautiful, and can be transformed equally well into everyday household articles or luxurious artistic objects.

Unfortunaly in the past, artists have rarely been free to do what they liked and have always had to comply, for cultural and economic reasons, with the wishes of their patrons and customers.

The history of marble developed hand in hand with the history of the Western World, but this does not mean that it was not known anywhere else, rather that no other country could boast such a rich, constant and complex production output. Western technology has been exported out of Europe only since markets have become world wide, and today marble is extracted from deposits all over the world.

How Marble was Used in the Past

In Prehistoric Ages man used numerous stone tools and although

173

173. Tomb of Saqqârah in the low Nile area built with blocks of squared calcareous marble (28th century B.C.).

174. Figures made of baked and enamelled different coloured bricks from the cyclopic walls of Babilonia (7th century B.C.).

174

none of them were made of marble, nonetheless they are an invaluable source of information; indirectly the history of marble is connected with magical representations, and small statues of goddesses made of soft stone are typical of this period. Prehistoric man also attached great importance to such representations, and had an exceptional knowledge of different stones and qualities.

The first Neolithic vases were probably used only to prepare and cook different kinds of agricultural produce, before pottery had been invented, and the rock was similar to that which later, buffed and polished, was used to make precious bowls and religious statues.

By the end of the Prehistoric Ages metal was used in large quantities in the newly established settlements, but marble was not as yet thought of as a precious stone, and only used to embellish and decorate traditional sacred objects. But the fact that it had been used was in itself important; all cultures develope in stages and rarely break away from their origins, although things alter beyond recognition in future times, and only too often what we herald as innovations are merely transformations. Prehistoric sculpture is a good example; the Paleolithic «Venus» was replaced by the Neolithic magical «Mother Godess»: they are both symbols of fertility, exalt birth and reproduction, and were executed in the same style; another school of thought upholds the view that these corpulent statues were copies of contemporary women whose diet was based on cereals, (or both).

The history of how stone (and later marble) came to be used for building is more complex.

The first Neolithic settlements were set up 8000 years ago in an area between Palestine and Anatolia, but they did not become proper political and cultural centres in the modern sense until 2000 years later. By the Bronze Age this new way of life was imported to the fertile alluvial planes of Mesopotamia and the Nile where monumental cities were built in comparatively short periods of time; these cities were governed by an all powerful, rich and literate theocracy. Like so many historical dilemmas, how marble became available and for what it was used is a riddle that cannot be answered: did man search for new kinds of raw material to put his ideas into practice, or did the available raw material influence production? It is not possible to draw conclusion from such scanty evidence, so it is better to examine each case individually: if prehistoric man had not discovered that hard stones could be shaped by chipping he would not have produced a range of functional lithic cutting tools. However, since he did, by trying out all the local stones, he soon found out how to trace the natural deposits and exploit them; some prehistoric communities used to trade stones for other goods.

The inhabitants of villages living far away from natural deposits made tools out of bamboo, bone and hardened wood, and continued to produce them, because it was cheaper, even after communication routes had been established and hard stone was easily available.

Local materials were used for private buildings, but imported materials were used for important religious or political constructions when the powers that be felt justified in using slaves and money lavishly. Until fairly recently only three varieties of building materials were used: wood and cane, mud and clay, stone and marble. Humble huts built in agricultural villages and belonging to the poorest section of the population were always

175. Red granite statue of
the Pharo Amenhotep II
(16th century B.C.)
(Archeological Museum in
Turin).

175

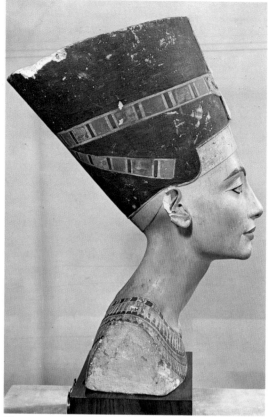

176

177

made with local materials, like the neolithic huts in primitive villages. Different materials were used in different areas, and traditional architecture varied from one region to another. Unfortunaty since these buildings were not designed or built by famous architects, and are not beautiful to look at, they are rarely mentioned in books and, it they are, merely as examples of backward and primitive settlements; the historical events and developments behind every type of building, in every region at all social levels are important, but, since they have been underestimated for so long, little is known about them.
The size and use of buildings did not depend on which materials were used, that in the case of monumental architecture were adapted to suit contemporary social needs.
Building techniques using local material rapidly improved after the start of the Egyptian Dinasties in Mesopotamia 4000 years B.C. Initially pressed clay and later sun-baked bricks were used for temples and huge vertical sepolchres. By the end of the IIIrd Dynasty small blocks of sandstone and calcareous rock from the hills near the Nile valley (see fig. 173) were used in Egypt, and by the IVth Dynasty (3500 B.C.) coloured marble from the desert was imported. Sun-baked bricks were still used for buildings on the Tigris and Euphrates until after 1000 B.C. Huge temples were built on old ruins and the construction sites looked like truncated pyramids and were called «zigurrat»: the temples were covered with a layer of fired bricks and bitumen fashioned like stones; occasionally the stones were decorated with coloured glazing imitating polychrome marble (see fig. 174), and during the Sumeric period small slabs

178. Sculpture in white marble called the «Lyre Player» from the isle of Keros in the Cyclades (2nd millenium B.C.) (National Museum of Athens).

178

3908

of coloured marble from the northen mountains were used for paving. Sun-baked bricks were used frequently for dome-shaped and vaulted roofs, since wood was not easily available.

How Marble was Used at the Beginning of History

Marble was first extracted and worked with metal tools at the beginning of the Bronze Age in the Eastern part of the Mediterranean. It was a coincidence that marble and metal started to be used at the same time; this is born out by the fact that hard marble was still cut by hammering it with harder kinds of rock. In Egypt and Mesopotamia and later in Anatolia and the Aegean, schools for artisans attached to temples and palaces were the first to use marble for building and decorating.

The traditional statues of the Paleolithic «witch-doctor-magicians», and the Neolithic «witch-doctor-priests» were still produced by artisans in the Iron Age. Artisans were not free to work as they are today, and were treated no better than slaves; their artistic production had to conform to the set of rules and models established by the high priests who were not allowed to do any kind of manual labour.

Marble was used mostly for sculpture; figure sculpture was less influenced by abstract rules and patterns, and, as urban civilization developed casting off many agricultural traditions, it became more naturalistic. All sculpture was formal and had frozen-like qualities since it was made to adorn dark temples and monumental tombs; solemn divinities and representations of sacred celebrations were the most popular themes executed in a style varying from Paleolithic magical naturalism to formal, purely aesthetic naturalism. The best examples were made in Egypt where anatomical moulds have been found: each working stage was depicted on the walls of workshops and even in some tombs (see figg. 115, 163): the figures were idealised and portrayed in stereotyped positions, especially during the Middle Kingdom. Initially, during the reign of the First King, sculpture was done in two dimensional flat-relief and only the profiles of figures were shown. Statues in full relief date back to the IIIrd Dynasty and were produced up to Roman times; there are three view-points: two side-views done in bi-dimensional flat-relief, and the dominant front view. The figures are life-size divinities in various shapes, or kings and the royal family, sometimes together with scribes and architects who held high social positions (see figg. 63, 175).

Dark grey-green basanite erroneously called «basalt», red granite known as syenite, pink or white quarzite and occasionally alabaster were used most frequently. They are all hard marble except alabaster and cannot be carved in high-relief. Partly because of this, and partly because there were only three view points the figures seem to be trapped in the marble. The prevailing dark colours, the polished surfaces and even the hardness of the marble had a precise religious significance, possibly immortality, since marble is not corrupted by time. Statues that had no religious significance were completly different: although they were still idealised and static the details were more realistic. Statues of calcareous marble did not take polish and were covered with plaster and then brightly coloured (see fig. 176).

In Egypt the same traditions were continued for 3000 years after the

179

country had been unified at the beginning of the Bronze Age.

In the land between the Caspian and Red Seas the different populations (Sumerians, Acadians, Babylonians, Helamites, Assyrians, Persians, Hittites, Phoenicians and Mytilenes) had given birth to heterogeneous cultures over the same period of time. For instance the most prestigious and influential class among the Sumerians, after the high priests and the court, were the merchants, and the military among the Assyrians.

The Sumeric style of architecture and sculpture influenced Mesopotamia and the near by areas for a long time. Sumeric society was more free and less based on agriculture than Egypt, and statues of gods, kings, princes and aristocrats were less naturalistic and greatly deformed by the established religious convention. The head was more important than the body, as the seat of expression and spirituality, and the eyes were extremely large and dominated the whole face.

There were two ways to work and select marble for statues in full relief; either tender, pale marbles, usually alabaster were used during the Archaic period, and carved in great detail: the eyes were brightly coloured either with paint or inlaid with pieces of shell and stone; dark, hard marble, usually green-black diorite from the northen mountains was carved in less detail and polished (see fig. 77); the deep abstracted gaze of these statues dominated the spectator even from afar, and as usual, the frontal view was the most impressive.

In the 3rd and 2nd millenium B.C. large cities were built in Anatolia, but, as in India and the Far East, marble was not used to build. It is interesting

180.

to try and establish the connections between Greek sculpture and the Colossus of Malatya that is made of white marble and is $3^1/_2$ metres high. Although it was made on the fringe of the Hittite area, the Mesopotamian influence is evident.

The Aegean Islands were not influenced by the main-land culture; urban settlements based on maritime commerce were built in the 3rd millenium B.C. exploiting the natural geographic advantages. The merchants of Tigris and Euphrates, were governed by rigid theocrates; but the ruling classes of the Aegean Islands were the merchants and consequently the artisans were relitively free. Sculpture of the first period was called «Cycladic», from the island of Cyclades were it originated. Many female idols were made, sometimes life-size, and although there were no representational affinities, they continue the Neolithic tradition of the «Great Mother». Cycladic statues were schematic because the artists wished to portray spirituality through

180. A painted statue in white marble of a Greecian girl (kore) (6th century B.C., The Acropolis Museum in Athens).

181. Marble relief of the «Ludovisi» throne depicting Aphrodite born from the sea (460 B.C. circa, National Roman Museum).

182. The little temple delicated to Athena Nike built on the Acropolis in Athens in 421 B.C. made of white marble from Mt. Pentelycus.

181.

160

harmonious geometric forms, rather than merely concentrate on the fertility theme.

The use of white calcareous marble for sculpture dates back to the Bronze Age in the isles of Naxos and Pyros, and apart from some exceptions like the «Lyra Player» was not fully exploited until later; figures were still formal and schematic, but no longer imprisoned in the stone (see fig. 178). Marble was first used for important works of art in the Eastern Mediterranean during the Bronze Age, and sacred statues of propitiary idols, gods and semi-gods were produced. Similar statues have been found in other areas with the same social background, in Indochina and Columbia for instance, but they were rarely made of stone that could take polish.

The architecture of this period in the Mediterranean area is known as «Megalithic»: the pyramids, the Egyptian and Mesopotamian temples, the Aegean false-dome tombs, dolmen and menhir in Western Europe. Apart from rare interior decorations and floors, marble was not yet used as an ornamental building material; granite from the Nile valley was used either for architraves, since it was flexurally stronger than calcareous rock or sandstone, or for vertical structures, obelisques and monolithis weighing hundreds of tons. These singular works of art were made to honour the «sun-god» and both the shape and texture had special symbolic value (see fig. 46).

Continuing the Neolithic tradition marble was used to make small vessels and other articles; everyday articles were of pottery which was lighter and easier to work. Stoneware was only used for important occasions and vessels were made of beautifully coloured, shiny hard stone (see fig. 179).

Architecture and Sculpture in the «Marble Peninsula»

Greece has been called the «Marble Peninsula» due to the astonishing quantity and variety of different marble; among these white and *statuario* marble were undoubtedly the most important.

The origins of classical art and architecture date back to the 2nd or 1st millenium B.C. after the collapse of the Cycladic civilization in the Aegean, Minoan in Crete, the Mycaenean civilization, and that of the war-like Achaeans (the conquerors of Troy) on the mainland: the urban populations migrated to the islands or to Jonia in Asia Minor, and Greece was over-run by barbarian tribes, the Dorics, who lived in rural villages, and for centuries only produced the most simple objects decorated with primitive patterns, similar to Neolithic art.

This lasted until the 7th century B.C. when a ruling class emerged and the Doric landed aristocracy and princes encouraged both military and artistic training, influenced no doubt by the Achaean and Eolian immigrants, who were more comopolitan and less attached to old traditions; architects and sculptors were no longer fettered by ancient religious dogma, and patrons began to commission works of art; stone was used instead of raw brick, and temples were crowded with statues of young men and women donated by the population (called *kurai* and *kuroi*).

Statues of athletes were set up in Olympia which had been the theatre of games between young aristocrats since the 8th century B.C.. Sculptors of the archaic period imitated the traditional Egyptian style and models, the four separate viewpoints dominated by the front view; the statues were still static and imprisoned

183

male figures in marble were portrayed naked, and in the Archaic period a mixture of oil and wax was used to cover the achromatic parts (see fig. 180).

Statues of young men and women were made as offerings to the gods: they were not portraits of individuals, rather an idealised picture of youth that lead sculptors to become obsessed with natural beauty, this was gratifying to the client but only too often an end in itself. The trend was encouraged by the Tyrants who seized power from the aristocratic landowners in the 6th century B.C.. The Tyrants originally belonged to the mercantile middle classes, and their court was a meeting place for artists and philisophers.

In the 5th century B.C. the ancient feuds between the old aristocracy and the urban middle classes, who were backed by the people, the war against Persia and the rivalry between Greek cities, helped create a more dynamic and intellectually free lifestyle that, specially in Athens, and stimulated new trends of thought. Neither architecture nor sculpture were immune to these changes and soon new classical artists began to emerge; their common aim was to abolish the dominant frontal view, the hard contours and the stereotype, souless smile and facial inertia.

This entailed setting aside all traditional symbolism in favour of a more worldly style that tried to capture a particular mood or action as it happened: figures were excuted in full relief and were more harmonius and natural, expressing feelings and emotions. It was not a coincidence that the first statues made at the time of the Greek victory over the Persians exhalted heroism, physical strength and valour.

In the 5th century B.C. Pericles commissioned Phydias to rebuild

in the block of stone, but no longer rigid and the stereotyped and symbolic facial expressions had changed too. It is significant that the fixed, unfathomable, god-like gaze of Egyptian statues was replaced by happy, satisfied and more human smiles.

Statuario marble could be carved in great detail as shown in the beautifully chiselled robes of the «Chytons» and the hair of the «Young Jonic Korai»: marble was not polished but the surfaces were made smooth and then brightly coloured. Colours made statues seem more life-like especially within the halflight of temples. Only

184

184. White marble corinthian columns of white marble in the temple of the Vesta in the Boario Forum in Rome (1st century B.C.).

185. The triumphal arch of Constantine in Rome, built in 315 B.C. with Luni and African marble, that had been carved in the 2nd century A.D. and was reutilized for the construction of the arch.

185

186. The first spirals of the figurative cycle of the Trajan Column in Rome, carved in Luni marble in the typical Roman narrative-realistic style (113 B.C.).

Athens on a grandiose scale: sculpture complements architecture in the Acropolis that was built at this time with marble from Mount Pentelicus, extracted and carved by thousands of slaves (see fig. 182).

Notwithstanding the fact that some artists were becoming well-known, sculpting was still thought of as manual labour, little better than slavery, and what's more, it was remunerated, hence not an honourable profession; a piece of sculpture was only appreciated for what is stood for in the community.

In the 4th century B.C. Athens fell and the Macedonians seized power, but there were no great social changes and Alexander thought highly of sculptors and architects in whose art he saw the means of glorifying his own victories.

The new Corinthian architecture was undoubtedly more elegant and graceful, and sculpture was influenced by the work of Myron who had tried to instil a feeling of energy and movement into his statues (School of Lysippus and Scopas); Praxiteles' sculpture overrode contemporary religious restrictions, and for the first time he portrayed chaste female nudes that were extremely graceful and comely.

Although most of the original statues have been lost, and only later copies survive, it is certain that the smooth surfaces of nude figure sculpture were covered with a thin layer of wax and oil to make them more life-like, while the heads and especially the eyes were painted in bright colours.

Another important trend dating back to the first representations of heroes in the 5th century B.C. was sculptured portraits. During this period marble was sawn into slabs and used for decorating the Mausoleum of Alycarnaxos, one of the seven wonders of the Ancient World. This technique was fully developed later during the Roman Empire. Until the Mausoleum of Alycarnaxos all marble used for building was in square, moulded blocks, or, as in the case of the «metope», in thick slabs that had been either split or squared.

As soon ad the empire founded by Alexander had been split up between his generals, the countries outside Greece was gradually hellenized. Co-existing with the more formal court-circles was a refined cosmopolitan class who loved classical sculpture of every school and period. Influenced by this new trend, sculpture became eclectic and artists were incessantly bombarded with commissions to reproduce the old classical masterpieces for public or court collections (see fig. 183). The technique used for copying was not new: during the classical period sculptors had already made clay models that could be altered and viewed from every angle before being reproduced in marble.

Marble was easily available in many parts of Greece (there was intensive and extensive quarrying activity), and it was used locally for everyday articles, but since the quality of painted and decorated pottery was high, there was not a tradition for precious marble vessels.

Rome and the First World-Wide Diffusion of Marble

Over the next thousand years the role of marble in the Eastern Mediterranean became more and more important. The trade of raw materials, especially tin, between the West and East, the different religious cults and ways of life, and other fragments of culture were absorbed by

187

Mediterranean populations in the pre-Roman period. Noteworthy are some «megalithic» monuments dedicated to spirits of the other world and astrological gods, made of monoliths weighing up to fifty tons and coming from areas more than fifty km. distant from where they were erected. These monuments were not usually made of marble, but of a specially chosen rock with a religious or symbolic meaning. The most sophisticated social structure of pre-Roman Western people were tribal monarchies wherein the priests held the most important non-governing offices. However huge, a sanctuary was never built in the centre of an urban settlement; villages were the centre of all activity and the economy was based on agriculture, sheep rearing and home-made craftwork.

The first proper cities were founded either by the Phoenicians for trade, or during the Archaic period in many Greek colonies.

Although the population of these cities were «isolated» among barbarians, they preserved their civilization and traditions, even competing with the motherland in architecture, sculpture and other forms of art; part of Southern Italy was called *Magna Grecia*.

Marble was not easily available in the Western colonies where huge monuments were constructed out of local stone, unless supplies and statues were brought from the East.

The relations between the local population and the colonizers were often difficult but trade connections were never entirely severed, and the former started reproducing imported articles.

The complex ethnic and cultural history of the Etruscans is a case in point; while preserving certain original characteristics, Etruscan architecture and sculpture in bronze and *terracotta* and sometimes white marble compares favorably with Grecian art. Soft marble called alabaster of Volterra was used only after the 3rd century B.C. for cinerary urns decorated with hellenistic bas-relief sculpture and lids shaped like people following the Italic tradition. The deceased ware portrayed lying on their sides, as if at a banquet.

Etruscan architectural models of wood and *terracotta* plastered with *tufo* were copied by the Romans even on the eve of their great expansion. No traces remain of the early statues decorating temples that commemorate the fathers of Roman history, but it is almost certain that they were of bronze or *terracotta* in the Etruscan fashion. The Romans came in contact with Greek civilization only after they had conquered *Magna Grecia*, Sicily and Greece itself in the 3nd and 2nd century B.C. According to contemporary sources hundreds of statues were taken from

Greece to Rome, even though, at the beginning, they were only thought of as trophies of war.

The Romans were among the most important clients of Greek sculptors and artisans who soon influenced Roman art and architecture. The new temples erected in Rome between the 2nd and 1st century B.C. were, for purely practical reasons, built like Greek ones (see fig. 184). Marble columns were brought from Athens to reconstruct the old Italic temple of Capitoline Jupiter that had been destroyed by fire. Carved Greek marble was used for private as well as for public buildings in Rome and other large cities. In 92 B.C. for instance Licinius Crassus redecorated the interior of his house on the Palatine with marble. An idea of the extent of the marble trade is given by the cargo of a ship that sunk in 100 B.C. off the coast of Tunisia: it was carrying Eastern columns and capitals, bronze and marble statues (see fig. 100).

The consequences of trade in the West during the late days of the Republic were of two kinds: firstly an economical one, deplored by a few stoics and old patricians with austere habits who viewed with distaste the fact that considerable riches were being squandered to follow the new fashion. An economic and technical solution was soon found in the 1st century B.C. after the near Lunensi marble deposits had been discovered and could be used instead of Greek marble quarries. Blocks were sawn into thin slabs for interior decorating which was much cheaper. Secondly the type of art and architecture produced by the Romans from the Ist century B.C. to the 2nd century A.D.; although the architectural patterns were hellenistic (see fig. 197), Roman architecture was practical, and included traditional Etruscan elements

188. Archeological digs in Luni (La Spezia): the floor of a costly house of the 1st century B.C. made of Luni Bardiglio and polychrome marble from the Eastern Mediterranean, Portasanta (Holygate) and Breccia of Theos.

188

168

189

189. The cript of Santa
Prassede in Rome.
Sarcophagi of white marble
dating back to the late
Empire; the central altar is
of medieval polychrome
inlaid marble and
polychrome marble taken
from Roman monuments.
190. The paleochristian
basilica of Sant'Apollinare in
Classe at Ravenna (4th
century A.D.) Cipollino of
Karystos marble columns.

190

like the arch and dome. Religious architecture did not play a very important role, and the new public buildings were usually forums, basilicas, amphitheatres and thermae, or civil engineering plans for bridges and acqueducts. Triumphal arches and mausoleums (see fig. 185) were not made before the Empire.

Roman architecture was not rythmical and harmonious like hellenistic art, rather functional and rationally planned; there were no great schools of sculpture but good, solid craftsmanship: the subject matter and technique were well handled but nothing exceptional was ever produced. Portraiture was important, executed in the formal, late hellenistic manner with an imperial background. There was a more realistic current without aesthetic pretentions stemming from the Latin tradition of keeping the likenessess of ancestors in ones home. Narrative bas-relief sculpture was the greatest change from Greek mythological bas-reilief, and was the story, in pictures (or in many parts of one picture) of the emperors' deeds; Trajan's column was the best work of art produced in this field (see figg. 29, 186); after Egypt had been conquered in the 1st century B.C. the Romans discovered new varieties of marble, brightly coloured and very different from Greek *statuario*. As the new fashion for coloured marble, decorated floors and walls rapidly spread, the Emperor ordered new deposits to be looked for and opened in all Roman provinces. The new quarries were an Imperial Monopoly, directed by procurators, worked by slaves, and the marble was mainly used for public buildings.

Every kind of marble was brought to Rome, and, according to Suetonios, Augustus boasted that he had found a city built of terracotta and left one made of marble.

191. Theodoric's Mausoleum in Ravenna. It has a monolithic cupola, and was built in the 6th century A.D. with white calcareous marble from the quarries of Istria.

Marble was used for building, even in the most distant cities, in *municipium*, colonies and provinces, and by every magistrate or private citizen who could afford a domus or a villa. Trade soon flourished specially by sea, and an efficient system of naval transport was developed. Work was organised on an industrial basis by craft-guilds, and *officinae* even catered for the mass-production markets. Obviously each city used marble from the nearest quarry, but it was a sign of economic power and wealth to import exotic marble for special purposes (see fig. 186).

In the 3rd century A.D. the structure of the Roman Empire changed radically influencing the architecture and sculpture of this period called *tardo-antico* (late-ancient). The colonials and lower middle classes (the plebeans) were hit hardest by ever increasing taxation and currency depreciation, and eventually with the help of the army, — (most soldiers were either barbarians or came from peripheric areas and rural districts), — the plebeans took over the public administration. Even in the West the pragmatic state religion was superceeded by new mysterious cults, Christianity and Neo-platonism.

The sculpture of the 2nd century A.D. was formal, commemorated the emperors' deeds, and was technically faultless; the hellenistic influence cherished by the old official sculptors and ruling classes gradually disappeared, and more popular elements were introduced; they were not decadent, rather the symbolic and irrational inner life prevailing over naturalism; this became an essential feature of Christian art after the fall of the Empire.

Official portaiture was still influenced by naturalism, but the statues expressed a deep inner life (see fig. 187). Bas-reilief, used to decorate

public monuments and marble sarcophagi, was executed according to new artistic canons, and was mass-produced and semi-manufactured for commercial reasons in special centres during the last days of the Empire (see fig. 189).

In architecture the most important changes happened when Christian art first became official in the 4th century A.D. and public basilicas started to be used as places of worship. The external structure was still of marble, and mosaics and affrescos decorated the interior. They better suited the new didactic al representational style that had its roots in narrative Roman bas-relief sculpture (see figg. 190, 233). Marble was used for everyday articles during the Roman age, like mortars and polished vessels and furniture in wealthy houses: tables, chairs and *arae* (see figg. 223, 224).

The Plunder of Roman Monuments During the High Middle Ages

During the last days of the Western Empire the so-called «provincial art» (hellenic-romano models imitated by local artisans) was influenced by the new, more spiritual conception of Christian life and by «barbaric» civilizations. Syrian, Copt, old Saxon and Gallo-Roman markets developed in small centres and gradually, because the means of transport were unreliable, started to expand. Many different materials were used and although the craftsmanship was good, marble articles were extremely rare. The Eastern Empire still held out against internal and external aggression, but apart from a huge mercenary army, had severed all links with the old Roman Empire. Absolute

civil and religious power was in the hands of theocrats who forbade all (both Christian and pagan) figurative representation; only decorative and symbolic bas-relief sculpture was produced, and the designs were only of animals, plants or abstract motifs. The symbols were similar to those used in the West during the High Middle Ages, and only religious architecture continued to flourish. Elaborate hellenic-corinthian columns and capitals were produced on a large scale using the old quarries in Greece and Asia Minor (in particular those on the Marmara sea) and exported to all the Imperial provinces. Pieces of sculpture have been found in the wrecks of Byzantine ships of the 6th and 7th centuries A.D.

The famous North African quarries fell into disuse in the 7th century A.D. after the Arab occupation; also Islam forbade all representation of the human form, although columns, mosques, palaces and «caravan serais» were built and decorated with marble. Old Roman monuments were systematically robbed of columns and capitals, that were redecorated by arab artisans; arab floors and walls were usually made of coloured ceramics in geometric patterns.

The only Western quarries that remained active until the Saracen invasion of the 8th century A.D. were those in the Pyrenées, used to make sarcophagi for Frankish kings: all others fell into disuse in the 4th and 5th centuries A.D.; Theodoric's Mausoleum in Ravenna was the last building for which blocks of white marble were ordered directly from the quarries of Istria in the 5th century A.D. (see fig. 191). This period of stagnation was the consequence of the economic recession that followed the great migrations of central and eastern Europe.

The greater part of monuments in

192. Syracuse. The doric temple of Minerva made of local calcareous marble was transformed into a Christian cathedral in the 7th century A.D. The floor made of white Carrara marble and red marble from Sicily was done in the post-Middle Ages.

193

193. Detail of a white
marble transennae (8th-9th
century) in the church of
Santa Maria of Castello in
Genoa.

194. Proto-romanesque
lunette of white marble in
the Church of Santa Maria
of Castello in Genoa.

194

174

Western cities had been destroyed after the first raids in the 3rd century, or used to erect fortifications. After the great invasions of the 5th century travelling became hazardous and many trade routes were cut off; public and state buildings were no longer kept up, and after the final collapse of the social structures quarries were definetly abandoned.

Cities degenerated into small agricultural centres catering only for the barest necessities of life (see fig. 192). Great monuments were left to crumble or used, among other things, as building material, and calcareous marble was baked to produce lime. New rural societies developed between the 5th and 9th centuries A.D. and gravitated round small regional markets; the refined techniques of ancient urban civilizations were gradually forgotten and superseded by domestic craftmanship, the remains of pre-Roman culture or that of the invaders, who still belonged to the Iron Age.

Throughout the High Middle Ages domestic and personal articles were made of wood, metal or pottery and decorated with geometric motifs and sketches of plants and animals: three-dimensional portraiture was completely forgotten.

There is no trace left of Carolingian and Longobard court architecture, even though other sources prove that Charlemagne rediscovered Paleochristian art; little remains of Christian churches built before the year 1000 but it is certain that they were built following the independent plan of Roman administrative institutions, and the churches represented the zenith of specialised craftsmanship. Artists who could sculpt in full-releief did not exist any longer; tombs and transenne made of Roman remains were decorated with flat geometric bas-relief, vegetable

195. Detail of the portal of the cathedral of San Lorenzo in Genoa carved by French artisans in white Carrara marble (end of the 12th century).

196. Abbey of San Siro in Struppa near Genoa (11th century). The surroundings are of austere local gray calcareous rock and the only marble object is a holy water stoup.

195

196

175

197 b

patterns and symbolic animals, similar to Byzantine iconoclastic art (see fig. 193). Church interiors were decorated with didactic affrescoes and mosaics using pieces of coloured marble, the remains of Roman slabs. Capitals and columns were also made from pieces of Roman monuments.

«Ecco che là, dove nessuno lo aveva immaginato, Tu persuadi gli animi degli uomini, fai scavare la terra, e Ti degni nella Tua misericordia di mostrare dei sorprendenti ammassi di pietre e di marmi» (Modena 1106). «Thou hast persuaded men to dig where no man has dug before, and in Thine infinite mercy hast disclosed wonderous piles of stone and marble» (Modena, 1106). Six centuries after the fall of the Western Empire there were no visible signs of ruins left on the surface and if a city was far away from marble quarries building materials were difficult to find: Divine Providence occasionally intervened and pagan marble ruins were discovered underground and exploited.

The last Hungarian and Saracen incursions of the 10th century mark the end of the Dark Ages, and in the West, particularly Italy, a period of urban and economic growth began brought about by the new commercial classes organised in self-governing communes called «Comuni».

Monastic institutions were reformed and became more strict enhancing the prestige and authority of the Church. At the same time a great number of Romanesque churches sprang up in feudal rural districts and cities; they were built in the same style of basilicas but were more solid (see figg. 2, 228, 229). Lithic building materials were in great demand, but since all quarries were still abandoned, supplies were scarce. Apart from castles, all houses even in towns, were made of wood; local stone quarries were quickly opened (see fig. 229), and wherever possible builders (lacking all technical know-how) searched and plundered Roman ruins taking away slabs and blocks of carved marble. Cities near rivers and the sea were in a priviledged position since it was easier to transport heavy loads by water and the roads were still unsafe. Coastal towns expanded rapidly despoiling what remained of the old Imperial cities. According to contemporary sources the Genoese and Venetians even took advantage of the Crusades to smuggle columns and marble slabs from Palestine and Constantinople (see figg. 2, 197).

All art was religious art, and as the quality of craftsmanship improved in large cities and monastries, the subject range increased and didactic, symbolic and ornamental statues were produced, poor folks bibles were inspired by everyday life, the four seasons and miniatures. Local bas-relief sculpture decorated stone door jambs and tympanum, and for the first time the columns of church façades. The figures were almost too expressive, rather archaic and child-like but revealed a more spiritual and serene approach to life, but it is

198. Orsanmichele church in Florence: high altar executed with «statuario» of Carrara and polychrome marquetry (half 14th century).

199. Dario Palace on the Grand Canal in Venice (1487). The architectural structure is of white calcareous marble of Istria (that was frequently used in Venice) and is enriched with coloured marbles: portasanta (holygate) and Verona red.

199

200

were called «*cosmateschi*» (from the name cosma) (see fig. 189). If marble was not easily available, decorations and furniture were embellished with inlays of coloured glass «tesseras».

The Rebirth of Quarries in the Late Middle Ages

Marble sculpture did not survive the iconoclastic crisis in the East; figure sculpture was dominated by three distinct viewpoints, and only ivory

200. Giovanni Pisano: Statue in white Carrara marble representing justice; originally it came from the funerary monument of Margherita of Brabante (1313, National Gallery of the Spinola Palace in Genoa).

201. Pace Gaggini: portrait in marble of Francesco Lomellino now in the Palace of the Banco of Saint George in Genova, (1509).

practically impossible to distinguish between the work done by trained artisans and that of gifted stone-cutters.

Stone taken from the ruins in Latium and Campanium were used for decorating interiors; the predominant geometric motifs inlaid with polychrome pieces of ancient marble

202

could boast a proper sculpting tradition.

Apart from the opulent Imperial palace decorations, marble was used less and less for church columns and capitals. The only articles produced in the West after the fall of the Empire were marble sarcophagi from the Pyrenées and Proconnesus on the Marmara sea. The roots of ancient Paleochristian tradition were so deep that even the nobles of the High Middle Age would not give them up, and the quarries of *Pietra di Finale* (Finale rock) were opened in Liguria only to supply sarcophagi in an area of a few hundered chilometres long. Sarcophagi made of *Sarizzo* marble from the Alps were sent to the Ticino, Pavia, Milan and other centres in the Po valley. This predilection for sarcophagi represents either a link with paganism and earthly life, or as Pliny believed, *lapis sarcophagus* a trachyte of Troas, used to make sarcophagi in ancient times, had special properties that helped the body dissolve quickly.

New varieties of marble unknown during Roman times were discovered in the 11th and 12th centuries in local quarries that had been opened to

203

*203. Michelangelo: a
«prisioner» now housed in
the Accademia Gallery in
Florence (1530).*

and pre-Romanesque buildings (see
fig. 228). Alters made of white
Pyreénean marble dating back to the
9th and 10th centuries have been
discovered in Acquitaine before the
Pyreénean quarries began working
again.

Ancient quarries were gradually
reopened; at Carrara for instance,
apart from a few rare cases, white
marble started to be extracted in small
quantities during the 12th century by
Genoese builders helped by the local
quarrymen.

In the 13th and 14th centuries
«masters» of the Great Tuscan Board
of Trustees (*grandi Fabbricerie delle
Cattedrali Toscane*) obtained the
authorities' permission to exploit
quarries, and the transport was
organised locally. By the 15th century
quarrymen could supply most kinds of
marble, and had drawn up their own
Statute. In the 15th and 16th centuries
the market expanded and quarries
started to operate on a supply and
demand basis rather than on
commission. As in Roman times a
market for special sized blocks and
semi-manufactured goods (mostly
slabs) developed.

Oddly enough measures protecting
ancient monuments were not taken
until the Renaissance, (and there was
not much left of them by the
beginning of the 15th century).
Marble from plundered monuments
and newly opened quarries was
exported for building. In Roman times
quarries were a state monopoly, but
during the late Middle Ages the
western social structures and life-style
changed; once again cities became the
centre of activity and the new
commercial middle classes started to
finance artisans, who up until then
had been dependent on feudal lords
and monks. This did not lead to better
economic conditions but craftsmen
enjoyed unprecedented creative

satisfy this increasing demand: black
calcareous marble from England,
Belgium and North France; alabaster
from England and Catalonia; Ligurian
ophicarbonate rock, limestone and
white marble from Mount Pisano.
Even old quarries that had been
abandoned after the fall of the Empire
were used for local supplies and
occasionally exported to satisfy special
requirements.

Lack of adequate techniques, proper
extraction schemes and reliable means
of transport had caused the quarries to
be shut-down in the first place and it
also explains why pillaged materials
were re-utilized in some Romanesque

204

freedom, a more dynamic life and a wider circle of clientèle. The new governing classes invested their wealth in the land, in private houses made of stone rather than wood, and in new churches that gradually became larger and more magnificent (see figg. 232, 236). By the 14th century, especially by the sea, a sophisticated network of transport had been developed. In north-west Europe the gothic style preferred by the middle classes replaced the monarchic and religious romanesque architecture. Italian gothic architecture was both elegant and practical (see fig. 198); statues in full-relief based on live models reappeared and religious sculpture became less formal and dogmatic. Portraiture was revived and although sculpture was limited to three or four dominant view-points it was becoming more plastic, and recognized artists started to emerge (see fig. 200).

The traditional patrons of art were kings, aristocrats and ecclesiastics who despotically controlled small armies of servants, masons and stone-cutters; by the 13th and 14th centuries they were superseeded by the communes or rich guilds of merchants. The trustees of large corporations kept accurate accounts and drew up detailed contracts with the «masters», acted as

205. Bartolomeo Ammanati:
the fountain of Neptune in
Piazza of the Signoria in
Florence (1563-75) with
statues of white marble and
bronze.

206. Detail of the Gallery of
Mirros in palace of
Versailles (17th century):
polychrome marbles are used
in abundance, especially
France red.

205

184

207. Church of Our Lady of
the Consolation in Genoa:
majolica Madonna by a
pupil of della Robbia set in a
baldachin of Spanish
Broccatello marble (17th
century).
208. Sanctuary of San
Francesco of Paola in
Genoa: marble polychrome
inlays in the Chapel of the
Saint (18th century).

207

186

supervisers for sculptors, decorative stone-cutters, masons, unskilled workers and apprentices. They obtained concessions to exploit stone and marble quarries and then sent «masters» to inspect the marble, the means of extraction and the transportation. Construction sites were structured hierarchically, and were generally very busy unless money run out (see fig. 204). Individual craftsmen moved about from one site to another, the overall organization was good and all undertakings were usually finished sooner or later. Some artisans set-up their own workshop as a fall-back in hard times and catered for small commissions and private clientéle.

Soon after the first Guilds of masons and stone-cutters called «Arti» appeared to safeguard the craftsmen's interests (see Appendix), and even the plans and drawings for new churches were in the hands of laymen, not ecclesistics.

The Italian urban tradition had deep roots, and continued throughout the High Middle Ages and during the feverish activities of the communes, which after much internal struggleing changed to Principalites and *Signorie* in the 15th century, small city-states ruled by one all-powerful family. Architecture and sculpture flourished at these courts and lords started to embellish private, public and religious buildings, and were soon followed by the rich middle classes. Collecting works of art became fashionable and enhanced the work of art as well as the artist; artisans no longer worked in order to earn their daily bread, but to make a name for themselves and profit by their newly acquired artistic freedom. Architects and sculptors had become «artists» in the modern sense of the word, signed their works and were better paid, but still depended on their patrons for work. The controversy over whether artists who create with their hands are on the same level as poets and musicians dates back to this period; initially only architecture and painting were acknowledged to be among the *Arti Gentili* (the noble arts), while sculptors had to wait until the 16th century, and even Leonardo said uncomplementary things about dirt sweat and toil.

Classical art was revived during the Renaissance, the natural sequel of gothic art that was predominant in Italy during the 13th and 14th centuries in intellectual circles; architecture was thought of as rational and scientific rather than purely artistic, and the first tract of modern times was written in this period. Architecture must be practical, linear and well proportioned, and building materials judiciously employed, the end result, elegant and simple. Rich and ostentatious families still preferred costly and opulent building materials, tangible proof of their economic power (see fig. 199) to the more austere new style. In Genoa for instance three marble columns cost the same as an old house in 1437, but trustees of unfinished gothic buildings were still placing orders notwithstanding: sculpting technique had greatly improved, and before a statue was executed in marble, life-size clay models were produced as well as drawings from the 4 main viewpoints. In the North sculpture was still part of French gothic architecture, while in Renaissance Italy it had attained artistic independence and no longer pertained to religious architecture. Princes wishing to emulate the courts of kings and emperors started to commission non-ecclesiastical works of art and portraits of nobles and aristocrats and the first profane paintings (see fig. 201). While architects and sculptors acquired higher social status, the traditional workshops were by no means abandoned; craftsmen imitated the

209. Pierre Puget: statue of
the Immacolata in statuario
marble of Carrara in the
oratory of San Filippo in
Genoa (1670).

209

189

new trends for less wealthy customers and although their work was less perceptive, the cratfmanship was good. By 1480 there were fifty-four stone-cutters' and marble workers' workshops, in Florence alone, and a quarter of them were run by well-known artists.

Ornamental and household articles and furniture (weights, mortars and vessels) columns, capitols, jambs and small pieces of sculpture were produced for ordinary houses.

The versatility and beauty of marble was again appreciated as in antiquity, and the ancient quarries that had been reopened by the Cathedral Trustees were now receiving numerous orders that guaranteed a regular productive output.

New Marble and How it Was Used in the Modern Age

Things became more unsettled as the changes of the late Middle Ages gathered momentum in the 16th and 17th centuries. Most European states were continually warring with each other, and tottering from one financial crisis to another. This caused the traditional gap between social classes to widen; the rich neglected commerce for international speculation, unemployment rose rapidly, the population increased, and starvation became endemic among the poor. The middle classes, who tried to emulate the way of life of the rich, were continually tormented with money worries and the possibility of loosing their life's earnings. In Germany discontent lead to Lutherism and the Ecclesiastical Reformation: Rome reacted with the rigid and dogmatic Counter Reformation and just managed to contain the spiritual and social changes.

210. Lercari Palace in Genoa: staircase leading up to the piano nobile (the most important floor) dating back to the second half of the 16th century. Carrara marble was still used for practical purposes, and the affrescos supply colour, even reproducing panels of coloured marble.

The thousand year old equilibrium of the Middle Ages was broken. These troubled times are reflected in the work of Michelangelo who was deeply touched by the religious and social problems of his day. He grew up in the late Medieval tradition, and his youthful work was influenced by humanistic ideals and natural beauty. He was a true man of the Renaissance, and for him formal beauty was above natural beauty and portraiture was contemptible. The work he did in Rome at the height of his career was influenced by the frailty of human beauty and by the contemporary social unrest and religious crises. The Council of Trent (see figg. 202, 203) shocked Michelangelo deeply, and although the old passionate fire still burnt within him, the work he did as an old man was more mystical and ethereal. Like other medieval artists he did not work from life-sized models, but he had the ability to envisage the finished statue within the virgin block of marble, and then create it without a flaw. He did not approve of mechanical or mathematical means applied to figure sculpture, but he was very careful which marble he used and even visited quarries to supervise extraction. Michelangelo also discovered a new deposit of *statuario* marble in the Apuan Alps, and according to a local legend he was nearly knocked down and killed by a block of marble the stoneboat workers had lost control of.

The Renaissance died with Michelangelo, and although a new generation of sculptors imitated his youthful manner they belonged to a new era. Artistically Mannerism represented the triumph of the body over the soul. It rapidly spread throughout Europe and as the first art dealers emerged, guild-trained artists set up academies to teach

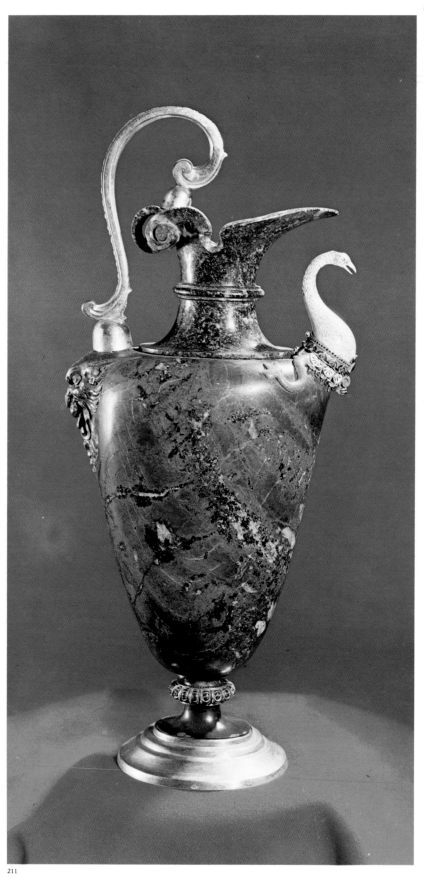

211

art-criticism and the classical manner. The hallmark of the 16th and 17th centuries priviledged classes were magnificent town palaces and sumptuous country villas (see figg. 206, 210). Many medieval urban areas were entirely rebuilt using coloured plaster on a white marble background instead of formal white stone. Michelangelo and the classical style were revived and artists like Palladio and Vignola, who adorned ceilings and domes with mythological and symbolic affrescoes celebrating power and riches, and imitation Roman statues in niches. Unfortunatly, the whole set-up, more often than not, appeared phoney rather than cultured. Baroque and Rococo geometric patterns of polychrome marble were used to decorate floors and walls instead of terracotta tiles; the basic conception and structure of palaces did not vary, but interior decorations and drawings were more lavish. Catholic religious architecture rigorously followed the artistic canons prescribed at the Council of Trent. Churches were attractive and functional and all profane decorations were abolished. Baroque painting and sculpture was meant (and succeeded) to uplift and inspire the congregation, and replaced the medieval narrative pictures and lay art that was an end in itself. During this period marble, plaster decoration and sumptuous organs were used to embellish churches and private palaces (see fig. 208).

Italian artists who had emigrated during the 16th century together with the first powerful commercial organizations exported *statuario* and white marble of Carrara to every corner of Western Europe. But long journeys doubled and even trebled the price of marble, and finally importing countries ended up by exploiting local quarries and even setting the fashion

212

211. A lapislazuli jug (end of the 16th century, Museum of Silver in Florence).

212. Germaine Soufflot: neoclassical pronaos from the Pantheon in Paris that was started in 1759.

to suit local material; hence the trend for black and grey marble in France and Belgium, and alabaster in Spain and Portugal.

Demand for brightly coloured marble and semi-preciuos stones increased tremendously, and by the end of the century goverments were literally bombarded with requests for quarrying concessions; some new quarries like that of the Languedoc for red marble, Sienna yellow and Spanish

Broccatello, were to become very famous (see figg. 27, 207).

The ancient quarries in Greece were reopened, and Roman monuments were despoiled again for marble from Egypt and Asia Minor that could not be found in any other way, unless forged. In the 16th century the Jesuits established a monopoly over lapislazuli a rare, precious stone from the mountains of central Asia (see fig. 45); together with white and black

213

centuries in order to build an inlaid polychrome altar in their church made by a famous artist who worked for powerful trusts and princes. When coloured marble was unavailable special artisans reproduced it with plaster starting a tradition that lasted until the 20th century (see fig. 210). However marble was not universally appreciated: some thought it to be too cold for interiors, not weatherproof if used for exteriors, and liable to be stolen. Erasmus of Rotterdam complained that people visited the Charterhouse of Pavia only to see the marble inlays and disturbed the religious atmosphere.

Marble was not only used for churches but also for furniture, ornamental vases, small chests and tables that, like all baroque art, were richly carved by specialised craftsmen. The most famous commissions for polychrome marble were from a semiprecious stone factory, that is still standing today, and was set-up in Florence during the reign of the granduke Cosimo I.

Everyday articles were mass-produced. In the Apuan Alps poor families living on the outskirts of the marble industry earned a scanty livelyhood by making thousands of mortars and floor tiles (see Ch. V) out of white or *brecciato* marble for merchants. Since no other material did as well, marble was also used for purely functional purposes in building, as well as for aesthetic reasons.

214

213. Antonio Canova: bust of Napoleon in statuario of Carrara (Gallery of the Accademia in Florence).

214. Monument of Cavour erected in Vercelli in 1864: the portrait and allegorical figures of Agriculture and Commerce are in white marble, resting on a pedestal of granite from Lake Maggiore.

Marble in the Industrial Age

People started to invest capital into machinery for the marble industry a hundred years after the English Industrial Revolution, but only recently has machinery been able to cope with all the stages of mass-

marble it was used to decorate their churches. As often happens the trend was exaggerated, and poor rural communities ran into debt for

215

215. The Academy of Fine Arts in Carrara: collection of chalk models for sculpting (beginning of the 20th century).

production, from extraction to the end product. The liberal and industrious middle classes tried to improve their financial and working conditions, and this change coincided with new discoveries in the field of applied science, the invention of the steam engine, illuministic rationalism, and Neoclassic sculpture and architecture. Neoclassicism was no mere re-elaboration of ancient art, as at the end of the Renaissance with Mannierism, rather a scientific discovery born from recent archeological finds that placed classical art high above the over-elaborate and sensual baroque style (see fig. 212).

Many buildings erected in the Confederation of North America were Neoclassic in style, that was adopted by the middle classes during the French Revolution, it was also fashionable at absolutist courts like Vienna and Saint Petersburgh. After the Restoration it became less fashionable, but still influenced building and sculpture until the beginning of the 20th century. Demand for coloured marbles ceased until after the Second World War and white marble was used instead. New deposits were discovered in the United States of America capable of satisfying the local demand. Western Europe had to face international competition for the first time, specially after the first exhibitions. This did the marble industry good, new techniques were developed both locally and abroad, and markets, that up until then had been the monopoly of powerful merchants, were liberalised.

The first industries capable of catering for every kind of order were set-up and marble was quarried and worked in the same place (if it was possible), and heavy loads were transported by

216

216. Palace of the Chambers
of Commerce in Carrara
(1961, functional marble
covering).

217. Detail of the head
office of the oil company
Nafta in Genoa (1935):
eclectic travertine external
covering.

217

196

railway rather than by water
(see fig. 171).

Nineteenth century architecture was eclectic, and although the market was booming, marble was only used for doorways, staircases and bathrooms in numerous middle class houses, and occasionally for Neoclassic public buildings.

Building techniques were revolutionised, and for the first time in history people started to appreciate the building potential of iron and steel and started to use it instead of wood, stone and marble (the Eiffel Tower for instance). In the beginning iron and

steel were only used for bridges, market places and railway stations, but it was the first step on the road towards reinforced-concrete that today is used instead of traditional building materials (see Ch. 6).

During the 20th century architecture became more simple and functional, and buildings were no longer embellished with heavy late liberty patterns in rienforced concrete, but rationally divided into well-proportioned volumes: beauty was in the structure rather than the decor. Marble suited this kind of architecture, and was used for walls and floors both inside and out (see fig. 216); the tough white or coloured granite marble was the most popular; marble still stood for power and prestige and industrial companies overdid the company buildings as in the past (see figg. 49, 217). Neoclassic mythological and commemorative sculpture was appreciated by the middle classes who started numerous private collections, specially during the Napoleonic Era (see fig. 213). Formal tombs and public monuments were part of 18th century urban planning, and were executed according to classical canons, and reflected the taste of the ruling classes who chose what they thought to be the most suitable designs among the many presented. At the same time other sculptors and artists were trying to revolutionise the traditional role of art, and free themselves of all social conventions and impositions; instead of working on commission they worked to please themselves (see fig. 214). The difficulty lay in placing their work with broad-minded art collectors and dealers, and for a long time new pieces of sculpture never got beyond clay or plaster models. Artists could not afford marble and were cut off from new technological discoveries that were only used in industry and in crafismens' workshops.

During the 19th century the concept of «art for art's sake» was universally recognised, and artists started to commission artisans to execute small models in marble (see fig. 218). Workshops also kept up a steady production of religious, profane and funerary subjects.

Artisans possessed great technical skill and were no mean artists, producing interesting individual pieces for special customers. They were unconventional, and in this mirrored the spirit of their age (see fig. 218). As well as the usual figure sculpture workshops produced large quantities of furniture and household articles for middle class homes such as fire places, small columns and ornamental vases; industrial machinery was used to produce wash-basins, mortars and marble slabs for furniture.

Chapter Four
The Marble of Carrara

219

The deposits of the Apuan Alps have already been mentioned in the Chapter on Geology.
The Carrara district has undoubtably been worked most, and provides the most complete historical background of marble production areas.
Marble from Carrara is called *Carrarino*, following the trend established by Gino Bottiglioni, who thought it was nearer the original version.

The Roman Colony of *Luna* and the Lunensi Marble

The marble of Carrara became famous during the Roman dominion because the pre-Roman populations, up until the Iron Age, were not interested in marble, although it was easy to locate the deposits. Torrents were (and are) full of pieces of marble used, as well as clues to the whereabouts of deposits, to make small articles. Rare beads from necklaces of white marble have been found in Neolithic tombs in the Lucido valley near Luni, and on

220

221

the northen side of the Tusco-Emilian Appenines. But this is an isolated example, and the Etruscans and later the Ligurians who settled in the Southern part of the Apuan Alps around the 5th century B.C. did not produce marble articles or exchange them with the neighbouring populations.

In 180 B.C. and 177 B.C. the Romans founded the colonies of *Luca* and *Luna* partly to protect the Apennine roads and partly to watch the area north of Pisa.

Luni was built on an overlaying quaternary terrace on the left bank of the estuary of the river Magra. The estuary formed a natural harbour known as *portus Lunae* by 195 B.C.; it was much older than the city of Luni and was used as a port of call between Pisa and Genoa on the Western routes first used by Greeks and Etruscans. The fact that a city had been built by the Romans, and not by the Ligurians near the harbour proves the Ligurians to have been uninterested in urban culture based on commerce, although the rich tombs near Ameglia prove that they did trade

with cities on the Tyrrhenian sea. The Romans had no experience of mountain warfare and found it difficult to subject the Apuan people, and they deported many, ravaged the land and quarries and Luni in 175 and 170 B.C. The Apuan population was finally subjected in 155 B.C. by consul Marcius Claudius Marcellus and the event was commemorated with a column the base of which was found in 1875. If the column really dates back to Marcius Claudius Marcellus' victory it is the oldest known specimen of Apuan marble sculpture. Other carved and moulded *abacus* dating back to the age of the Republic (see fig. 221) confirm the fact that marble was used in Luni before Rome. It is not known when marble started to be extracted from the Apuan area; Pliny and later Renaissance tract writers said that Apuan marble replaced the famous Greek *statuario* of Pharos in the West.

Unfortunatly many works of art were taken away from Luni after the 18th century and now are in museums or private collections. Luni was

219. Archeological digs in ancient Luni (La Spezia): aereal view of part of the Forum and of the «Cardine Massimo» that leads to the port.
220. Archeological planimetry of Luni in Roman times showing the most important monuments and the port (A. Frova).
221. National Museum of Luni (La Spezia): an Apuan marble abacus with an inscription dedicated to Claudius Marcellus.

222

plane near the city and were used as building material (see fig. 219); larger lithic blocks either come from the mountains behind Luni — calcareous marble and sandstone — or from the right bank of the river Magra — polychrome crystalline schists — only three kilometres away across the river estuary (see fig. 59).

The Carrione river born in the valley of Carrara was full of pieces of white and grey marble; it flowed four kilometres south of the city and lunensi builders probably discoverd the first marble deposits by going upstream about six kilometres; *statuario* marble was discovered later. Meanwhile Greek marble was still used in Rome; statues and architectural elements were imported after the 2nd century B.C. and virgin blocks for local artisans after the 1st century B.C; coloured marbles from the East were so fashionable that they were even used at Luni for floors and walls together with the local white and *Bardiglio* marble (see fig. 188).

It was only a question of time before the Luni quarries were exploited commercially.

According to Pliny, Mamurra one of Caesar's prefects, was the first to commission Karystos and Lunense marble columns for his Roman house in 48 B.C.; by 40 B.C. marble was well-known throughout Rome, and during the reign of Augustus huge quantities were used to modernise the city. It is unnecessary to make a list of all the works of art of this period: up until the 1st century A.D. everything was made of Luni marble.

Above all Luni marble was used in Italy and southern Gaul, and the wreck of a ship loaded with columns from the *lunensi area* was found off St. Tropez in Provence. At this time Strabo wrote about the quarries of

rediscovered in the 15th century and was the theatre of questionable archeological research for two centuries; proper scientific means were only used after 1970. Small pieces of alluvial sandstone from the quaternary terrace have been found on the coastal

223

white and *Bardiglio nuvolato* marble, what the *portus Lunae* looked like, and described the *navis lapidariae* that carried loads up the Tiber. In 109 B.C. a consular-road was built between Luni and Pisa, and, as the colonial population increased the city was entirely rebuilt.

Luni exported wood, wine and cheese, and crasftsmanship flourished. The population of Luni included wealthy Roman knights, the contracting classes, colonials, natives and many freedmen with Greek names; they were either artisans who had come to Luni to ply their trade during the reign of Augustus or technicians who worked in the quarries.

Marble was used locally for furniture, floors and walls but the rapport between the city and the quarries was ambiguous. Locally marble was used for building as well as furniture and household articles (see fig. 224). During the Roman Republic quarries

were public property and freely exploited by the Luni settlers, but during the reign of Tiberius they became a state monopoly.

The quarries were twelve kilometres from the city and the quarrymen, slaves and freedmen lived in settlements built on the site; ruins and burial inscriptions have been found at Torano and Vezzale in the marble valleys.

Archeologists first began to study ancient quarrying methods in the 19th century, and recent research financed by the Carrara Town Council has given a complete picture of how the Roman quarries of Luni were run. Traces of terrace exploitation have been found in fourteen quarries: the blocks were first separated with trenches then broken away with pickaxas, chisels and wedges (see fig. 73). All tools ranging from sledgehammers, hammers and pickaxes to wedges and levers have been classified (see fig. 72). Blocks

224

224. *Archeological Museum of Turin: marble throne called of the «Alessandri» (end of the 2nd century A.D.) found in the archeological digs of Luni.*

were numbered and initialled by the foreman and occasionally even marked with the cutting sector and quarry area.

COL (*Colonia Lunae*) was carved on the blocks until 16 A.D. during the reign of Tiberius, together with the name of the officer belonging to the *collegium* of Luni, an institution similar to the Medieval guilds, was another followed by *Augustus servus* (the servant of Augustus).

Roughly hewn remains of vessels, pieces of sculpture and columns have been found along with the more interesting burial inscriptions that prove the existence of a corporation headed by one Hilario in 22 A.D., as well as altars and sacred *aediculae* built by the quarrymen.

Sylvan, guardian of woods and fields was the most popular god, and was worshipped by slaves and the lower classes. A votive altar to *Mens Bona* was erected by the superintendent

Felice in the 1st century A.D. (see fig. 223) and Artemis, Luna, Jupiter and the nymphs were honoured. The votive aedicula called *Fantiscritti* (children with inscriptions) in Carrara dialect is the most famous; it was carved in the mountainside (see fig. 225) and dedicated to Jupiter, Hercules and Bacchus. It gave its name to the surrounding valley and became fashionable in the Renaissance when many visitors, (among whom Giambologna and Canova) (see fig. 226) used to carve their name and the date of their visit on the surface.

As in other Imperial quarries, compared with the number of initialled blocks, there are few traces of locally produced articles left. Blocks of marble were usually only squared, or at the most rough hewn in large marble centres. Cutting, sawing, carving and sculpting was done at destination by craftsmen working in workshops. A Roman inscription mentions *tabulari marmorum lunensium* (Lunensi marble sawers). *Arae* and *aediculae* were the only finished product manufactured in quarries by the workmen; they date back to the 1st and 2nd century A.D. and not being influenced by the contemporary official style, were less sophisticated.

Transport was another problem; following the Greek tradition blocks were loaded on to carts at the foot of the quarry and then taken to the loading posts. The Carrione river was nearer but it is more probable that marble was shipped from Luni harbour. The poet Servius mentions a temple dedicated to Apollo in Rome built «of solid marble that had been brought from Luni harbour». There was a *«marmorata»* toponym near Luni similar to that on the Tiber in Rome used to load and unload marble. According to others the toponym *«le Marmore»* of which no trace remains, was used as a deposit for useless blocks. The Carrione river is also very shallow and it would have been difficult to load and unload ships without proper hoisting machinery; it was used with great difficulty in the Middle Ages after Luni harbour had been completly buried by mud.

Under the marble floor of the Imperial Forum in Rome there were chippings of Apuan schists that did not belong to the Carrione river area. The chippings were probably used for packing and were available in Luni. Geografically Luni could not have been better placed, and soon became an important stopping centre for traffic travelling by land and sea, it was the last harbour of the Tyrrhenian sea with a direct trade route to the Po Valley and it could be reached overland from the West. For this very reason it was difficult to

defend, and recent archeological studies have shown how in the 5th century A.D. during the barbaric invasions, statues and monuments were smashed to pieces to make primitive fortifications.

There are no traces of large buildings in the Luni area after the 2nd century A.D.; the amphitheatre, the staircase and portico of the great temple of white marble from Punta Bianca were older; the most obvious explanation is that the new buildings were the first to be plundered: for instance by the 6th century the marble covering the floor and walls of the Forum in Luni (see fig. 227) had been spoiled and wooden and clay huts built there, but the quarries were not abandoned, and Luni marble was used in Rome for a long time yet. During the latter part of the Roman Empire many changes contributed to upset the marble market; quarries were run on a new juridic system, and the position of slaves and the lower classes altered after the barbaric invasions in Italy. In the 4th century the price of marble rocketed, but Rutilius Namatianus, an imperial official, who visited Luni in 416 still talked about quarry rubble heaps «whiter than snow». The last monument of Luni marble was the Foca column built in the Forum in 608: by that time Luni was no more than a wooden village overshadowed by ancient ruins. But in Rome marble was still used since for centuries great hoards had been stored up.

The Origins of Carrara and the Reopening of Quarries

During the Middle Ages the standard of living dropped tremendously compared with the level of prosperity achieved by Luni during the first years

225

225. S. Salvioni: the ancient
quarry of the «Fantiscritti»
near Carrara (beginning of
the 18th century).

226. The Fine Arts Academy
of Carrara: sacred Aedicula
called of the «Fantiscritti»
removed from the wall the
«Fantiscritti» quarry.

226

227

227. *Archeological digs in Luni: the remains of the white marble floor of the Forum: most of it was removed in the 6th century.*

of the Empire. Notwithstanding, Roman laws and institutions survived and the religious and social crises improved the position of the lower classes. Fortunatly the invaders did not settle in Luni until after the 7th century and the administrative traditions were kept up by the religious community that included the old Roman colonies and rural parishes that were gradually replacing the ancient villages called «*Pagi*» (see fig. 230).

A basilica had been built in Luni after the Edict of Constantine and the bishops of Luni had it enlarged and restored at different periods and decorated with marble sculpture and bas-relief. Scattered fragments have been found in more recent houses, but it is difficult to say whether they are

Roman or quarried specifically for the basilica.

In the 6th century the dioceses was on the eastern boader of the *Maritima Italorum*, a part of Liguria that had been conquered by the Byzantines as a stronghold against the Longobards; but by the 7th century the Longobards overrun Luni and other Roman provinces pillaging as they went.

By the end of the 8th century Luni had become part of the *Marca Toscana* the borderlands created by Charlemagne to defend the Imperial territorial waters; the Bishop became an important public figure and his prestige increased under the new *Marca Obertenga* created by Emperor Otto I in the 10th century between Luni and Genoa; Genoa soon became an independent commune governed by a merchantile oligarchy which transformed the city into a great sea power. But the days of Luni as an important urban centre were over. The city had been crippled by the Norman and Saracen invasions and worst of all the geography of the area was changing. By the end of the Western Empire the large quantities of alluvial debris from the river Magra were no longer carried out to sea, and the harbour was gradually silting up and Luni was surrounded by unhealthy marshlands that have only been drained recently with the help of modern technology (see figg. 61, 220, 230); the climate got gradually worse and in the 12th century the bishopric was moved to Sarzana. The small river port of San Maurizio still functioned and the remains of Luni harbour was mentioned in a 17th century atlas although the city itself had been abandoned in the 13th century.

Nothing concerning the history of the old imperial quarries was found until the 10th century: they were on the border between the lands conquered by the Longobards and the Roman Byzantine Empire: military Roman outposts were scattered about the area, and around the year 1000 the *milites*, descendants of old Lunensi families, still held certain priviledges. Agriculture replaced quarrying and small new towns, among which Carrara, were built on the more fertile plains far from the old centres (like Vezzale) and the marble routes. After the break-up of the *Marca Obertenga* in 963, Otto I decreed that small comunities were to be governed by Bishops and organized into *corti* (courts) entirely controlled by the Emperor. Nothing was left out: houses, settlements, fields, vinyards, meadows, planes, valleys, alps,

pasture lands, woods, water and rivers, mills, fishing, servants and entire families. Once again quarries had become part of the financial potential of the Luni district, but only in 1185, when the Bishop of Luni was created a count by Frederick Barbarossa, were quarries included in the list of church revenues. After Barbarossa's appointment, the Bishop-count of Luni had jurisdiction over the land and people of Carrara and was granted the imperial priviledge to exploit the subsoil.

A few years later quarries started functioning again, but it is difficult to say whether this depended on the new regime or on the incessant demands to obtain mining concessions.

The first written sources are deeds under the seal of a notary concerning a load of Carrara marble columns and capitals shipped to Genoa. Another is about a boy sent as an apprentice to Antelamo, a genoese artisan. In Genoa stone was used for building instead of wood, and the Bishop-count only charged a token-fee for each block extracted. In the Lunense area local stone — mostly calcareous rock and sandstone — was used to build romanesque churches and castles and even for bas-relief sculpture; in the 12th century Carrara was rebuilt in marble (see fig. 228). Marble was still thought of as a luxury in the Lunense area, and although the quarries were so near, it was rarely used for building.

Bas-relief sculpture was probably executed by the local stone cutters (see fig. 229) who started a tradition that lasted on in the Lunense area even after the quarries of Carrara had been reopened: the subject matter was conventional and the style fairly rudimental.

The legend of Luni died as other

228. *Interior of the cathedral of Sant'Andrea in Carrara (12th to 15th century) where even the ashlars are made of marble.*
229. *Remains of the Romanesque church of Saint George in Pontremoli near Luni, that was entirely built of local sandstone.*

Italian cities developed, but, at first, no other centre took its place: the deep rooted antipathy the Apuan people felt for the Roman colonizers died hard and prevented them from keeping-up a Roman tradition. For this reason the marching feudal lords of Pisa, Lucca, Genoa, Florence and Milan, and the Fieschi and Malaspina families and the communes tried to annex the Lunense area, and during the Middle Ages the descendents of Count Obertenghi tried to size it from the Bishop-count.

By the 13th Carrara had become and indipendent commune, roughly divided into two classes, the consuls (the descendents of the ancient *milites*) and the *populus* (the common people). At first it seems that the Bishop-count backed the commune to keep the Malaspina's territorial pretensions in check.

But as the smaller rural centres sent their representatives to join the commune, a large percentage of the total population ceased to pay homage to the feudal overlord, and by the middle of the century the revenues were divided equally between the commune and church that still dealt with judicial administration (see fig. 242). Among the smaller communities there was a particular arrangement about the division of land, the origins of which are unknown. It developed as the power of feudal lords diminished; the heads of families living in the same districts (called *vicinanze*) were automatically business partners and collectively owned a certain acreage of land (called *agre*) that could not be divided or transferred: often quarries were part of an *agre*. The *vicinanze* could exploit the land, but the subsoil could only be exploited by the Bishop-count, who had been granted the priviledge by the Emperor

(this priviledge was called «*regalia*»). In 1273 Bishop Henry tried to restore the Church to its ancient splendour. He reorganised the customs in the port of San Maurizio and on the roads to Pisa and Rome at Avenza, Genoa and Piacenza at Santo Stefano, Parma at Caprigliola and the marble routes from Carrara. He also tried to alter the laws about marble extraction and to control the quarries more closely. This documentation is collected in the *Codice Pelavicino* (Pelavicino Codex) at Sarzana and provides unique information on Lunense economy and the goods in transit: oddly enough however the profits on marble were no higher than those from the Avenza customs, and less than the Curia's agricultural revenue.

Henry's plan was short lived since the region was given to Pisa in 1313 by Henry VII and changed overlords eight times in the next 150 years (Castruccio Castracani, Spinetta Malaspina, Milan, Lucca, Florence, Campofregoso of Genoa); in the 15th century Carrara and the *vicinanze* were given to the Marquis Malaspina of Massa.

Customs duties on marble continued to be paid, and after the 14th century the profits went on the upkeep of the marble routes. The oldest known orders of Carrara marble documented by notarial deeds date back to the 12th century in Genoa. There were earlier orders not documented by notarial deeds for capitals of Carrara marble for the church of Santa Maria di Castello in Genoa made between 1130 and 1137. Genoese orders were mainly for white marble used for building, the precious *statuario* of Carrara was used only after 1265. Niccolò Pisano was commissioned to make the pulpit for the cathedral of Sienna: he should have used slabs and

VALLE della MAGRA

Alterze dei principali punti

Alpe di Camporaghena Tise fr. .... 1025.5.
Alpe di Mommio .... 982.8.
Pizzo d'Uccello .... 961.8.
Monte Cornoviglio .... 596.5.
M. Rotondo (Com. di Zeri) .... 594.3.
La Cisa .... 534.0.
Pontremoli, Torre del Pubblico .... 136.9.
Filattiera som: del Campanile .... 129.3.
N.B. La Tesa francese è brac: fior. 3. 6. 9.½

Spiegazione dei Segni.
◉ Capiluoghi di Comunità
● Terre principali
⊙ Castelli
○ Borghi e Villaggi
⌂ Chiese parrocchiali
= Santuarj
◇ Rocche antiche
═ Strade regie
Strade provinciali
Strade comunitative rotabili
Strade com: pedonali
Confini granducali
Confini di Stati esteri
⊗ Poste

Scala di Miglia 10. Toscane
1 2 3 4 5 6 7 8 9 10
Chilometri 16. e Metri 536.
1 2 3 4 5 6 7 8 9 10 11 12 13 14 15 16

Zuccagni fece. Angeli perfezionò. Grassi incise.

231

232

blocks of Carrara marble and work it at Pisa; but he used Carrara marble only for the pulpit, and the columns are made of granite from Assuan, diorite, breccia of Theos, *cipollino* and other pieces left over from Roman times (see fig. 233).

For the next two hundred years the quarries of Carrara, Pietrasanta, Campiglia, Monte Pisano and Montagnola Senese worked mainly for the great Tuscan cathedral trusts: white marble was the most popular; Pisa had set the fashion in the 13th century, and on the façade of the cathedral was written: «*Non ha eguali questo tempio, bianco come la neve*», («none can rival this temple that is as white as snow»). Even during the Gothic period, when church exteriors were decorated with coloured (see fig. 114) as well as white marble, Carrara still continued to supply white and *statuario* marble for sculpture.

Giovanni Pisano was sent to Carrara in the 14th century to choose marble for the pulpit of the cathedral of Pisa, all expenses he incurred were refunded by the Cathedral Trust and the blocks were rough hewn by the local quarrymen and made ready for transport.

In the late 14th century Pisa placed a large order of Carrara marble for the churchyard, and hired a group of workers, stone cutters and a blacksmith to look after the tools, who were paid on a daily basis.

After the 15th century orders were placed directly; Master Maffiolo da Como, a Lombard stone cutter who had come from Genoa to Carrara, looked after the orders and organised transport by land and water. He hired boats from the ship owners of La Spezia on the eastern Riviera, that could transport a cargo of 15 tons and were loaded in the small harbour of Avenza. In the 16th century the boats were pulled up on to the beach because the coastline was straight, the water shallow and the natural harbour of Avenza had been silted up; the port of San Maurizio could not be reached easily overland and up until the last century it was difficult to load and unload blocks of marble, a great problem for merchants (see fig. 149). The feudal system of «regalie» meant that those who expoited the subsoil did not have to own the land itself. Florentine trusts, that had first ordered Carrara marble in 1319, obtained the Bishop-count's permission to extract marble for the Campanile of Giotto and the cathedral of Santa Reparata. Orsanmichele and the chancels by Donatello and Luca della Robbia were made of marble from the new quarry of Sponda; hundreds of tons of marble were used each year for Brunelleschi's dome, and in Florentine workshops. The Florentines re-launched the quarries of Carrara in the 14th and 15th centuries, and their fame attracted good stone cutters and quarrymen who wanted to become specialised workmen.

Commerce and industry were the backbone of Florentine society, and both the workshops and trusts could find agents called «conductores marmi albi de Carrara», capable of supervising the extracting, squaring, rough-hewing and transporting of blocks at a fixed price according to weight.

However sometimes supplies were delayed or held up for technical (usually transport) and political reasons. The blocks were shipped to Pisa where they were transferred to special flat boats. They sailed up the Arno to Signa and from there were taken to Florence on carts built like the ones used at Carrara. Sometimes the flat bottomed boats sailed directly to Avenza, or marble was transported all the way by cart to avoid Pisa. Carrara marble, and marble pillaged from Roman monuments was used to build the Cathedral of Orvieto. The great cornice was taken seperatly to the port of Corneto near Tarquinia and then loaded on thirty two-wheeled carts.

In 1400 Jacopo della Quercia used Carrara marble for the Fonte Gaia and the Loggia della Mercanzia in Sienna although there were quarries nearby. The Genoese had been the first to use Carrara marble, and unlike the Florentines, went on improving mass produced articles — pillars and columns for private houses — from the quarries of Pietrasanta and Carrara.

It was inevitable that Milan should use Genoa harbour, and many masters from Lombardy came to Genoa and

Carrara looking for work, and infact the medieval part of Carrara is similar to Ligurian towns.

By the end of the Middle Ages Carrara had become very prosperous and the first tourists who passed through on their way to Luni seem to have been impressed: it was overflowing with blocks of marble and half finished marble articles.

The marble industry was not the most important, but it was certainly one of the most profitable; during the Gothic period public and private buildings, as well as the entire urban centre, were lavishly decorated with marble. The parish church of S. Andrea and a few private houses are tipical of this period (see figs. 231, 232). The art of stonecutting was soon picked up by the local artisans who became as good as their foreign masters and were capable of executing any order.

Masters and Marble Merchants

Genoese notary deeds prove that by the end of the 12th century there were *marmorari* in Carrara capable of rough-hewing columns and capitals, as in Roman times; probably they could also finish-off columns for stair-cases and windows that were frequently used in Genoese buildings of that period. The same school of artisans worked for the master craftsmen of Pisa in the 13th century and for the Florentine *operarii* in the 14th century. Documents of the Florentine Trusts do not mention local craftsmen after this (except for transport and manual labour) until 1420 when the Pisans commissioned master Maffiolo da Como to choose marble for the graveyard. The Florentines continued to work on their own up until 1452. It is difficult to

explain why there were no local masters at this period, possibly they had moved to other centres for political reasons, especially after the blood-thirsty conflicts between the Guelph and Ghibelline fractions that caused Vezzale to be destroyed.

But Genoese documents of this period have not yet been studied in detail or published, so the explanation could be different. During the 13th, 14th and 15th centuries Genoa imported large quantities of columns, capitals and white slabs of marble for floors and walls; these operations, by 1464, tally with those of Carrara and the many palaces standing in Genoa today prove this (see fig 236): throughout this period the quantity of imported goods undoubtedly increased. Different groups of quarrymen must have worked in the Carrara quarries during the 14th and 15th centuries: native masters together with Lombard *marmorari* looked after mass produced articles made specially for the Genoese market. The masters working for Florentine contractors specialised in white marble for walls and floor coverings made to measure, and in smaller quantity *statuario* for sculpting. The Florentines and Pisans had chosen to work on their own and cater for one section only of the market only: architecture. In the long run this helped the Carrara masters who had learned new trade secrets, to cater for individual orders.

The masters of Carrara founded a marble guild round 1450, but we do not know much about it since the statutes have been lost.

Meanwhile fewer orders were coming in from Florentine agents and trusts, and by the end of the century, customers contacted local masters directly without the help of a middleman. The number of sculptors working for private patrons or trusts increased; they used to travel to Carrara to choose blocks of *statuario* themselves as Donatello, Pisano and Jacopo della Quercia had done before them. They arrived in Carrara with letters of introduction from their patrons and even from the Marchese of Malaspina, selected the suitable blocks of marble and engaged quarrymen to extract, rough-hew and make ready for transport.

Some sculptors worked alone, others set-up partnerships modelled on the *Botteghe Genovesi* (Genoese workshops); occasionally transport costs were too high and the work had to abandoned half-way; for instance the huge statue of Polvaccio marble started by Agostino Antonio Guccio was used in 1510 by Michelangelo to sculpt his David, Michelangelo himself had travelled to Carrara about a dozen times to choose a siutable block.

By the end of the 15th century there were about fifty masters belonging to the marble workers guild called «*Arte del Marmo*» all making the same sort of mass produced traditional articles like columns, capitals, holy-water stoups, slabs for walls and floors, oil jars, vessels, mortars, candlesticks and cannon balls. Demand for this kind of article steadily increased and in the next 30 years (from 1443 to 1474) the profits from custom duties more than doubled (from 200 tons to 500 tons of marble).

In 1473 the commune of Carrara lost its independence and became part of the Signoria Malaspina of Massa. In the long run the absolutist regime was beneficial to the organization of marble industry; Alberigo II Malaspina, a humanist and personal friend of Michelangelo, re-organised the workers' schedule, but in 1491 he

came to an agreement with the marble guild to increase the customs duties which were doubled and in consequence transport costs weighed less on the market price, and all profits went to Carrara. In 1519 the people of Carrara begged Alberigo's widow to go back to the old system of taxation, and forbid all foreigners to extract and work marble in Vicaria either for themselves or on the behalf of others. Lucrezia Malaspina and her daughter Ricciarda did nor want to alienate either the Pope or Florence so they merely forbade foreigners to enter the quarries without official permission, while the citizens of Carrara were authorised automatically (See Appendix).

The oldest quarries belonged to the Malaspinas who had let the Zampone and Sponda quarries to the first Lombard settlers, the Maffioli and da Bassano families. The Zampone quarry had been opened by the Florentines in the 14th century; the new quarries — Polvaccio, Porcinacchia, Grotta, Colombaro, Miseglia, Bedizzano, etc. — were run by families who belonged to the «*vicinanze*» and owned an «*agre*», and were occasionally sub-let.

From the middle of the 15th century notary deeds provide a clear picture of the marble production and economic situation at the beginning of the Modern era.

Only members of the local families, and specially those who lived near the quarries, were allowed to become members of the marble guild: even the Lombard masters and manual workers who had settled in Carrara were excluded. Members of a guild came from all social levels and their standing depended partly on their professional ability and technique but above all on their financial means; the

234. The Malaspina castle in Massa: the courtyard and north wing of the Renaissance palace.

hierarchy was rigid: master quarrymen, stone cutters and sculptors.

Quarries were organised in different ways, either as family businesses where costs and profits were divided equally among the associates, unless the owner of the quarry insisted on a larger share of money or more blocks of marble and this invariably ended by reducing his partners to being financially dependent on him. Occasionally quarries were let to *cottimisti*, quarrymen who worked for themselves and paid rent in marble rather than in money. Michelangelo's partnership with a group of local masters was exceptional, and the Marquis himself had granted special permission (see fig. 235). Masters who had rented a quarry to an apprentice or an employee either ran a town workshop — alone or in partnership — or emigrated to Central or Southern Italian cities where they found work as skilled craftsmen, imported large supplies of marble or both. Finally some masters who did not belong to a *«vicinanza»* worked for a fee, but since production was not stable they were often out of work and obliged to earn their living as agricultural labourers.

As an institution the marble guilds were ruthless; after foreigners had been banned from working in the quarries it became impossible for an apprentice to pick up the trade by working with Florentine manual labourers or Genoese stone cutters. Poor families could only just afford to send a son to work with a master, and after ten years training he would become a member of the guild. Unskilled adult workers were rarely employed, their wages were inadequate and they had no prospects. Apprentice sculptors usually belonged to the urban lower classes, while apprentice stone cutters and dressers were peasant stock from the Lunense mountains.

The purely commercial outlook of the 16th century altered things for the worse; apprentices were treated like labourers or servants and forced to mass produce small articles that were finished off in workshops: the shadow of the Industrial Revolution loomed on the horizen. Over the centuries the marble market had changed too; *statuario* marble from Carrara, used mainly for sculpture, Tuscan cathedrals and Genoese palaces (see fig. 236), had become famous in many parts of Europe. English and French visitors wrote enthusiastic reports about it, and the Lombard masters advertised it in the Po Valley as far as Venice and Sicily where it was used in preference to local marble and marble from the Alps. Genoese merchants exported it specially to Southern Italy and Spain. The best customers were Genoa, Naples and Rome; ancient Roman monuments were no longer pillaged and the fame Michelangelo had acquired in Rome reached the Apuan area.

The cities that imported the smallest quantities of marble were far from rivers and the sea. The marble used in Milan came from the Valle d'Ossola, and was shipped over Lake Maggiore and along the river Ticino. Transporting marble overland to Milan would have cost as much as to ship it to England. Blocks of marble never weighed more than 9 tons so the 10-15 ton *«leuti»* and *«cimbi»* boats of Lavagna used to transport slate could be loaded easily on the beaches in front of Avenza. *«Leuti»* and *«cimbi»* boats never travelled further than Genoa or Rome and for longer journeys the marble was loaded on 20-60 ton *«navigli»* ships at la Spezia.

235

The costs varied according to how long the journey was, how heavy the cargo, and whether special equipment was needed for loading and unloading. Marble was loaded along with other goods and was frequently smashed or cracked during the journey. When this happened both parties tried to place the blame at each other's door, specially if the rent had been paid beforehand. In the 14th century to transport a small block of marble from Genoa to Rome, cost as much as the marble itself including deposit, customs, transport overland and loading, and if all went well the master's profit was 10% at most. He could earn more if he owned his own carts and bullocks and hoisting equipment. The producer could benefit from the so-called *«Prestito Marittimo»* (a maritime loan) where the ship owner became a sort of middleman. The owner advanced two thirds of the price that, together with the buyer's deposit, defrayed the master's fee once the marble had been loaded on board. At destination the ship owner was paid back the two thirds he had advanced plus costs, and in case of disagreements he sold the marble himself. The risks were reduced but the producer's profits were reduced also.

In 1528 the plague broke out and, as a result, new families became members of the *«vicinanze»*. By the middle of the century producers started to sell directly to the large centres to increase their profits.

However they lacked the necessary funds to launch a large commecial entreprise and could not always guarantee supplies to satisfy the ever increasing demand. Orders were late, or not carried out which damaged the good name of Carrara.

Alberigo Cybo Malaspina, son of

Ricciarda Malaspina and the Genoese Lorenzo Cybo, created Prince of Massa and Marquis of Carrara by Emperor Charles V, was a learned ambitious man, a typical product of the old Genoese aristocracy. In 1564 in order to restore the good name of the city he came to an agreement with sixteen producers; all orders were sent directly to the *Offitium Màrmoris* run by the Prince's confidential agents and an equal share of work was given to each producer who had to deliver the articles by boat. The agreement only lasted ten years, and times were changing rapidly; the Prince worried by lack of money let the gabelle out on contract to powerful Genoese financers. Their confidential agent in Carrara, Diana, a very shrewd man who eventually inhereted the *Offitium Marmoris*, acted as middleman for all the most important orders. To increase his profits Diana had ships suitable for marble transport fitted out, and bought excessively large blocks of marble that he sold directly in large cities (usually Genoa) where they were cut in local workshops, packed and shipped again. The finished products, parapets, columns and pillars were sent to Spain; in this way Genoese financers indirectly controlled marble extracting, transporting, carving and marketing. In Seville alone there were 30.000 Genoese columns during this period. To crown it all the agent Diana took advantage of the chaotic situation regarding concessions and bought quarries to sub-let.
In the 16th century marble production dropped from twenty to fifteen tons a year partly because the producers were incapable of running the commercial and production sides of the business, as well as playing the part of confidential agents for sculptors and architects, and partly because of the pointless and harmful competition among rival firms, and because the middlemen exploited the producers ruthlessly to made the largest possible profits.

The commune and *vicinanze* were liable for the upkeep of marble roads and occasionally had to alienate the individual *agri* to meet the costs. Times were unsettled and owners provided capital while the others provided manpower, and consequently the economic and social standing of manual labourers was diminshed in the eyes of society.
Quarrymen and stonecutters were not called «masters» any longer since their job was repetitive and mechanical. Quarry owners were socially above the workers, master sculptors produced figure and decorative sculpture and finished off articles, like columns and mortars, that had been rough-hewn by stone cutters in their homes. Marble tiles called «*marmette*», «*quadrette*» or «*ambrosette*» were also produced at home by the poorest workmen and their children; the Genoese merchants had cornered the market and paid a fixed amount (a mere pittance) per tile.
Nine hundred and fifty tons of marble were exported in 1583, and in 1564 only four hundred tons had been exported; these figures do not include mortars that were not liable for taxation until 1574. Diana catered for all sections of the market exporting large columns and huge blocks called «*all'azzardo*» (hazard blocks), standard sized blocks and all sorts of finished articles.
The increase of productivity did not better the standard of living of the lower classes because at the end of the 16th century the population increased tremendously and the cost of labour

236. San Salvatore of Cogorno (Genoa): detail of the Fieschi palace with the typical white marble and gray calcareous rock external covering (1252).

237

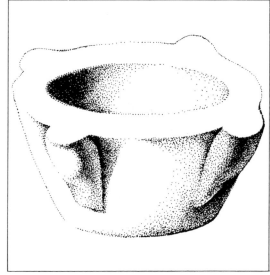

238

239

dropped — many families were forced to emigrate — partly because the marble market was in the hands of a small group of businessmen who paid the workers as little as possible. In the smaller urban centres of the Marquisate of Carrara marble was used to replace stone, but the houses were still very simple (see fig. 240); Massa, the capital of the Marquisate, on the other hand, was being rebuilt on a lavish scale. In 1574 the Prince, worried by the increasing mismanagement of public affairs and of the natural resources, issued laws

forbidding the alienation of collective and communal «vicinanze». But the situation did not improve notwithstanding later laws forbidding usury and the illegal exploitation of the marble industry by agents not at par. Fundementally things had not changed since 1386, except that an authoritarian prince was ruling Carrara instead of a group of priviledged families.

After the 1550's it becomes more difficult to follow the new social developments; the number of notary deeds dropped and public writs do not provide adequate information. The crisis of the 17th and 18th centuries was not as bad as it first seemed, and in part was probably caused by internal social changes and production organization. New technologies were not discovered until the 19th century, apart from the water powered saw.
At the end of the 16th century demand for coloured marble increased tremendously while orders for white marble, streaked white marble and

Bardiglio of Carrara, dropped. *Statuario* was still used for sculpture, but the old Sponda quarry was worked out and the Polvaccio quarry was more expensive to run. Cosimo I de Medici had opened a rival quarry of *statuario* marble on Mount Altissimo using the same techniques as the Carrara masters. The quarry had been discovered by Michelangelo (see fig. 241). Cosimo also exploited the *mischi* of *Seravezza*, a brightly coloured breccia rock similar to *Paonazzetto* from Asia Minor used in Roman times. Alberigo I had difficulty keeping up friendly relations with Florence and preventing Carrara marble workers from going to the Versilia region; demand for white marble dropped in Venice also. New quarries of coloured marble were discovered and opened in many parts of Europe to cater for the new baroque style. Carrara still supplied slabs of white marble called «*lapidi*» cut with the first water powered saws ever used, and demand for mass produced articles like «*quadrette*» and mortars did not drop during the 17th century. «*Quadrette*» and mortars were easily shipped from Leghorn harbour and it was not necessary to drag the boats on to the beach for loading. Occasionally empty ships carried tiles and mortars as ballast, free of charge, and many merchants dealt in grain and wheat with marble as a sideline. The same ships transported Lunense marble to the South, and Southern wheat to Liguria; the wreck of a 17th century ship carrying ceramics from Pisa, and mortars from Carrara has been found of Saint Marguerite in Provence (see fig. 238). White and coloured «*quadrette*» were made using differently shaped standard models, and had great decorative value.

Suitable pieces of marble were broken away from small blocks with wedges and then shaped with serrated or straight chisels and hand polished with sand and water (see fig. 5). Carrara merchants supplied poor families and manual workers without regular jobs with blocks of marble after having fixed a price that varied according to the type and number of tiles produced. The finished product was sold directly to Genoese merchants and provided Carrara businessmen with a regular income. In 1634 «*quadrette*» became a state monopoly but merchants still continued to sell them at cut prices. Finally the workers managed to convince the Prince to fine all merchants who sold «*quadrette*» for less than a certain amount, but the monopoly was not abolished. In 1657 Carlo I Cybo of Malaspina granted the monopoly to a group of Flemish merchants who held it until the end of the century exporting mainly to England and Belgium where the fashion for Carrara marble had been imported from Spain during the reign of Philip II. On the return journey marble ships were used to transport wool, textiles and wheat to Italy, and occasionally blocks of veined marble were sent North on the out-going voyages.

In the 17th century there was not enough work in the quarries of Carrara partly because there was no market for certain products and partly because «*quadrette*» could be made from small left over blocks; many quarrymen moved from the marble valleys to agricultural areas where they worked as peasants; the best sculptors and stonecutters emigrated to large cities where they worked coloured marble.

Notwithstanding the outbreaks of plague the population continued to

241

241. Todays view of
Michelangelo's quarry on
Mt. Altissimo near
Seravezza.

increase throughout the 18th century, and all over Europe the poorer classes did not have enough food or money. In the Marquisate of Carrara the worst famine followed the floods caused by incessant rain and deforestation of the hills; precautionary measures were taken, edicts called «bandite» were issued in the 16th century and the *Ufficio dei Fossi e dei Canali* (the Office of

Ditches and Canals) was established in the 18th century, but neither of these measures were effective.

In 1717 there was an uprising in Carrara caused by the high price of bread, the result of European wars and international tension and marble sales dropped considerably. In 1710 Prince Charles II Cybo Malaspina complained about it in a letter to the Emperor. The situation went from bad to worse and groups of quarrymen called *«guastamestieri»* (unfair competitors) started to sell articles directly to foreign buyers who exploited the situation and prices dropped even further. The prince intervened and forbade owners of boats to buy marble except from the *Publici Negozianti di Carrara* (the Public Vendors of Carrara) a group of families who had agreed to keep the price of marble up.

Unfortunatly the organization never succeded in doing what had been planned and was influenced by the ups and downs of the market. Also many quarries had been worked too deep, and to prevent the walls from caving in, the quarry owners would go beyond their legal territorial limits causing interminable wrangling and quarrels.

Around the middle of the 18th century during the reign of Maria Teresa Cybo Malaspina wife of the Duke of Modena's son, Ercole D'Este, the marble industry recovered slightly. Large quantities of marble were exported, to England in particular, where Neoclassical art had become fashionable. Maria Teresa tried to re-organise production and encourage foreign trade so that ships could bring food back on their return voyages specially during the famines of 1764 and 1766. Duke Francesco started building a harbour at Avenza, but it was never finished and was soon silted up by the sea. In 1767 Maria Teresa divided the members of the marble guild into three categories, merchants, sculptors and manual workers. Trade became the priviledge of the rich and wealthy, but in 1772 she lifted the ban. Following the advice of Giovanni Domenico Oliviero who had worked in Spain for a long time, Maria Teresa set up the fashionable and prestigious

Accademia delle Belle Arti di Carrara (Academy of Art of Carrara) in 1769. This institution gave the marble industry a substantial boost: *statuario* became fashionable, and young local artists were no longer forced to emigrate to earn a living.

The edict of 1751 concerning *«agri»* concessions was fundemental for the future of the marble industry. Laws about concessions had become confused, the feudal system of *«regalie»* had deteriorated, and members of *«vicinanze»* were continually accusing one another and breaking the traditional laws and statutes. The new edict abolished all feudal rights over the exploitation of the undersoil and entitled the *«vicinanze»* to grant quarrying concessions of their *«agri»* to any person belonging to a *«livello perpetuo»* of the *«vicinanza»*, a sort of everlasting contract, to avoid quarrels, and the routine procedure for granting quarrying concessions and researching new quarries was described in detail and codified. The marble *gabella* that ever since the reign of Alberigo I Cybo Malaspina had been let out on contract was again run by the Duke's office called *Camera Ducale* that was also responsable for the upkeep of the marble roads. There were two sorts of roads, *«carraccie»* used to transport large blocks and *«carezzabili»* used to transport finished products. Between 1749 and 1753 an Italian engineer Vandelli used mines for the first time to build a grandiose if impracticable road along the cliffs of the Apuan Alps and Apennines joining Massa to Modena. A few years later mines started to be used for quarrying.

The first water powered *«frulloni»* (blenders) for smoothing marble were built in 1778, but only after much hesitation, since the people feared it

242

would increase unemployment. At the
same time the quarries in the Carrara
area were counted, and the total land
registrary office was 450, a huge
figure compared with the number in
the 16th century. On the whole the
new legislation was beneficial and
encouraged independent enterprise; in
most cases quarries were run by two
or three quarrymen and one
stonecutter at most. The economy of
the Principality of Carrara was still
unstable, changes had come too late to
solve the most pressing social
problems like poverty and
malnutrition. Like other italian princes
the Malaspina wanted to be *Assolutisti
Illuminati* (enlightened authoritarian
rulers) even though the old ideas of an
infallible aristocracy still lingered on
and their inability to change became
evident during a crisis, for instance
during the American War of
independence the quantity of marble
imported to England dropped
tremendously, but d'Estensi forbade
marble workers to leave the country.
It was even worth sending chips of
marble to Holland where it was used
for painting since any job was
better than none. Later the
American Confederation became

one of Carrara's best customers. European wars and political instability eventually caused the marble market to collapse; Maria Beatrice the wife of Ferdinand of Austria reigned in Carrara for 6 years and was ousted in 1790 by the Cisalpine Republic.

The Industrialization of Marble

In 1796 the «liberal, egalitarian and fraternal» French arrived in Carrara and promptly confiscated all marble production as a contribution to the liberation army. This was received with mixed feelings even by the lower classes who naturally hoped to improve their standard of living under the new regime; eventually the population revolted against French monopoly, but a French officer Alexander Henraux had already settled in Carrara as an agent of the French goverment. He was to send marble for monuments glorifying the Republic to France, but by 1800 the whole productive organization was paralized and exportation was held up by the Napoleonic wars. In 1806 Carrara became part of the Principality of Lucca under Elisa Bonaparte Baciocchi; it was typical that she re-organised the Academy on Neoclassical lines, moved the seat to the Ducal Palace and encouraged well-known masters to come and teach there.

The aim of the new goverment was to destroy all traces of the Medieval institutions that still lingered in Carrara; in 1808 the Napoleonic mining legislation replaced Maria Teresa's edict, and the concessions of «agri» and «vicinanze» were abolished between 1809 and 1812, becoming part of the commune.

Maria Beatrice returned to Carrara after the Restoration and revived the old d'Este system. The «vicinanze» were still part of the commune, but according to the procedure established in 1751 all citizens had a right to exploit the «agri».

As soon as peace had been restored throughout Europe the marble quarries started to function again, but this was not the beginning of a new Renaissance for Carrara since the political institutions had not changed, and the ideals of the French Revolution had not been forgotten. Workers were no longer prepared to accept their condition without a murmur and a new independent business spirit developed among the middle classes.

The process of industrialization in the Carrara area was one of the most complex in Italian history; it was very difficult to plan and organise production on a factory basis even though a certain number of articles had been mass-produced for a long time. This turned out to be a great advantage since the new middle class businessmen could rely on skilled workers and artisans whose experience and know-how was invaluable when it came to setting up and using new machinery and, as production costs diminished, more capital was invested and engineers designed new pieces of machinery (although they did not know anything about the art of quarrying and working marble).

Two years after the Congress of Vienna the marble industry began to flourish with the help of capital from industrialised France and Great Britain. During his stay in Carrara the ex-Napoleonic officer Henraux had realised the great potential of the marble industry in the modern world, and in 1815 went into partnership

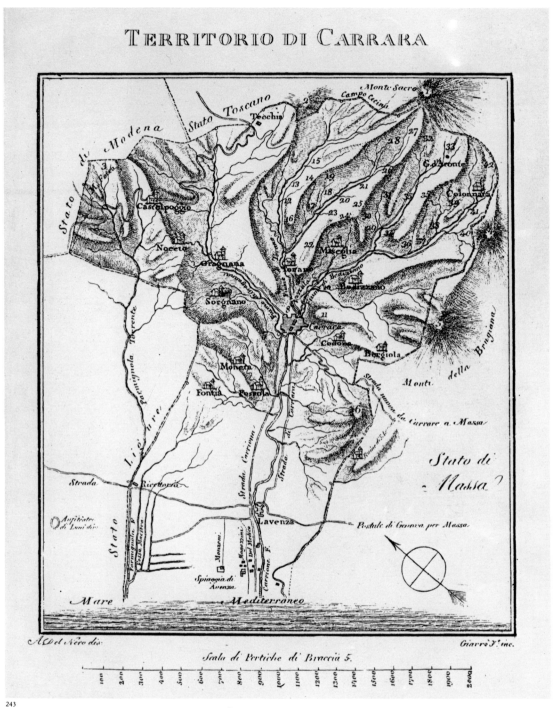

TERRITORIO DI CARRARA

243. Repetti's chart of the Carrara district (1820); the marble roads and the depots on the Avenza beach are clearly marked, and the numbers refer to the number of working quarries and the type of marble extracted.

243

with Borrini of Seravezza, but he did not work in Carrara since he had been unpopular during the French domination. A few years later the marble roads built by Cosimo I and the *statuario* quarry on Mount Altissimo were re-opened and blenders, the «frulloni» (see fig. 161) and saw-mills were set up. Saw-mills, hung from mobile trusses invented by Tonini, were powered by horizontal water wheels designed by the Swiss engineer Charles Muller; his water wheels were used until 1831 when they were replaced by eight iron frames designed by a Frenchman, Narier. Narier also instructed local mechanics, and in 1866 a slab of

244

marble one centimetre thick won a prize at the International Exhibition of Paris.

Carrara still exported only rough blocks of marble; in 1816 an Englishman, Thomas Robson, settled in Leghorn and then moved to Carrara where he financed quarrying and sold the blocks to English customers. Another Englishman, William Walton, moved from Leghorn to Seravezza in 1830 and then to Carrara where he made his fortune during the '48 crisis by selling left-over blocks of marble to a group of financers. As well as investing his capital in a landing stage

with a mobile crane on the Avenza coast, (see figs. 150, 151) to avoid having to drag the boats on to the beach, he invested in a saw-mill larger and more modern than the one owned by Henraux, and became a member of the association to build a marble railroad to Carrara.

There were many Italian businessmen as well, but foreign capitalists had greater experience and pursued a far-sighted policy, that in the end was more profitable; the local businessmen also lacked adequate financial backing and as soon as the initial difficulties had been overcome they tried to

244. Colonnata (Carrara): A monument dedicated to Mazzini with the mine dumps in the background.
245. A «loading post» of the Ravaccione quarry at the beginning of the 20th century; the blocks of marble were hoisted from the stoneboats to the marble railway wagons.

232

245

boycott foreign merchants. The marble industry gathered momentum and in 1869 another landing stage was built by local industrialists. By 1583 one thousand tons of marble were extracted every year, and by 1838 production had increased to nine thousand tons, and to forty thousand tons in 1857. By the middle of the 19th century three hundred out of six hundred quarries were functioning together with thirty two saw-mills, sixty workshops and fourteen «frulloni», and three thousand men were employed. But the equipment was old-fashioned: Waltons' saw-mill was not finished until 1861 and the most important industrial developments date back to the last quarter of the century.

In 1820 Emanuele Repetti published the first book ever on the marble quarries of Massa and Carrara (see fig. 243), and a fairly accurate description of the pre-industrial population of Carrara and of the surrounding valleys was given by the census of 1819; quarrymen, agricultural labourers, shepherds and blacksmiths were the poorest and did not earn enough to support a family; fathers and sons usually worked as quarrymen or stone cutters, the wives worked in the fields or were weavers and daughters looked after sheep. Industrialization merely widened the gap between the business orientated middle classes and the workers. Compared to other parts of Italy Carrara marble workers developed an early interest in politics, and unlike the majority of Italians, held definite views about the unification of Italy. Francesco IV and Francesco V d'Este were completely out of touch with the working classes; in 1846 quarrying concessions were reformed, non-functioning quarries were declared

246. Borgo of Bedizzano and the «Fantiscritti» valley that is crossed by a section of the marble railway.

247

247. Interior of the
workshop for moulding
architectural pieces in
Carrara (beginning of the
20th century).

obsolete, the growth of functioning
ones was restricted, and the two year
trial period was abolished.

The inhabitants of the Lunense area
and Carrara were mostly good
republicans and hated the oppressive
d'Este and Piedmontese goverments.
The first popular upraising occured in
1848 and the successive rebellions of
1853, 1854 and 1856 were violently
quelled by the Austrian-Estense army.
Finally in 1859 the republicans half-
heartedly joined the Piedmontese; after
the d'Este family had been ousted
Cavour wrote to the people of Carrara
«praising them for their energy and

love of independence and guaranteed a
better future under the dictatorship of
King Vittorio Emanuele».

Republican ideals had been abandoned
in favour of the Piedmontese, but
things did not improve and only the
rich middle classes, who wanted to
create a new national market,
benefited from the change.

The nobilty were opposed to the new
regime that had deprived them of their
traditional rights and priviledges (this
however did not last long) and the
clergy up-held the old institutions in
the name of religion and tried to
exploit popular discontent. The people

248

248. The outside of a sculpture workshop at Valle of Carrara (beginning of the 20th century); on the left there are some workers' houses.

were divided: some were faithful to Mazzini (see fig. 244) and others, after the unification of Italy, became freemasons or anarchists, a perpetual thorne in the side of the Prefect. Over the next fifty years, however biased, prefects' reports are the best source of information on living conditions.

As businessmen had foreseen, the unification of Italy boosted the national market and production steadily increased from 40,000 tons of marble in 1886 to 1,150,000 tons in 1914. The process of industrialization was speeded up by foreign enterprise: in 1874 there were twenty «frulloni»

and fifty three saw-mills in Carrara totalling more than 3,000 blades, 2,100 more than in 1864. Saw-mills had been greatly improved by the beginning of the 20th century, fly-wheel correctors had been introduced and the flow of sand water was controlled automatically (see figg. 157, 158). During the Seventies and Eighties the middle classes rebuilt or restored numerous urban areas that had not been changed since the Middle Ages.

The domestic market was not as profitable but was more stable than foreign ones; marble was used as

237

249

249. Torano (Carrara): tombstone of the Bertogli quarry placed at the entrance of the «Quarrymen's League» commemorating the ten victims of the disaster that happened in 1911.

250. S. Vatteroni: «The chain» painted in the seat of the Chamber of Commerce in Carrara during the Sixties.

250

251

ballast and exported to the United States, but the American Wars of Succession and heavy import taxation caused sales to drop tremendously in the Sixties. Producers approached other potential international buyers — England, France and Belgium — but each country invariably imposed restrictions on imported goods. Exportation taxes were abolished so businessmen tried to limit the costs of extraction, working and transportation; this meant that wages froze for fifty years (from 1860 to 1910) even though food was becoming more and more expensive.

In 1871 a group of financiers agreed to build a marble railroad; the first stretch was completed in five years while the whole was finished in 1881 and it soon became the backbone of the marble industry.

Production costs were reduced by 10% and quarry deposits were linked

directly to the saw mills, landing stages (see fig. 245) and the national railroad network; by 1910 80% of transport was done by rail (see figg. 144, 246). Quarrying methods were still backward and inefficient, pre-industrial methods were costly and long drawn out, and the mines used mostly for the «grandi varate», dislodging large blocks, were neither practical nor safe. In 1894 an engineer from to the local mining district summed up the situation in a written report; quarries were unsafe and the quarry floors were gradually being smothered by debris, and, worse still, one third of the marble was wasted because of the use of mines. A new law limiting the «grandi varate» was issued in 1895; in the same year Adolfo Corsi designed the first wire saw (see fig. 81) powered by a combustion engine, and two years later he adopted the *Monticolo*

251. *The solitary meal of a quarryman with two huts in the background.*

253

252. *Coming home from work at the time when the marble roads did not reach the quarries.*

253. *Colonnata: one of the oldest settlements in the valley behind Carrara, nearly hidden by the blinding whitness of the quarry dumps.*

penetrating pulley (see fig. 83). But it took another twenty years for mines to be used selectively together with pneumatic quarrying machines (see fig. 86). At the same time the first funiculars and cableways (see figg. 138, 139) connecting the quarry floor to the loading stages were designed to replace the traditional stoneboats; they were already used for supplies in high up quarries (see fig. 140).

In 1907 Walton, Goody and Crips built the first edition of the Balzone cableway that could carry blocks weighing up to five tons down Mount Sagro. In 1930 its carrying capacity was increased to twenty tons, the greatest ever (see figg. 141, 142, 143). After 1904 most saw mills and wire saw plants were powered by electricity and six years later, in 1910, the Hydroelectric Apuan Company was set up. The number of active quarries increased from 400 in 1880 to 650 in 1914 after the slight set-back of the nineties, but the existing infrastructures were inadequate and could not keep up with production. In 1919 sixteen of the most wealthy industrialists went into partnership; between them they owned more than half the equipment to extract, transport and work marble; small companies and family businesses were not equipped to deal with all stages of production and became dependent on them. Large companies used to sub-let the least promising quarries in exchange of 1/7 of production, but most tenants who had no knowledge of the market were compelled to hand over the entire stock. The middle class myth of the self-made man meant a great deal to hardworking and ambitious quarrymen who, unfortunatly, were the first to come to grief during a period of crisis because they could not rely on adequate financial backing. In thirty years — from 1870 to 1900 — the number of hired workers doubled from 5,000 to 10,000 men.

After the unification of Italy the urban population increased partly because young stone cutters and quarrymen emigrated to the marble centres from the surrounding rural districts, that were gradually being swallowed up by quarries and mine dumps; workshops, saw-mills and deposits were being built in the small centres at the bottom

254

254. The public fountain of Giuncugnano (Lucca): it was made during the Thirties by a quarrymen with a rural background.

255. The Professional School of Carrara: (beginning of the 20th century) modelled on Academic lines.

255

242

of the valleys (see fig. 247). By the end of the 19th century rural property had been broken up and the lower classes had lost all contact with an agricultural society that was becoming more and more depressed.

Quarrymen were still excluded from exploiting the marble «agri» although, in theory, they enjoyed the same priviledges as the middle classes. Old men, children and farmers worked as manual labourers, had no prospects, grew prematurely old through sheer physical exhaustion before they qualified as skilled workers. Many jobs still had to be done by hand and no proper measures were taken to safeguard the workers: more lives were lost at Carrara than in any other part of Italy (see figg. 249, 250).

The organization of marble production differed greatly from normal industrial routine, firstly because men worked in small isolated groups and this caused a certain amount of rivalry (see fig. 251), and secondly because the traditional hierarchy had never died out. It was too far for some quarrymen who lived in old villages perched on mountain-tops (see figg. 252, 253) to walk to work in the morning and home at night, so they were forced to spend the week in old huts built near the quarries. This explains why most local hands had abandoned the old republican ideals in favour of anarchy. The situation came to a head during the economic crisis of 1894 but the uprising was brutally repressed by military courts.

The quarrymen persevered and in 1902 they won their first great victory, a regular labour contract that placed them among the avant-guarde of the Italian working classes. The workers were roughly divided in to two ideological camps, the idealistic

256. *Cava Carbonera stoneboat for a monolith to be sent to the New Forum in Rome (1929).*

256

243

257

individuals and the pragmatists, and
this distinction is still true today.
During the worst years of the crisis the
state and local administration backed
by influential families and a few
ambitious citizens organised the first
public welfare institutions; a
kindergarten, a welfare fund, a health
insurance fund, a poor house, a state
hospital and a vocational training
school were started. In 1923 the
vocational school became an industrial
school for arts and crafts to train
marble workers and master builders,
the Industrial School for Artists and
Master Craftsmen (*Scuola Industriale*

di Arti e Mestieri) (see fig. 255), and
undoubtably this was a step in the
right direction.
The study of linguistics and
etnography of the marble area, and
the traditional and industrial
production methods by Gino
Bottiglioni was published at this time
in a foreign magazine but was not
appreciated in Italy till much later.
Between 1911 and 1914 the workers
fought to obtain pension schemes and
better working hours; everything came
to a standstill during the First World
War, but picked up again soon after;
in 1920-21 fascist squads started

*257. A modern depot:
together with local blocks of
marble there are foreign ones
that are also worked and
sold in Carrara.*

persecuting union leaders, and the workers' association was closed down. However the new regime organised a housing corporation and a corporation to record income and expenditure, and a welfare service for sick people and pregnant women.

The market for raw and manufactured marble collapsed during the First World War, and only 60.000 tons of marble were produced in 1918. Things gradually improved, and by 1926 production reached 340.000 tons a year; three quarters of this was exported, but after the re-evaluation of the lira it was no longer economically viable for many countries to purchase Carrara marble. Local businessmen formed an association to assess the amount of unsold stock, and to control future out-put of initialled blocks. The operation failed, and during the great slump of the Thirties production was cut by half. The economic sanctions imposed on Italy after the Ethiopian war caused foreign sales to drop further; the fascist regime tried to make good their losses and started to use marble for all national building (see fig. 256). Discarded material like calcium carbonate was used by chemical industries in order to try and diminish the increasing number of mine dumps called «ravaneti». The unions had been abolished, but social insurance was compulsory; however this did not prevent the health authorities from asserting, in 1934, that marble dust was free from silice and did not damage the lungs because the new

protective equipment and insurance fees were too expensive.

Production dropped again during the Second World War and battles were fought in 1944-45 along the «Gothic Line» near Carrara. The Apuan Alps were no-man's-land, and many workers had joined the Resistance movements while others suffered hunger: groups of women and children with all their wordly possessions packed into rudimentary carts walked as far as the Po valley in search of food.

By 1946 most of the equipment had been repaired and quarries started to function again. International sales increased, and marble for the building industry was in great demand, and production reached 500.000 tons a year by 1960. Adequate infrastructures had been built, and all quarries could be reached by road avoiding complicated loading and unloading operations — transfers from cableways, «lizze» and rail-roads. Efficient semi-mobile machinery had been introduced and although it facilitated production, experienced quarrymen were still the backbone of the marble industry.

Nowadays Carrara marble and the artisan school of Carrara have become famous all over the world: craftsmen work and sell every kind of marble product (see fig. 257), technicians and engineers design and build new sophisticated pieces of equipment and machinery, and skilled workers are trained in the most advanced marble centre ever.

Chapter Five

The Future of Marble

Socio-economic, enviromental, commercial and technological changes have influenced marble production throughout history. Except in production areas, where marble was used as a common building material, it was unknown in rural districts. Traditionally it has always been used for urban architecture, and still is today, both in countries with industrial and agricultural economies. In the past the marble market expanded in concomittance with periods of middle class urban prosperity, and in theory marble production should increase in the future, since the lower and middle classes are gradually becoming more wealthy.

Many intellectuals are campaining against excessive urbanization and are for a re-evaluation of rural life; there has never been a great return to an agricultural way of life in the past, except during periods of economic crises. Without exception, war and revolutions damage trade, specially that of heavy goods like marble, but it is impossible to foretell what could happen in the future. Large quantities of marble have always been exported throughout the Western World specially during periods of political stability, while, in the past, the organization of trade has always been the greatest problem. Demand varied according to current fashion and cultural developments, but has been fairly stable since the Middle Ages and the trend should continue. New technologies are essential to the development of new means of production, transportation and research. Things have changed tremendously during the past hundred and fifty years: new materials like iron structures and reinforced concrete were produced to compete with marble, but have been developed alongside new pieces of machinery — railroads, mechanic frames and wire saws — designed to reduce costs and improve the standard of production. The individual historical, social, economic and technological factors were brought together during the Industrial Age: urbanism, economic crisis and international wars, commercial organization, the mechanization of transport and production, competition and better social conditions.

On the whole marble production has increased all over the world, and, if the present trend continues, new

258. A. Aalto: Kultur-Zentrum of Wolfsburh in Western Germany. The external marble covering has architectural as well as protective functions.

258

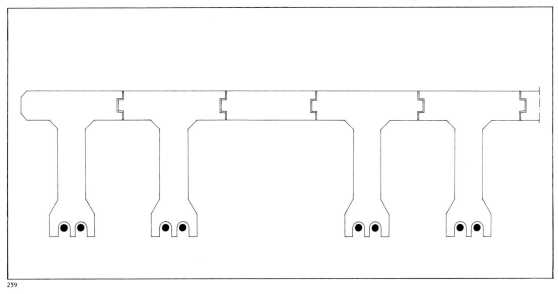

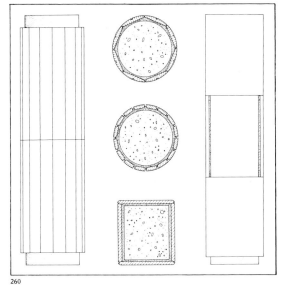

extraction and working methods, as
well as new materials, will soon be
produced. It is possible that man does
not yet possess the technological
know-how to produce new materials,
although he is capable of planning and
building new equipment. Man-made
materials can compete with marble on
a technical or economic level, but
from an aesthetic and prestigious point
of view marble has no rival. Marble
has always been expensive, more so in
the past than now, even though the
cost of labour has increased. In 1320
Melchiorre of Coppo Stefani recorded

that the altar of Orsanmichele in
Florence was initially to have been of
silver, but in the end, Carrara marble
from the Sponda quarry was decided
on, not because it was cheaper, but
because it was not so easy to steal.
Melchiorre wrote: «E costò il
tabernacolo così lavorato di marmo
grandissimo denaro — e fu gran
lavoro». «The marble tabernacle was
very expensive and took a long time to
make». King Carlo Alberto bought
eighty two granite columns from the
quarry of Mount Orfano near the
Lake Maggiore to rebuild the basilica
of Saint Paul in Rome that had been
destroyed by fire in 1823. The
columns were transported in four
loads down the rivers Po and Ticino
and then by sea to Rome; each
column cost 6,000 lira (£ 11.000
pound sterling of today). Efficient
means of transport helped cut
production costs more than anything
else, and new equipment compensated
the increasing cost of labour. New
products often enjoy instant
commercial success, but do not last,
since many buyers revert back to
traditional materials that never date
and last longer. Marble has great
symbolic value, as it has always been

identified with the powerful, rich and priviledged classes; some traditions die hard and there is no reason why this should not be true for the future as well as for the past.

Marble and Building

Marble is one of the most versatile building materials; it is functional and beautiful and can be used for practically anything: columns, architraves and steps and balconies, floors and interior and exterior decorations — baths, fireplaces, sculpture and to partition buildings — parapets etc. —. The present and future use of marble for building is the result of a complex historical process. Marble is up to ten times more resistant to compression than to traction, and the structure of some marble is so compact that it is stronger than concrete and even cast-iron. Flawless marble columns are better than most other building materials if cut along the horizontal axis plane, and not longer than eight or ten times their own diameter to avoid mechanic stress. Marble is practically timeless, but unfortunatly, contemporary architects and engineers have more faith in modern materials, and they drill holes in the marble to restore antique monuments and insert pieces of other material, like iron, to prevent decay: iron, however, is less enduring than marble. This is just one of the many cases when harm is done for the sake of a trend and this is becoming more and more widespread. Other materials have been studied in greater detail than marble about which not much is known as yet. Until recently marble was not used for supporting structures, because it was too expensive; reinforced concrete

pillars were often covered with marble slabs and made to look as if they were solid (see fig. 260). Marble monoliths have always been very expensive, and in the past supporting structures were either coverd with slabs, white-washed or plastered.

Horizontal marble structures like architraves are not very strong, since the compression strength of marble is much greater than the tensile strength. Fibrous materials are more suitable: the tensile strength of wood for instance is ten times greater than that of marble; cast iron is twenty times greater and steel a hundred. Architraves built by the Egyptians, Greeks and later by the Romans were short in proportion to the height of the columns that were placed close together; but this would not be possible in modern architecture (see figg. 182, 184). Eventually the Romans copied Etruscan arches which allowed for greater open spaces, and were exploited for public buildings, therefore the marble structure was not under tensile stress. Houses with wooden beams and arches were built up to the 19th century when they were replaced by iron that had great tensile and compression strength.

Draw pieces of iron were produced industrially, but costs were high, and soon new a mixed building material was invented, cast iron, that possessed great tensile and compression strength (see figg. 2, 185, 190, 198, 210, 228). Reinforced concrete structures can be shaped directly on the costruction site, and production costs are relitively low. During the 20th century traditional building materials nearly all disappeared from the market. Iron is still occasionally used for large constructions. During the Sixties experiments were carried out to exploit marble in the same way as

261

261. *G. Michelucci: interior of the church of San Giovanni Battista (Saint John the Baptist's) in Florence; it is made of stone, rock and reinforced concrete.*

reinforced concrete for horizontal structures. Two life sized models were shown at the «*1° Mostra del Marmo e delle Tecniche d'impiego del Marmo nell'edilizia Industriale*» at Carrara in 1965. The first was a pedestrian foot-bridge made with joists eight metres long and twentyfive centimetres thick reinforced with steel beaded moulding, fixed into grooves with epoxide resin (see fig. 259). The second was a hollow joist ten metres long and twentyfive centimetres thick pre-tensioned with nine harmonic steel wires capable of carrying a central load of one ton. These are exceptions and have not been followed up; it

proves that marble has great building potential, but for the time being production costs are too high.

On the whole, in industrialised societies, apart from a few monuments, it is unlikely that marble will be used once again for supporting structures; it is still used for doors, architraves and window frames but has a purely decorative, non-functional value. Marble is irreplaceable for stairs, doorsteps and floors and stands up to wear and tear better than any other material; in the past, stairs were part of the supporting structure — the steps functioned as joists — but today the structure is of reinforced concrete and marble is only used as a facing. It is still used in all buildings, even the most economical. Following the old tradition marble is used in public buildings and in the more opulent private houses (see fig. 261). In poorer houses granulated marble mixed with a kind of cement is used instead of ceramics, or small roughly cut pieces from discarded blocks (see fig. 159). These methods are comparatively cheap since extraction and squaring costs nothing and there is no shortage of raw material in quarrying areas, where, otherwise mine dumps would grow rapidly. To reduce production costs small mass-produced marble tiles called «marmette», in one or two standard sizes, have been put on the market. The same method was used by the great pre-Industrial Revolution merchants who supplied churches and patrician houses with «quadrette» (see Ch. V); in the past production costs were low because labour was cheap: new automatic equipment has helped keep prices down today. To reduce costs further mable tiles measuring ten centimetre by ten centimetre and one centimetre thick have been produced: «marmette», the traditional tiles, are usually two centimetres thick. Industrialised producers are trying to capture the less wealthy but larger middle class market, and in the past twenty years demand has gone up tremendously, but only in one sector and this means the market is vulnerable if a economic crisis occurs. The housing crisis has nothing to do with the expansion of the marble market and while certain household marble decorations are taken for granted and seem commonplace, no other building material has taken their place for thousands of years. Probably, in the future machinery

capable of cutting rough blocks of marble into standard sized, ready made «marmette» will be devised, and experienced marble technitians will choose the most suitable blocks and select the finished product.
Initially the exteriors of Roman buildings were covered with terracotta tiles or bricks to protect the walls, and marble facings were introduced later on. During the Middle Ages marble had a purely prestigious and aesthetic function since the walls were made of stone; in the Renaissance marble facings were used for two reasons, to decorate the walls and protect them better than plaster (see fig. 199). This is true today and costly marble facings have a purely symbolic value in expensive modern buildings; in poorer houses marble is only used on the ground floor or for skirting boards to protect the most vulnerable areas. Some architects have rediscovered the decorative as well as functional value of marble and its great architectural harmony. These three trends will no doubt develop in the future; in the first case industrial production will gradually become standardized, and costs will diminish further, while the other two trends depend on individual demand, and laying marble is one of the most costly operations as each slab must be fixed individually to avoid stress (see fig. 236). In the past builders fixed each slab with iron cramps, but pre-fabricated parts will probably be used in the future.

Marble and Sculpture

The amount of marble used for sculpture has always been less than for building. Only 5% of the marble extracted at Carrara in the 5th century

was sent to sculptors' workshops and there is no reason to assume that things will change in the future. On the contrary, due to mass-production, demand will probably decrease further.

Marble used for sculpture is one of the most precious, and extraction costs increase continually. *Statuario* marble is extracted underground and it is not possible to reduce the cost of labour as for open-air extraction using selective mines. However the increasing cost of *statuario* is not the only reason why artists no longer use it; the roots are much deeper and go back to the reaction of avant-guarde movements to academic classicism, and artists' desertion of workshops. Twenty-one major Italian sculptors have been asked why, and their answers differ greatly. Some say that marble belongs to the past and must be re-discovered, some that it is beautiful but arrogant, others that it is difficult to work unless the artist loves and understands it deeply, or that it has purely cerimonial and religious connotations and does not belong to our century; that it has been replaced by more functional materials; that it goes against todays rapid productive and broadcasting methods; that it reached its zenith with Michelangelo; that it is eternal, unlike other materials, that it suits sculpture «the art of taking away», that it is dying. There is a great tradition of plastic as well as artistic sculpture that will be examined in the next paragraph.

Craftsmanship

Industrialised societies have altered the traditional concept of craftsmanship and its meaning has become ambiguous. On the one hand one talks about the number of workers and the kind of work executed, that is mostly manual, and on the other, that each article is manufactured individually, and the way in which the business is managed. None of these aspects are typical of pre-industrial craftsmanship: the socio-economic fabric of society has changed, and the type of production has changed with it. In the case of marble there are two main problems; firstly pre-industrial mass-production and the dependence of large numbers of workers on small groups of merchants, and the existance of machinery, however primitive; secondly the impossibility to start up new industries capable of mass-producing standard size articles. Nowadays large and medium size industrial concerns cater for what was once the artisan's market, and small family businesses have specialised in ornamental pieces or everyday household articles. Apart from the type of equipment and business that do not vary much, modern artisans belong to neither of the above categories. In the past twenty or thirty years new man-made materials for interior decorating have been launched on the market to replace marble, and all that is new — specially if made in U.S.A. — enjoys immediate success, but sooner or later is replaced by the old traditional materials. Society is changing rapidly and this could be beneficial for the marble industry and market. The higher the standard of living, the greater the need for marble to be used for tombstones, headstones and memorial tablets, and no substitutes have yet appeared on the market.

Modern commercial organizations are most careful to exploit every new trend, but put much less effort into scientific research, that would help

263. Studio Nicoli (Carrara):
an abstract piece of modern
sculpture executed in white
marble.

263

increase new working techniques, reduce production costs and discover new means of using marble, than into marketing the product. The future of marble cannot be seperated from its past; knowledge of the properties of marble, and above all centuries of experience are as vital today as they were in 500 years ago. Also it is imperative that traditional techniques are kept up to restore and refurbish the vast quantity of large and small beautiful buildings in historical centres.

Chapter Six

Marble in the U.S.A.

Valuable or inexpensive, marble has been used for building in the United States from the time of the Declaration of Independence, and it is still in great demand today. White marble was used for monumental buildings, designed in the Neoclassical style fashionable in Europe at the time of the new American republic's inception. Initially marble was imported from the Mediterranean basin, but soon domestic veins were discovered and quarried, giving rise to the modern American dimensional stone industry (dealt with in greater detail later).

In a loose sense, the word «marble» is applied to all the types of stone that take polish well; however in the American dimensional stone industry the following distinctions are made:

1) Marble: a) true marble: generated by the metamorphic recrystallization of limestone; b) onyx marble, that is, calcareous onyx; c) verd antiques, a serpentine based rock (hydrous magnesium silicate); d) travertine, classified as marble for commercial reasons, although not easily polished

2) Granite: true granite: a hard natural igneous rock that takes polish, such as quartz-diorite, syenite, porphyry, gabbro or siliceous metamorphic rock like gneiss

3) Other stones: limestone, slate and sandstone; sandstone, especially when hard, is erroneously known as quartzite

All the above-mentioned types of rock are available in large quantity from domestic deposits. Certain types of true marble, travertine and granite, for example, are still imported from abroad whenever demand exceeds supply, or when domestic deposits do not yield material with the desired chromatic characteristics. In this case the dimensional stone industry's policy is to import raw blocks from foreign quarries that are later sawed and polished in the United States.

A huge continuous deposit of true marble is situated along the central axis of the Appalachian mountain chain formed by Paleozoic limestone transformed by regional metamorphosis caused by the folds of the Appalachian orogeny. However, since the chain is very old, the mountains have been eroded to a great extent and marble now outcrops on the surface. The marble is 93 to 98% calcium carbonate in large and small crystals, according to the degree it was transformed by the regional metamorphism. The remaining impure substances (graphite, iron or manganese oxides, mica, etc.) give different colorings to the marble. White marble is the purest. Colored marbles take different tones of black, yellow, red and green.

The Appalachian marble deposit starts in Vermont near the Canadian border and stretches as far as Alabama; the marble belt is 1/4 of a mile to four miles wide. Drill cores have shown the veins to be three hundred to eight hundred feet deep, allowing large compact blocks of homogeneous color and grain to be extracted by modern methods.

The Vermont quarries are among the oldest and most exploited in the United States. Some are even among the largest in the country, like the Imperial quarries near Dunby, in Dorset Mountain, that produce a well-known variety of white marble. Sometimes the marble is faintly cream, hard and translucent, veined, or mottled and clouded with gray or green. Other important quarries are situated in West Rutland; reddish marble is extracted near Swanton; bluish-gray near Proctor; verd near Rochester and Roxbury; and black with white fossil casts on Isle La Motte in Lake Champlain.

There is a long sequence of smaller

264. Monticello: Thomas Jefferson's Neoclassical style house in Virginia.

258

quarries situated along the Appalachian mountains that produces true marble. It crosses Massachusetts, New York, New Jersey, Maryland, Virginia and North Carolina.

However, the most interesting deposits are in Tennessee and, above all, Georgia and Alabama.

Marble from the South, quarried since the last century, is frequently translucent, making it suitable for sculpture, and possesses high strength and low absorption, ideal for external facing.

The most important quarries in Georgia are near Tate, in Pickens County, where the depth of the deposits is less than two hundred feet. The marble extracted is usually coarse grained and its color varies from white, occasionally veined with green or pink, to dark or pale gray. The largest quarries in Alabama are still in the Sylacauga and Gnatts Quarry areas in Talladega County, where the deposits are about two hundred feet deep. The marble is finer grained and some beds are translucent; it is usually white or creamy white and occasionally veined with light green.

In the Rocky Mountains and along the Coast ranges the metamorphism of limestone has produced true marble, but since the mountains are still geologically young, there are no great outcrops as on the Appalachian chain. Moreover the outcrops are always situated at great altitudes, and consequently are not easily accessible. The white marble, faintly clouded and golden-veined, quarried near Marble, Colorado, is very famous and used for important national monuments. Another well-known variety of marble is the pink, yellow and gray marble of Tuolumne County in California. True marble is also quarried in Missouri and Alaska where the contact metamorphism was generated by granitic magma. Onyx marble is

extracted in Arizona, while green serpentine marble is quarried along the Susquehanna river in Maryland, as well as in Rochester, Vermont.

The continental plates are principally made up of granite, a type of silicate rock. Granite has high strength and low absorption, but is often altered or fractured by dynamometamorphism. An extensive and high level of regional metamorphism in geologic time transformed granite into gneiss, a type of rock that is equally strong and compact. Relatively recently igneous rock surfaced on the continental crust after the formation of mountain chains. This includes diorites, syenites and porphyries, as well as granites, that are usually well preserved and can be extracted in large blocks. It is essential when opening a new quarry to take the following elements into account: the size of the crystals, the color of the feldspar and the location of the deposit.

The most important quarries of granite and other igneous rock in the United States are in Grant County, South Dakota; Washington County, Vermont; Hillsborough County, New Hampshire; Sterns County, Minnesota; and Madison County, Georgia. Other quarries boasting high production levels are located in Alabama, Massachusetts, North and South Carolina, Pennsylvania, Texas and Wisconsin.

Several types of stone used for building belong to the family of sedimentary rocks produced by the consolidation of carbonaceous or siliceous materials deposited in lakes or seas throughout the different geologic ages.

The most important are limestone, sandstone and slate. Generally they possess less strength and more absorption than marble and granite, and do not take polish well, although there are rare exceptions. Limestone in

265

265. The Capitol in
Washington, started in 1793
and finished in 1863
following a plan by Thomas
V. Walter.
266. The Library of the
Congress, Washington, is
rich in chiseled marbles.

266

particular is, in some cases, as brightly colored as marble.

Lawrence and Monroe counties in Indiana are important centers of limestone quarrying. Slate quarries are found in Rutland County, Vermont, and Northampton, Pennsylvania. Other limestone and sandstone quarries producing building materials are located in Alabama, Minnesota, New York, Ohio, Texas and Virginia. The use of marble for architecture and sculpture was derived from Europe. In the 18th century most distinguished colonial architecture was influenced by the Georgian style, and modeled on the work of Andrea Palladio and Inigo Jones. In the following hundred years, the design of public buildings and private houses in the new republic was based on Neoclassical artistic canons. Large quantities of white true marble and limestone were required for this kind of architecture and sculpture.

In fact Washington can be compared to ancient Rome in its architects lavish use of marble.

Since Roman times the most famous and highly commercialized variety of marble in Italy was that of Carrara. A whole chapter of this book has been devoted to its history. But by the 19th century American public trusts and private citizens were employing white marble from Vermont, Alabama, Georgia and Colorado. The classical style continued to be favored for commemorative art and architecture until the 20th century. However from the middle of the 19th century materials belonging to the new technological era, iron and reinforced concrete, started to be used for load bearing structures. The cupola of the Capitol in Washington, for instance, erected between 1851 and 1863, was built using a cast iron load bearing structure.

By the end of the century architects like Sullivan, Burnham and Root started a new trend wherein load bearing structures were no longer hidden by external coverings but were part of the architecture of the building, as in the Reliance and Guaranty Building in Chicago. This marked the beginning of a new era that was to lead to the «glass towers» of the postwar period.

These changes have depend ed depended on the cultural and economic evolution of American society. The rational architecture of the 20th century has banished all non-functional decoration, though marble, for time immemorial the symbol of wealth and power, solidity and solemnity, has found its way to the head offices and reception rooms of banks and others companies, if only on the inside. However the mood of the times has changed and efficiency, functionalism and rationalism have replaced opulence. This new aesthetic is better expressed by man-made materials that are lighter and more brightly colored. There is yet another, more practical reason: man-made materials produced by industrial means are more flexible than stone and, above all, cost (or used to cost) much less than marble. The physical properties of marble make it difficult to extract and apply on an industrial basis, and for over a century no significant improvements in production, either technical or economic, offset the increasing cost of labor.

Things were made worse by the economic crisis of 1929, and the first signs of improvement came only fifty years later, at the end of the seventies. The overall production of dimensional stone in the United States dropped gradually from five million tons in 1928 to 1.4 million in 1978, excluding the peak of 2.5 million tons reached in the fifties. On the other hand the production of crushed and

267

267. The Supreme Court in Washington: a classical temple.

268. The Abraham Lincoln Memorial in Washington, built in 1917 after a plan by Henry Bacon.

268

269

broken stone used for reinforced concrete, plaster, mortar and paving has increased, as has agricultural stone and fluxing stone used for metallurgic processing.

Economic, technological and cultural trends have shifted over the years, and recently such changes have led to an increase in the demand for dimensional stone. The energy crisis, particularly, has caused the price of many materials to increase substantially. The first products to be affected were synthetics derived from oil, followed by glass and aluminum, since their production costs rose drastically. The public, however, is becoming more and more disenchanted with man-made products and consequently is rediscovering natural materials.

In the case of marble, and of all dimensional stone in general, the greater initial cost (notwithstanding the price increases of man-made products) is nearly always compensated by the fact that it is long lasting and requires a minimal up-keep.

Meanwhile machines for extracting and working marble have been perfected; in some cases production

269. *The New York Public Library.*
270. *The New York Stock Exchange, where some representative marbles from Georgia have been employed.*

270

265

271

has become standard, as in the case of slabs for floors and external and internal coverings. The new machinery has also helped to keep prices down. The marble industry has been given further impulse by recycling the debris from quarries and sawmills. Large grained debris is utilized for terrazzo, stucco dash, agricultural stone and fluxing stone. White marble dust with a high percentage of calcium carbonate is used for industrial products: cosmetics, liquid detergents, glue, rubber, asphalt, stucco, paint, plastic, glass, paper, pencils, insulants, fitted carpets, animal foods, chewing gum, etc. In the future it is probable that some white marble from white limestone quarries will be used exclusively to produce calcium carbonate dust.

Statistics show that more dimensional stone is being used presently than in the past.

According to figures provided to us courtesy of the Marble Institute of America, between 1980 and 1984 demand for finished marble products increased 232%; demand for travertine increased 424%; and demand for granite increased 675%, surpassing by a long shot the highest levels of production in the past.

271. The Massachusetts Institute of Technology, built at Cambridge in 1915.
272. An array of styles and materials: Grand Central Station and the Pan American Building, New York.

American Ballet Theatre—Spring Season   Ballet Nacional de Cuba—Alicia Alonso   Martha Graham Dance Company   ...rforming Arts—People's Republic of China   ...ondon Festival Ballet—Rudolf Nureyev

273

273. Lincoln Center,
New York. On the left, the
Metropolitan Opera House;
on the right, Avery Fisher
Hall.

274. A contemporary marble
structure: the East Building
of the National Gallery,
Washington; a detail of the
exterior.

274

275

275. *The East Building of
the National Gallery,
Washington: detail of the
interior.*

Appendix

Written and Oral Sources

Plinii Naturalis Historiae
(from Book XXXVI)

(Concerning the quarries of Paros and Luni; the origins and technique of marble sawing and when it was first introduced into Rome).

Omnes autem candido tantum marmore usi sunt e Paro insula; quem lapidem coepere lychniten appellare, quoniam ad lucernas in cuniculis caederetur, ut auctor est Varro, multis postea candidioribus repertis, nuper vero etiam in Lunensium lapicidinis, sed in Pariorum mirabile proditur, glaeba lapidis unius cuneis dividentium soluta, imaginem Sileni intus extitisse.

. . . .

Secandi in crustas nescio an Cariae fuerit inventum. antiquissima, quod equidem inveniam, Halicarnasi domus Mausoli Proconnesio marmore exculta est latericiis parietibus. is obiit olympiadis CVII anno secundo, urbis Romae CDIII.

Primum Romae parietes crusta marmoris operuisse totos domus suae in Caelio monte Cornelius Nepos tradit Mamurram, Formiis natum equitem Romanum, praefectum fabrum C. Caesaris in Gallia, ne quid indignitati desit, tali auctore inventa re. hic namque est Mamurra Catulli Veroniensis carminibus proscissus, quem, ut res est, domus ipsius.

. . . .

Sed quisquis primus invenit secare luxuriamque dividere inportuni ingenii fuit. harena hoc fit et ferro videtur fieri, serra in praetenui linea premente harenas versandoque tractu ipso secante.

(D. E. EICHHOLZ, *Pliny Natural History,* vol. X, Books XXXVI-XXXVII, Harvard University Press, London, 1962).

Genoese Deeds of the Year 1191 concerning Marble

Duranto, son of Giordano of Carrara, has undertaken to deliver a column of marble to Guglielmo Fondichiere. The 20th June 1191.

Wililemi Fundigarij].
Testes Iohannes Boletus, Bernition Scotus, Dominicus magister. Sub volta Fornariorum, ea die. Promittit Durantus filius Gordiani de Carraira se daturum Wilielmo fundigario columpnam .I. marmoris longam palmorum .VIIII $^1/_2$. et grossam palmorum .IIII. et sumissi .I., sanam et integram, in portu Ianue, ad medium augustum pro sol. .XL., et quietus est, sub pena dupli. Et Wido de Cunizo et Bonus Vi-

cinus filius Alberti ed Bellotus de Marchesello debitores et pagatores, in solidum, sub pena dupli, abrenunciantes iuri solidi et iuri quo cavetur principalem debitorem primo conveniri.

Stefano Zartex has undertaken to deliver various goods to Lanfranco Ricerio at the port of Deiva by the middle of December. The 16th October 1191.

Lafranci Ricerij].
Promittit Stephanus de Zartex se daturum Lafranco Ricerio, in portu de Deva usque ad medium decembrim, columpnellos .XII. petre vermilie de Paxano, pro sol. .IIII $^1/_2$.columpnellum, longos palmorum .V. et grossos sumissi .I., et capitellos .XII. pro den. .XIII. capitellum, sub pena dupli in suis bonis. Et sol. .XX. confitetur se recepisse ab eo. Et magister Guarnerius debitor et pagator, sub pena dupli, abrenuncians iuri quo cavetur principalem debitorem primo conveniri. Sub volta Fornariorum, ea die. Testes Bonus Vasallus de Cartagenia, Obertus Boletus.

Ottobono comes to an agreement with Oberto Boleto about the masonry to be done in his (Ottobono's) house. The 14th December 1191.

[fo. 74 r.] Oberti Boleti, p.].
Ottobonus de Sola[la]rio promittit Oberto Boleto levare domum eius a base columpne usque in pedes .XXXIII. ex parte vie, et ingrossare murum ab utraque parte si necesse fuerit, et facere scalam et mezanum cum voltis et picare columpnam et facere usque ad lixare et capitellos et columpnellos vermilios et laborare marmora et facere murum de opera picata, simili operi Wilielmi Zirbini de Petris, et facere balconatam .I. in mezano et murum et portas et duas balconatas superius et sportam de archetis. Hec omnia promittit facere usque ad sanctum Michaelem, cum suis expensis, pro lib. .XLV. Et Obertus dare promittit lib. .XLV. et calcinam et marmora et columpnam et capitellos et ligna necessaria et ferra necessaria operi in opera ponenda. Et ut supra promittunt attendere ad invicem, sub pena lib. .XLV. vicissim stipulata in suis bonis. Sub porticu Ottonis ferrarij, die .XIII. decembris .MCLXXXXI., indictione .VIIII.

(M.W. HALL, H.C. KRUEGER, R.L. REYNOLDS, *Ligurian Notaries of the 12th century, Guglielmo Cassinese (1191-1191),* Genoa, 1938).

Bishop Henry's Autobiography

(Concerning the establishment of the marble customs at Carrara in 1273).

In Dei nomine, amen. Anno Domini MCCLXXIII, in quo anno assumpti fuimus, nos Henricus, natione de Ficeculo, in ep. lun. per dominum Gregorium Papam X apud Urbem Veterem mense aprilis, et mense madii intravimus episcupatum primo in die beati Marci Evangeliste.

. . . .

Item, in Carraria fecimus fieri domos apud Vezale que constiterunt nobis ultra II libr. imp., et recuperavimus fabricas, de quibus in nullo respondebant ep. lun., et de quibus modo habemus bene L. libras imp., et plus haberemus si nobis fideliter responderent.

Item, recuperavimus magistros marmorum, qui quasi in nullo respondebant lun. ep., et fecimus fieri doanam marmorum, de quibus habet emolumentum et utilitatem ep. lun. ultra L. libras imp. annuatim. Item, revocavimus doanam salis ab hom. de Sarzana, qui dicebant se habere medietatem in ipsa et litigavimus cum eis in curia Romana et alibi, et habuimus multas brigas et guerras cum eis propter hoc: tamen cum Dei auxilio eos superavimus, ita quod nihil habent facere ibi, nec possunt aliquid vindicare in ea de iure de cetero. In qua lite et discordia expendimus ultra II m. libras imp.

(M. LUPO GENTILE, *The regest of the Pelavicino Codex*, in «Atti della Società Ligure di Storia Patria», vol. XLIV, Genoa 1912).

Public Notaries of 15th century Carrara

Tomeo of Gaddo rents out for four years three quarries situated at Aponda, near Torano, to Giovanni, son of Paolo Martini of Sorgnano, and to Giovanni of Castellino from Gragnana, including a hut with the necessary tools, for a fee equal to 1/6 of the profits. From the NOTARIAL ARCHIVE OF CARRARA, Public Notary Nicolao Parlonciotto, 1475-1477).

In Christi nomine, amen. Anno eisdem Millesimo CCCCLXXV°, Indictione VIII[a], die XIII° mensis septembris. Thomeus quondam Gaddi de Carraria hoc publico instrumento, locavit et concessit Iohanni filio Pauli Martini de Soregnano et Iohanni quondam Castellini de Gragnana et cuilibet eorum insolidum presentibus stipulantibus et recipientibus, ad utendum et fruendum pro certo affictu et reddittu, caveas tres marmorum [cum capanna et una maza ferri ponderis librarum 22, uno picono ponderis librarum 7$^{1/2}$, uno martelletto ponderis librarum 6, una squadra ponderis librarum 6$^{1/2}$, quatordecim libras mollettarum, decem cuneis librarum 60$^{1/2}$, una zappa librarum 6, uno palo fereo librarum 43, una seghetta librarum 7], sitas in pertinentiis Torani in loco dicto a Sponda, iuxta Bernabovem Dominici de Carraria, dictum locatorem, et canale, vel siqui, etc. et ipsam capannam et omnes et singulos ferros et armamenta suprascripta, hinc ad annos quatuor proxime futuros.

. . . .

Actum Carrarie in domo mei notarii infrascripti. Presentibus Iacobo filio magistri Adornini de Clavaro, habitatore Carrarie, et Bertozo quondam Dominici Muccetti de Aventia, testibus, etc.

(C. KLAPLISCH ZUBER, *Carrara and the marble «masters»* (1100-1300), «Deputazione di Storia Patria per le Antiche Provincie Modenesi», Massa 1973).

The Statute of the Genoese «Maestri» (Masters) in the 15th Century

Capitula Magistrorum Dominorum sculptorum marmarorum et lapidium (sic).

In nomine Sancte et Individue Trinitatis Patris et Filii et Spiritus Sancti ac Beatorum Iohannis Baptiste martiris Iohannis Evangeliste ac Beatorum Simonis et Iude apostolorum Beati Laurentii martiris protectoris Ecclesie majoris Ianuensis ac Beati Georgii vexilliferi Communis Ianue ac Beatorum Quatuor Incoronatorum protectorum et defensorum infrascripte artis magistrorum sculptorum *(sic)* marmarorum et lapidium ac totius Curie celestis: *Amen.*

De Consulibus eligendis. — Statuimus et ordinamus quod singulis annis eligantur per omnes homines dicte artis duo Consules dicte artis qui curam habeant totius artis prout solent facere et habere Consules artium hujus Civitatis et quod eligantur tempore quo solent eligi in presenti Civitate alii Consules artium et qui Consules eligi debeant ad voces ita quod illi qui habebunt plures voces sint et esse debeant Consules.

De obediendo Consulibus et juramento. — Item ordinamus quod omnes homines dicte artis et de ipsa laboratores teneantur et debeant in ingressu Officii Consulum jurare singulis annis de parere mandatis ipsorum Consulum eorum videlicet que ad ipsam artem spectabunt et pertinebunt et que erunt licita et honesta sub pena peyurii et ultra soldorum quinque usque in decem arbitrio Consulum.

De festivitatibus celebrandis. — Item ordinamus quod omnes dicte artis teneantur et debeant celebrare festa infrascripta et ipsorum apothecas clausas tenere sub pena librarum duarum usque in quinque arbitrio Consulum nisi cum licentia dictorum Consulum: festum *Beatorum Quatuor Incoronatorum:* festum *S. Sebastiani:* festum *S. Ambrosii:* festum *S. Georgii:* festum *S. Laurentii:* festum *S. Rochi:* festum *S. Michaelis:* festum *S. Martini:* festum *S. Lucie:* festum *S. Antonii* et omnia festa Apostolorum.

De quantitate solvenda pro ingressu dicte artis. — Statuimus quod omnes forestos *(sic)* qui de cetero venerint ad habitandum in presenti Civitate causa laborandi pro arte qui aggregati erunt dicte arti per Consules et Consiliarios ipsius solvere debeant ipsis Consulibus libras sex januinorum quorum dimidia detur et applicetur Spectabilibus DD. Patribus Communis et reliqua dimidia dicte arti.

De famulis exercentibus dictam artem ad terminum annorum sex. — Statuimus quod de cetero per rectum vel per indirectum quoquo modo aliquis tam januensis quam extraneus non possit nec debeat in presenti Civitate exercere ipsam artem sculptoriam marmoreorum et lapidium nisi ipse talis steterit per annos sex continuos ad exercendum dictam artem cum aliquo ex magistris dicte artis presentis Civitatis cum instrumento quo tempore annorum sex finito ipse talis qui addiscerit dictam artem debeat aggregari in ipsam artem et solvat pro ingressu dicte artis soldos decem eo salvo quod filii magistrorum et filii fratrum et fratres fratrum possint intrare dictam artem libere et sine instrumento et sine aliqua solutione fienda nec aliquis de dicta arte possit societatem seu compagniam facere cum aliqua persona que non sit de dicta arte et qui de ea non sciat laborare judicio Consulum sub pena librarum vigintiquinque a quolibet contrafaciente exigenda per ipsos Consules totiens quotiens contrafecerit applicata pro dimidia DD. Patribus Communis et pro reliqua dimidia dicte arti.

De marmoris (sic) *et lapidibus que conducentur in Ianua.* — Item ordinamus quod illi lapides marmorei qui conducentur de cetero in presentem Civitatem et venduntur debeant per Consules dicte artis contribuere inter homines dicte artis qui de ipsi voluerint pretio quo ipsos emerint sub pena librarum quinque exigenda a quolibet dicte artis qui presenti capitulo stare recusaret applicanda ut supra: salvo tamen quod si aliquis civis aut mercator aut dominus ipsos marmores *(sic)* et lapides faceret venire pro suo usu aut ad suam instantiam de eis non possit fieri contributio inter homines dicte artis.

De non incantando opus vel se impediendo de opere incepto vel promisso alicui ex magistris dicte artis. — Item quod nemo de dicta arte possit et valeat se impedire de aliquo laborerio quod inceperit aliquis ex dicta arte nec ipsum finire nisi de consensu illius magistri qui ipsum laborerium inceperit sub pena florenorum quatuor et ultra arbitrio Consulum dicte artis applicata ut supra.

De balia Consulum in questionibus decidendis. — Statuimus quod Consules dicte artis baliam habeant decidendi omnem controversiam que forte contingeret intra homines dicte artis de summa videlicet librarum duarum cum dimidia et quilibet *(sic)* ordinationi faciende per ipsos Consules stare teneatur nec ab ea possit appellare et Consules teneantur ipsos rixantes et contendentes infra dies octo expedire et concordare sub pena soldorum quadraginta pro quolibet Consule contrafaciente applicata et supra.

De non incantando domos et apothecas. Statuimus soqud nemo dicte artis possit aut valeat pro se aut alia persona incantare seu incantari facere vel impedire aliquam domum seu apothecam quam conduceret alius magister dicte artis nisi de consensu conductoris sub pena librarum vigintiquinque applicata ut supra et ultra dicta domus aut apotheca claudatur et clausa remanere debeat per annos duos et ille talis qui eam incantaverit solvere teneatur domino dicte apothece pensionem.

De societate facienda pre sepulturis. — Ordinamus quod semper quocumque decesserit aliquis de dicta arte seu uxor vel filii aut famuli etatis videlicet annorum duodecim supra quilibet de dicta arte si requisitus fuerit teneatur ipsum talem defunctum associare ad sepulturam sub pena soldorum quinque applicata ut supra.

De Missa celebranda. — Ordinamus quod omnes magistri et laboratores dicte artis teneantur omni ultima Dominica cujuslibet mensis se convenisse in .... ad audiendam Missam et hoc pro devotione et bono usu dicte artis sub pena soldorum duorum applicata ut supra et si aliquis ex Consulibus aut Consiliariis negligentes fuerint ad audiendum *(sic)* ipsam Missam cadat quisque ipsorum Consulum in penam soldorum decem et Consiliariorum quinque nisi si interveniret causa legitima judicio Consulum.

De electione Consiliariorum et Massariorum. — Ordinamus quod postquam electi fuerint Consules debeant eligi per eosdem Consules tam de novo quam de vetero sex Consiliarios *(sic)* dicte artis et Massarios unus ac etiam duo alii Massarii qui duo tantum curam habeant capelle dicte artis.

De condemnationibus exigendis. — Ordinamus quod Consules teneantur exigere omnes condemnationes que fuerint facte tempore sui Consulatus et dimidiam ipsarum dare DD. Patribus Communis sub pena solvendi de suo proprio.

De eundo ad pallium festum SS. Simonis et Iude. — Ordinamus quod Consules et Consiliarii ac homines dicte artis ire debeant cum aliis artistis ad associandum palium prout solet fieri omni anno cum suis brandonis videlicet duobus sub pena soldorum viginti arbitrio Consulum applicata ut supra.

De associando Corpore Christi. — Ordinamus quod omni anno Consules ire debeant in processione Corporis Christi cum duobus brandonis de pondere librarum trium pro singulo.

Contra falsificantes petras. — Si aliquis de dicta arte promitteret alicui civi aut alio cujusvis *(sic)* aliquam quantitatem petre et postea illam permutaret vel non attenderet possit condemnari per Consules in valorem illarum lapidium quas falsificasset aut non attendisset et preterea cadat in penam librarum quatuor. *(Archiv. Govern. — Fogliaz. Artium 1424-1703).*

(F. ALIZERI, *Notes by Professors of drawing from the origins up to the 16th century*, vol. IV «Scultura», Luigi Sambolino, Genoa 1877).

The Statute of Carrara: Chapters Written in 1519

(Establishing the marble gabelle and forbidding all foreigners to extract marble from the quarries of Carrara).

XXXVIII

Item petunt quod homines predicti Vicariatus, tam marmorarii quam alii, quibus in futuris exportari continget extra ipsum Vicariatum aliquam quantitatem marmorum, tam rudium quam laboratorum, cuiusvis qualitatis et conditionis existant, non teneantur solvere pro gabella nisi ad rationem solidorum quindicim Imperialium monete currentis pro singula carratia; excepits mortariis pro quorum singulo solvi debeant pro gabella quatrini tres tantum dicte monete currentis; et quod pro qualibet sarcina, seu salma marmorum, solvi debeat gabella ad ratam gabelle limitate super carrata, ut supra, et quod nulla persona forensis possit, per se nec per alium, fabricare nec laborare aliqua marmora alicuius qualitatis et conditionis in lapidiciniis seu caveis marmoreis aut in aliis locis in dicta Vicaria consistentibus. Prefati Domini concesserunt quod quicunque conducentes marmora extra territorium Carrarie solvere teneantur ad rationem solidorum XXIV imper. monete currentis tantum pro singula carrata; pro singulis vero mortariis solvere debeant quatrinos sex dicte monete. Et quod nemo forensis possit fodere nec laborare marmora in dicto territorio Carrarie, nisi habita speciali licentia ab ipsis Dominis. In ceteris vero respicientibus dictam gabellam marmorum et mortariorum, serventur consuetudines et capitula super ipsis disponentia.

(A. ANGELI, *Carrara in the Middle Ages, Statutes and ordinances*, «Atti della Società Ligure di Storia Patria», vol. LIV, Genoa 1929).

The Republic of Genoa's Concession to Extract Coloured Marble

Relatione degli Ill.mi della m. da farsi al Collegio Ill.mo supra la supplica del mastro Gio: Morello, li 1626 a 6 luglio

Gli Ill.mi SS. Aless.o Giust.no, e Gio Batta squarcia.o della mattina letta la supplica del mastro Gio:, et una notta de diversi luoghi dove dice di haver ritrovato cave di diversi qualità da registrarsi in appresso, et al tutto havuta consideratione sono di parere riferire al Coll.o Ill.mo quanto in appresso.
Che si conceda a detto supplicante et a suoi heredi previleggio per venticinque anni prossimi de poter lavorare, e cavar marmi, e mischi in ogniuna delle suddette cave come meglio le parerà, restando per questo tempo prohibito ad ogni persona dal poter mettere mano in dette cave sotto pena arbitraria al Serenissimo Senato e perche buona parte di dette cave sono situate ne beni de particolari se intenda che in queste non possa travagliare ne far lavorare se prima non si sarà agiustato con li patroni delle terre, o luoghi dove saranno simili cave, senza il consenso di quali si dichiara che non le sia lecito farvi lavorare, e quanto a quelle che non sono in terre sue particolari se le concede e che possa travagliarci senz'altro, dandone pero prima parte al Giudicente, accioche se vi conoscesse qualche inconveniente possa darne parte al predetto Ser.mo Senato.
Di tutto quello utile che detto maestro Gio: o altro per lui haverà ogn'anno dalle cave ne quali lavorerà, o farà lavorare, sia esso, o li suoi heredi come sopra ubligato, o ubligati, a dar buono, fedele e legal conto in Camera de gli Illustrissimi Procuratori, et al cadere di essa pagare la decima parte di esso utile sotto pena in caso di contraventione arbitraria al Ser.mo Senato e di restar privo della Concessione sul presente privilegio il quale voglia e se intenda concesso con conditione che sino al presente non sia ad altri stata fatta simile concessione e non altrimente.
Che debba metter mano fra un anno prossimo e travagliarvi poi continuamente a Giudizio del Coll.o Ill.mo. Che non possa extrahere fuori del Dominio senza alcuna de detti marmi, e mischi senza Licenza del Ser.mo Senato o Ill.mi Procuratori sotto pena a detto Ser.mo Senato arbitraria.

die 13 detto

• approbata detta relatio, et metà iam decretum
• referendumque Ser.mo Senatui
• ad calculos...

La notta, e luoghi delle cave suddette sono come in appresso
Una cava d'alabastro orientale a herono nelle montagne di monte marcello
un'altra nelle montagne di Lerice di alabastro Cristalino
un'altra di marmo giallo assomigliante all'antico di Roma
un'altra di negro, e giallo a una cava che si domanda ceri di Castello di Trebiano, o vero di Lerice
Un'altra nelle montagne di Caprione a Lerice diportasanta come l'antico di Roma, bianco, rosso, e di molti altri colori
Un'altra di negro e giallo sull'Isola della Palmaria di Porto venere
Un'altra di negro e bianco nella medesima Isola
Un'altra di negro argentato e due altre di alabastro cristalino di color delle corniole, e delle ambre, e del Calcidonio color di latte sulla medesima Isola
Un'altra su l'Isolotto che si domanda il Tino di Portovenere di marmo negro color argentato
Un'altra sopra la fortezza di Portovenere di negro, e giallo, o cavando le dette pietre si giova alla fortezza perche si slarga il fosso e saffonda
Un'altra tra Portovenere, e Remaggiore di breccia Brocca Broccatelato come il Broccatello di Spagna Al Biassa villa della Spezza, e Pegassano villa pure della Spezza vi è una cava di Portasanta di diversi colori ce un'altra a Breccia a broccatelata assomigliata al meglio broccatello di Spagna nel medesimo luogo Nel territorio della Spezza una cava di negro fatta o occhi bianchi su la foce della Spezza per venire a Ricò vicino a una chiesa che si domanda
S. Benedetto una cava di verde, e bianco fatta a ochietti
A Pignone una cava di marmi gialli
A Casà una cava di aspri corallini, e bianchi, un altro rosso corallina senza macchia nel medesimo luogo
Un'altra a Scogna villa di Brignata, o vero alla Podestaria di Guam negro e turchino
Un'altra di negro e torchino, chiaro, e oscuro nel medesimo luogo al groppo moresco
Su la giurisdizione di Brignè nel fiume che viene dalla Rochetta una cava di marmi rossi, verdi, bianchi e di molti altri colori
Un'altra di verde fatta a ochietti, che si domanda verde ochiatello pure a brignè
A Levante una cava di bianchi e rossi nel medesimo luogo un'altra di verde rosso e bianco
Al Montaretto nella valle del Saligè in loco detto Salara una cava di diversi colori
Un'altra sotto anli, bianca, nera, e rossa
Nella valle di Castagnola in luogo detto in acqua fredda una cava di marmo verde, giallo e nero, un'altro di diaspro di diversi colori come l'arco celeste nel medesimo luogo
Un'altra sopra alla villa di Piassa verso Levante cioè dove si leva il sole di negro e turchino color di aqua di mare
Un'altra tra Castagnola e Framura, appresso al fiume dove sono certi molini di color rosso come il diaspro, corallino, color del ginapro, e molti altri colori
Un'altra nella giurisdizione di nervi di color bianco, e negro, o vero giurisdizione di quarto e di quinto non so li confini
Un'altro di bianco e nero nel fiume di bisagno
Nella giurisdizione di Sestri di Ponente in un fiume che si domanda Chiaravagna una cava di marmi verdi
Un'altro di alabastro sopra il medesimo fiume di color orientale come quello di Roma de diversi colori
Nelle montagne del Gagge vi sono di molte cave di diversi colori ma la maggior parte del colore delle Castagne
Nel fiume di Varena a Pegli nelle montagne di montio a S. Alberto in luogo detto Reguma una cava di marmi negri, verdi, e bianchi
Un'altra cava sopra li edificij della Cartera in un bosco di Castagne che è di Benedetto Traversa, di verde, negro, e bianco
Un'altra tra il detto Traversa e la Cartera in luoghi incolti campagna rara in luogo del comune verde, negro, e bianco
Un'altra alla radice della Istessa montagna, verde, negro, e bianco e dura fino in cima della montagna
Un'altra giù per il fiume di Varena, verde Straparena
Un'altra di negro amachiato di madre perla nelle montagne Spantalono cioè nel Canale e questi sono colori verdi che si domanda Parma di Smeraldo
Un'altra nella giurisdizione di Prà verde parma di smeraldi
Nelle montagne di Varalo di diaspro di diversi colori Calcidonii di varij colori
Un'altro sotto anli, sotto Framura alla marina de diversi colori
Nel fiume di Varena a Pegi, Pietre bianche nere e verde dure come il

porfido, ed altre nere sensa altre machie, et altre negre e color di madreperla
Nel fiume Paravagna a Sestri Pietre dure como il detto porfido di diversi colori

Li 1626 a 28 Agosto

Gli Ill.mi SS. Procuratori commissionati come sopra del Ser.mo Senato havuto de nuovo consideratione a quanto è stato a lor SS. Ill.me esposto dà detto mastro Giò: Morelli, sono di parere riferire oltre a quanto si antiene nella relatione fatta sotto li 13 luglio passato; d'imporre pena a chi si intromettesse nelle cave nominate sopra in pregiuditio di detto mastro Giò. di lire cento ogni volta che fusse contrafatto da aplicarsi come stimarà il Ser.mo Senato.

(THE STATE ARCHIVE OF GENOA, *Public Finance Acts,* f. 175). (*Ref. Edoardo Grendi*).

Parish Archive of Senarega (Genoa)
Filza M (25th, June 1744)

(*Extract of a letter from Francesco Campora to the rector Arpe, concerning the church altar, and a contract to be drawn up between the above and Alessandro Aprile, sculptor*).

...che il marmo di tutto il complesso dell'Altare è balaustrata, sia bianco statuario, e che la predella faccia dell'urna, e fianchi e piano della Mensa, siano tutti in un pezzo intiero per ciascheduno, si come pure li gradini, sino al principio del suo gharibo, tanto il fronte quanto il piano o cornice con vista di fianco, sia in due pezzi formati, il Tabernacolo finito con cuppolino levaticcio, e due collonette di brugatello, li sclini si dell'altare come di ballaustrata sino alli suoi dritti né i piani come ne fronti i quali saranno di bardiglio in un pezzo per ognuno, li balaustri, ogn'uno intiero senza tacchi con suoi mischi alla guisa del dissegno, si come li piedistalletti pure, ed'uno scalino solo, li due Termini a fianchi sutto gradini, in busti di Serrafino, in un pezzo per ogn'uno, le altre Teste d'Angioli, che si vedono a suoi posti, come d'urna a fianchi e mezzo, siano sculpite nel medesmo pezzo, e non rapportate, si come quelle di gradini ancora li mischi connessi e distribuiti a suoi posti, secondo mostra il dissegno, siano lavorati a basso riglievo, si nell'urna che ne gradini è Tabernacolo ed in piano solo, quelli della predella, e sarano, brucatello di Spagna, e saravezza, giallo di Verona, e qualche pezzetto di verde antico, ed'allabastro di Sestri, indove stimerà far bene il buon gusto dell'Artefice, a ciò vengha l'oppera, al possibile vagha e con buona sodezza ornata, si come non si può dubbitare, della Perizia ed'Honorato Nome del Sig. Allesandro Aprile, facendo tutto questo solo per una formalità consueta e per rendere pago la cortezza de Massari e parocchiani di S.ta M.a di Senaregha, che così bramano sia fatto, per loro sodisfazione...

(*Researched and transcribed by Paolo Giardelli*)

The legend of mount Pisanino (Apuan Alps)

Quando Pisa (la) era già una città forte e (essa) trafficava tutto per arricchirsi anche di più, nel posto dove (la) è (era) accesso (-a) questo (-a) fatto (cosa) c'era sempre tutto piano.
In questo piano (ci) vivevano (stavano) [dei] pastori con le loro pecore ed i cani da guardia, in tanto che i lupi non gliele mangiassero.
Una sera, il pastore che (egli) abitava più in alto, (nel) mentre (che egli) era [intento] a mettere dentro le sue pecore, (egli) vide un bel giovinotto che (egli) andò ad incontrare (scontrarlo). (Egli) Era tutto sudato, stanco e pieno di polvere; (egli) avrà avuto trent'anni, (egli) era alto (grande), col naso aquilino, coi capelli (neri) e con gli occhi neri; e dai suoi occhi tristi si conosceva che (egli) era pieno di dolore; in tutto l'insieme (questo uomo egli) metteva soggezione e dalla sua fierezza (dal suo petto) si (ri-)conosceva che (egli) era una persona nobile.
Quest'uomo, insieme a suo padre, (egli) era scappato da Pisa (da) dove (egli) era nato, [Colà] suo padre (egli) rivestiva funzioni di comando (comandava), ma dato che la gente [a lui sottoposta] non faceva sempre (facevano) il suo dovere, egli venne scoperto e allora gli toccò scappare. I soldati gli andarono dietro, (e) gli uccisero il padre e (lui) lo ferirono. (Ma) Tuttavia gli riuscì (a) scappare ed (egli) arrivò fin lassù da quel pastore. Questo pastore lo mise nella sua capanna, gli fasciò la (sua) ferita e non gli domandò nulla.
Il pastore (egli) aveva una figlia che (essa) era tanto bella. Anche lei (ella) aveva due occhi belli e chiari ed una bocca rossa ed un personale che bisognava vedere (-la). Lei lo curò con amore e con pazienza. Dopo qualche giorno il malato si fece togliere (cavare) le tende dalla finestra per guardare fuori e (egli) guardava sempre verso Pisa. (Questa) La ragazza (essa) capì che (egli) era pisano e quando lei e (il) suo padre (essi) parlavano insieme, lo chiamavano il Pisanino.
La figlia del pastore (essa) aveva tanti innamorati, ma lei non ne guardava nessuno. Solo questo giovanotto le fece conoscere che cos'era (qual che era) l'amore. Ma con tutte le sue cure non fu capace (buona) di guarirlo.
Anche lui le voleva bene e (egli) avrebbe voluto essere il padrono di Pisa per regalargliela. (Ma) Invece (lui) morì.
I pastori gli fecero una bara (barella) e lo seppellirono nel prato; gli fecero una tomba di pietra (sasso) che credettero degna di lui e (essi) pregarono il Signore per lui che (egli) potesse andare in paradiso. Quella giovanotta (essa) pianse tanto sulla (nella sua) tomba. Tutte le sere (notti) vi si recava (ci andava) e le (sue) lagrime le lavavano il viso, le bagnavano i vestiti e (ella bagnò) tutta la (sua) tomba; i suoi lamenti (essi) commossero anche le belve. Una notte perfino (infino) le stelle (esse) piansero a dirotto e (esse) erano lagrime di sasso infocato. Quella ragazza le vedeva cadere e le parevano [tante] goccie d'oro sulla (incima alla) tomba del suo amoroso. Alla mattina non c'era più la tomba ma una grande montagna (un grande monte) che chiamarono (e le misero nome) Pisanino per ricordare il giovanotto. E le lagrime della ragazza (esse) diventarono dei sassi bianchi come la neve: (che) oggi sono (egli è) i marmi (il marmo) di Gorfi gliano.

(E.BONIN, *Beiträge zur Mundart und Volkskunde von Gorfigliano (Garfagnana) und Nachbarorte,* München 1952).

Various Antique and Modern Marbles Classified According to Colour

Name	Other names	Place of origin	Country	First used in	Structure	Notes	Figure
1. White Marbles							
Pyros	Hard Grechetto	Isle of Pyros	Greece	2nd millenium B.C.	true marble	statuario	
Naxos		Isle of Naxos	Greece	2nd millenium B.C.	true marble		
Thaxos	Hard Greco	Isle of Thaxos	Greece	1st millennium B.C.	true marble		
Pentelycus		Mt. Pentelycus	Greece	1st millennium B.C.	true marble		182
Proconnexus		Isle of Marmara	Turkey	1st millennium B.C.	true marble		
White Carrara	Lunense	Apuan Alps	Italy	2nd century B..C.	true marble		197, 208
Aurisina		Istria	Italy	1st century A.C.	hard calcareous rock		191, 199
Pyrenees		St. Beat	France	2nd century A.D.	hard calcareous rock		
Altissimo	Michelangelo	Apuan Alps	Italy	16th century A.D.	hard calcareous rock	statuario	40
Vermont		Vermont	U.S.A.	19th century A.D.	hard calcareous rock		
White Onyx		Tehuacan	Mexico		calcareous alabaster	translucent	
Indian		Mandalay	India		true marble		
2. Streaked White Marbles							
Karystos	Cipollino (onion shaped)	Karystos	Greece	4th century A.D.	true marble	green stripes	32, 190
Streaked Carrara	Lunense	Apuan Alps	Italy	1st century B.C.	true marble	green streaks	15
Statuario of Carrara	Lunense	Apuan Alps	Italy	1st century B.C.	true marble	statuario	22, 34
Calacatta		Apuan Alps	Italy	14th century A.D.?	true marble	yellowish streaks	45
Arabesqued		Apuan Alps	Italy	14th century A..D.	true marble	grey links	169
Candoglia		Ossola	Italy	14th century A..D.?	true marble	pink stripes	
3. Pale Marbles							
Chiampo		Vicenza	Italy	13th century A.D.?	hard calcareous rock	hazel	
Botticino		Brescia	Italy	1st century A.D.	hard calcareous rock	hazel	
Perlato		Trapani	Italy		hard calcareous rock	hazel	
Travertine		Rome	Italy	15th century A.D.	soft calcareous rock	hazel	43
Aurora			Portugal		true marble	pale pink	
Onyx	Golden-Amber		Marocco		calcareous alabaster	pale yellow	
Onyx	Cotognino	Hatnub	Egypt	1st century A.D.	calcareous alabaster	hazel stripes	
4. Yellow Marbles							
Antique Yellow	Numidian	Chemton	Tunisia	2nd century B..C.	true marble	uniform or speckled	26
Sienna Yellow		Sienna	Italy	14th century A.D.?	true marble	uniform or streaked	15, 27
Gialletto		Verona	Italy	1st century A.D.?	hard calcareous rock	finely streaked	
France Yellow	Serrancolin	Pyrenees	France	16th century A.D.?	true marble	streaked	
Onyx	Nacarado		Peru		calcareous alabaster	mottled	
5. Red, Brown and Violet Marbles							
Antique Red	Tenario	Cape Matapan	Greece	2nd millenium B.C.	true marble	bright red	37
Syenite	Stone of Ethiopia	Assuan	Egypt	2nd millenium B.C	granite	light red	46
Porphyry		Gebel Dokhan	Egypt	2nd century B.C.	porphyry	purple	48
Granitello	Stone of Trades	Kestambol	Turkey	2nd century A.D.	granite	violet	
Red Cipollino	Karia marble	Alykarnaxos	Turkey	3rd century A.D.	true marble	red stripes	
Verona Red	Ammonitic	Verona	Italy	1st century A.D.	hard calcareous rock	mottled orange	42, 199
Levanto Red		Eastern Liguria	Italy	12th century A.D	ophicarbonate rock	speckled or streaked	44
Pecorella		Orano	Algeria	2nd century A.D.	calcareous alabaster	mottled, red	
Baveno		Lake Maggiore	Italy		granite	rose coloured	
Balma		Vercelli	Italy		syenite	brownish-violet	47
Collemandina		Garfagnana	Italy	19th century A.D.	hard calcareous rock	streaks of red	
French Red		Languedoc	France	16th century A.D.	true marble	streaks of red	33, 206
Royal Red			Belgium	16th century A.D.	hard calcareous rock	streaks of brown	
Deutschrot Mittel			Germany		hard calcareous rock	streaks of brown	
Solberga	Rapakiwi	Kalmstad	Sweden		granite	red	49
Red Granite			Brasil		granite	red	
6. Green Marbles							
Basanite	Bronzino/Basalt	Bekhen	Egypt	2nd millenium B.C.	graywacke	grey-green	39
Serpentine	Lacedemonio	Sparta	Greece	2nd Millenium B.C.	porphyry	olive green	51
Ophite	Granite of the chair	Uadi Atallah	Egypt	1st century B.C.	dioritic gabbro	grey-green	
Serpentine		Uadi Atallah	Egypt	1st century A.D.	peridotite	mottled	
Antique Green		Larissa	Greece	2nd century A.D.	ophicarbonate rock	striped	25, 40
Ieracite	Green Porphyry	Gebel Dokhan	Egypt	2nd century A.D.	porphyry	violet-green	
Polcevera		Genoa	Italy	16th century A.D.	ophicarbonate rock	striped	41
Alps	Cesana	Turin	Italy		serpentinite	streaked	
Vert Antique		Barcelonette	France		serpentinite	streaked	
Tynos		Isle of Tynos	Greece		serpentinite	streaked	
Malachite		Katanga	Zaire	19th century A.D.	copper carbonate	striped	

Name	Other names	Place of origin	Country	First used in	Structure	Notes	Figure
7. Black-Green marbles							
Bardiglio		Carrara	Italy	3rd century A.D.	gneiss	grey	10, 188
Antique Black	Numidic	Gebel Azelza	Tunisia	1st century A.D.	true marble	finely streaked	
Dark Bigio	Tenario	Cape Matapan	Greece	2nd century A.D.	true marble	mottled	
Granite of the Forum	Claudiano	Gebel Fatiruh	Egypt	1st century A.D.	diorite grain	dark grey	50
Black Porphyry	Serpentine	Gebel Dokhan	Egypt	1st century A.D.	porphyry	black with green streaks	
Bigio Granite	Graphic	Fontaine do Genie	Algeria	1st century A.D.	granite	brownish grey	
Antique Granitello		Isle of Elba	Italy	1st century A.D.	granite	grey	
Bigio Porphyry	Morvigione	Frejus	France	2nd century A.D.	porphyry	grey	
Ardesia	Lavagna	Genoa	Italy	12th century A.D.	argillaceous schist	black	38
Portoro		La Spezia	Italy	16th century A.D.	hard calcareous rock	black with yellow streaks	15, 28
Sarizzo		Central Alps	Italy		gneiss	grey	
Black Diorite	Anzola	Lake Orta	Italy		diorite	dark grey	
Montorfano		Lake Maggiore	Italy		granite	light grey	
Belgium Black		Namur	Belgium	15th century A.D.?	hard calcareous rock	black	27, 45
Noir		Faugeres	France		true marble	mottled	
Schwarz		Schupbach	Germany		hard calcareous rock	grey streaks	
Labrador			Norway		syenite	iridescent	
Cornish Granite		Cornwall	England		granite	grey	
Black Granitello	Germany	Odenwalt	Germany	2nd century A.D.	granite	mottled	
8. Polychrome Marbles							
African	Luculleo	Theos	Turkey	1st century A.D.	breccia	black, green, red	36, 188
Pavonazzetto	Phrygian-Synnadic	Afyon	Turkey	1st century A.D.	breccia	black, green, red	
Portasanta (Holygate)	of Chyos	Isle of Chyos	Greece	1st century A.D.	calcareous breccia	red, yellow, white	25, 35
Green Breccia	Hecatontalithos	Oriental Desert	Egypt	1st millenuim B.C.	conglomerate	black, grey, green	
Peach Blossom		Chacys	Greece	1st century A.D.	calcareous breccia	red, violet, white	
Broccatello		Tortosa	Spain	2nd century A.D.	fossilised calcareous rock	red, yellow, grey	207
Oriental Lumachella	Egypt	Thuburbo	Tunisia	1st century A.D.	fossilised calcareous rock	pink, grey, yellow	
Breccia of Aleppo		Aleppo	Syria	1st century A.D.	calcareous breccia	red, yellow, black	
Ceppo		Bergamo	Italy		conglomerate	green, black, white	
Serravezza	Medicea	Apuan Alps	Italy	16th century A.D.	calcareous breccia	white, red, violet	30
Rouge Melange	Campan	Pyrenees	France		calcareous breccia	red, green, white	

Physical and Mechanical Properties of Different Families of Marbles

	Breaking load (Kg/cm²)			Minimum height (cm)	Wear (mm)
	Compression	Traction	Flexure	Shock caused by a sphere of 1 kg	Sliding friction
True Marbles	1080-2100	40	120-260	35- 75	1,8-5,3
Hard Calcareous rock	1500-2500	50	100-200	25- 40	0,6-3,0
Calcareous Breccie	975-1800		85-115	40- 50	2,6-8,0
Travertines and Alabasters	575-1300		25-155	25- 35	2,0-7,5
Conglomerates	210-350	20	45- 70	35	3,8-9,5
Ardesia	1490		585	95	8,8
Ophicarbonate rock	950-1320		50- 90	45- 52	1,8-5,5
Serpentine	1430-2300	80	205-355	50-105	0,7-1,6
Granites and Syenites	1620-2440	40	115-190	58- 72	0,2-0,5
Porphyry	2830-3025	60	245-315	60- 64	0,3-0,9
Sarizzo	1680-1960		110-215	70-100	0,6-1,3

Bibliography

Chapter One

General

F. CORSI, *Delle pietre antiche*, Rome 1845.

H.W. PULLEN, *Handbook of ancient roman marble*, London 1894.

CORPO REALE DELLE MINIERE, *Guida all'Ufficio Geologico. Collezioni di pietre decorative antiche*, Rome 1904.

M. PIERI, *I marmi d'Italia*, U. Hoepli, Milan 1950.

M. PIERI, *I marmi esteri*, U. Hoepli, Milan 1952.

F. RODOLICO, *Le pietre delle città d'Italia*, Le Monnier, Florence 1953.

M. PIERI, *Pigmentazioni e tonalità cromatica nei marmi*, U. Hoepli, Milan 1957.

F. CALVINO, *Lezioni di Litologia applicata*, CEDAM, Padua 1963.

Nel mondo della Natura, Enciclopedia Motta di Scienze Naturali, vol. IX e X, F. Motta Publisher, Milan 1963.

E. ARTINI, *Le rocce*, U. Hoepli, Milan 1964.

A. BIANCHI, *Corso di tecnologia dei Marmi e delle Pietre*, University of Padua 1964.

Minerali e rocce, Enciclopedia Italiana delle Scienze, Istituto Geografico De Agostini, Novara 1968.

G.B. CARULLI, R. ONOFRI, *I marmi del Carso*, Venezia Giulia district, Udine 1969.

R. GNOLI, *Marmora romana*, Edizione dell'elefante, Rome 1971.

Guida Tecnica per l'impiego razionale del marmo, edited by the Italian Industry of Marble, Milan 1972.

P. MALESANI, S. VANNUCCI, *Ricerche sulla degradazione delle «pietre»*, L.S. Olschki, Florence 1974.

Tettonica a zolle e continenti alla deriva, edited by F. IPPOLITO, from «Le Scienze», the Italian edition of «Scientific American», Milan 1974.

P. PIEPOLI, *Materiali naturali da costruzione: Le rocce*, V. Veschi, Rome 1975.

L. TREVISAN, G. GIGLIA, *Geologia*, Vallerini Publisher, Pisa 1976.

The Conservation of Stone, edited by the Centre for the preservation of sculpture in the open air, Bologna 1976.

L. TREVISAN, E. TONGIORGI, *La Terra*, U.T.E.T., Turin 1977.

P. PENSABENE, D. MONNA, *Marmi dell'Asia Minore*, C.N.R., Rome 1977.

Deterioramento e Conservazione della Pietra, G. Cini Foundation, Venice 1979.

ISTITUTO DEL COMMERCIO ESTERO, *Marmi Italiani*, Vallardi, Florence 1980.

AUTORI VARI, *I marmi della Montagnola Senese*, Province of Sienna 1981.

M. FRANZINI, C. GRATZIU, *Meccanismi di degradazione fisica dei marmi*; IDEM, *Il marmo cotto in natura e nei monumenti*, from «Rendiconti della Società Italiana di Mineralogia e Petrologia», 1984 (in printing).

Apuan the Alps

D. ZACCAGNA, *Descrizione geologica delle Alpi Apuane*, from «Memorie descrittive della Carta Geologica d'Italia», vol. XXV, R. Geogical Office, Rome 1932.

S. BONATTI, *Studio petrografico delle Alpi Apuane*, from «Memorie descrittive della Carta Geologica d'Italia», vol. XXVI, R. Geogical Office, Rome 1938.

R. NARDI, *Bibliografia geologica delle Alpi Apuane*, in «Atti della Società Toscana di Scienze Naturali», vol. LXX, Pisa 1963.

1ª Mostra nazionale del marmo e delle tecniche d'impiego del marmo nell'edilizia industrializzata, edited by the Chamber of Commerce, Industry and Agriculture of Massa and Carrara, 1965.

F. BALDACCI, P. ELTER, E. GIANNINI, G. GIGLIA, A. LAZZAROTTO, R. NARDI, M. TONGIORGI, *Nuove osservazioni sul problema della falda toscana e sulla interpretazione dei flysch arenacei tipo «macigno» dell'Appennino settentrionale*, from «Memorie della Società Geologica Italiana», vol. VI, Pisa 1967.

M. BOCCALETTI, G. GUAZZONE, *La migrazione terziaria dei bacini toscani e la rotazione dell'Appennino settentrionale in una «Zona di torsione» per deriva continentale*, from «Memorie della Società Geologica Italiana», vol. IX, Pisa 1970.

M. BOCCALETTI, P. ELTER, G. GUAZZONE, *Plate tectonic models for the development of the Western Alps and Northern Apennines*, from «Nature Physical Sciences», vol. 234, New York 1971.

M. BOCCALETTI, P. ELTER, G. GUAZZONE, *Polarità strutturali delle Alpi e dell'Appennino settentrionale in rapporto all'invasione di una zona di subduzione nord-tirrenica*, from «Memorie della Società Geologica Italiana», vol. X, Pisa 1971.

L. DALLAN NARDI, R. NARDI, *Schema stratigrafico e strutturale dell'Appennino settentrionale,* from «Memorie dell'Accademia lunigianese di Scienze G. Capellini», vol. XLII, La Spezia 1972.

G.M. CRISCI, L. LEONI, A. SBRANA, *La formazione dei marmi delle Alpi Apuane. Studio petrografico, mineralogico e chimico,* from «Atti della Soc. Toscana di Scienze Naturali», A, LXXXII, Pisa 1976, pp. 199-236.

A. THEY, *Guida ai minerali del marmo di Carrara e Massa,* Cantucci Publisher, Bologna 1977.

REGIONE TOSCANA, *I Marmi Apuani. Schede merceologiche,* Ertag, Florence 1980.

Chapter Two

Antiquity

B. GALIANI, *L'architettura di Marco Vitruvio Pollione,* Sienna 1790.

C. DUBOIS, *Etude sur l'administration et l'exploitation des carrières dans le mond romain,* Paris 1908.

G. DE ANGELI D'OSSAT, *I marmi di Roma antica,* from «Atti del I Congresso Nazionale di Studi Romani», Rome 1931.

L. MADDALENA, *I marmi dei fori imperiali,* from «Atti del III Congresso Nazionale di Studi Romani», Rome 1934, pp. 5-10.

C. D'AMBROSI, *La cava romana di Aurisina presso Trieste,* Institute of Mineralogy n. 3, Trieste 1955.

C.N. BROMEHEAD, *Coltivazione delle miniere e delle cave,* from «Storia della tecnologia», vol. I, Boringhieri, Turin 1961.

S. LLOYD, *Costruzioni in mattoni e pietra,* in «Storia della Tecnologia», vol. I, Boringhieri, Turin 1961.

A.G. DRACHMAN, *The mechanical technology of Greek and Roman Antiquity,* Copenhagen 1963.

R. MARTIN, *Manuel d'architecture Greque,* vol. I, J. Picard et C., Paris 1965.

R.J. FORBES, *Studies in ancient technology,* vol. VII, E.J. Brill, Leida 1966.

J.B. WARD-PERKINS, *Quarrying in Antiquity, Technology, Tradition and Social Change,* from «Proceeding of the British Academy», vol. LVII, Oxford University Press, London 1971.

R. GNOLI, *Marmora romana,* Ediz. dell'Elefante, Rome 1971.

D.E. EICHHOLZ, *Pliny Natural History,* vol. X, books XXXVI-XXXVII, Harvard University Press, London 1972.

P. PENSABENE, *Considerazioni sul trasporto di manufatti marmorei in età imperiale a Roma e in altri centri occidentali,* from «Dialoghi di Archeologia», vol. VI, 2-3, Rome 1972.

D.E. EICHHOLZ, *Teophrasthus De Lapidibus,* Claredon Press, London 1975.

H. HODGES, *Artifacts. An introduction to early materials and technology,* J. Baker, London 1976.

P. BACCINI LEOTARDI, *Marmi di cava rinvenuti ad Ostia e considerazioni sul commercio dei marmi in età romana,* Ostia X Digs, Rome 1979.

E. DOLCI, *Carrara Cave Antiche,* Commune of Carrara 1980.

The Middle Ages

L.B. ALBERTI, *De Statua,* from «Opuscoli morali di L.B. Alberti» C. Bartoli, Venice 1568.

L. CAROVE, *Il castello di Musso e le sue cave di marmo,* Cairoli, Como 1960.

B. GILLE, *Macchine,* from «Storia della tecnologia», vol. II, Boringhieri, Turin 1961.

C.N. BROMEHEAD, *La tecnica delle miniere e delle cave fino al XVII secolo,* from «Storia della tecnologia», vol. II, Boringhieri, Turin 1961.

R.H.G. THOMSON, *L'artigianato medievale,* from «Storia della tecnologia», vol. II, Boringhieri, Turin 1961.

N. DAVEY, *Storia del materiale da costruzione,* Il Saggiatore, Milan 1965.

J.B. WARD-PERKINS, *Quarries and stoneworking in the Early Middle Ages,* from «Artigianato e tecnica della società dell'Alto Medioevo Occidentale», Italian Centre of Studies on the High Middle Ages, Spoleto 1971.

C. KLAPISCH-ZUBER, *Carrara e i maestri del marmo; 1300-1600,* Deputation of the Italian Centre of Studies on the High Middle Ages, Massa 1973.

E. BACCHESCHI E ALTRI, *Le tecniche artistiche,* Mursia, Milan 1973.

P. VARÈNE, *Sur la taille de la pierre antique médiévale et moderne,* University of Dijon, 1974.

P. BAROCCHI, *Agostino del Riccio, Istoria delle Pietre,* SPES, Florence 1979.

The Industrial Age

V. SANTINI E C. ZOLFANELLI, *Della segatura del marmo,* Carrara 1874.

G. TENDERINI, *Delle Segherie dei marmi in Massa Carrara,* Carrara 1874.

G. BOTTIGLIONI, *Die Terminologie der Marmorindustrie in Carrara,* in «Wörter und Sachen», band VI, heft 1, Heidelberg 1914.

A. CONSIGLIO, *Il marmo,* Nistri, Pisa 1949.

C. MANARESI, *La lavorazione dei marmi dalla cava alla posa in opera,* Görlich, Milan 1960.

L. ROSSATO, *Appunti sulla lavorazione e sul commercio del marmo,* Verona 1963.

G. TORTORA, *L'estrazione e la lavorazione del marmo,* vol. I, Publisher S. Marco, Bergamo 1967.

«Carrara Marmi», quarterly review edited by the Commune of Carrara, n. 1-23, Carrara 1975-82.

«Marmi, Graniti, Pietre», review specializing in the Marble Industry; 1-131, Milan (1961-83).

Chapter Three

Prehistory and the Early Ages

A.C. BLANC, *Dall'astrazione all'organicità,* De Luca publishers, Rome 1958.

AUTORI VARI, *Alba della Civiltà,* A. Mondadori, Milan 1961.

V.G. CHILDE, *L'alba della civiltà europea,* G. Einaudi, Turin 1972.

Antiquity

M.W. PORTER, *What Rome was built with,* London-Oxford 1907.

G. LA FAYE, heading *Marmor, Marmorarius,* from «Dictionnaire des Antiquités grecques et romaines», Paris 1918.

M.E. BLAKE, *The pavements of the roman buildings of the Republic and carly Empire,* from «Memoir of the American Academy in Rome», VIII, Rome 1930.

P. DUCATI, *La scultura greca dei tempi aurei,* Memi, Florence 1943.

C. BLUEMEL, *Greek sculptors at work*, London 1955.

G. LUGLI, *La tecnica edilizia romana,* Rome 1957.

I. CALABI LIMENTANI, voce *Marmorario* from «Enciclopedia dell'Arte Antica», Rome 1958.

A. RIEGL, *Arte tardoromana,* G. Einaudi, Turin 1959.

ISTITUTO DELLA ENCICLOPEDIA ITALIANA, *Enciclopedia dell'Arte Antica classica e orientale,* Rome 1965.

A. FROVA, *L'arte di Roma e del mondo romano,* UTET, Turin 1961.

B. ADAM, *The technique of Greek Sculpture in the archaic and classical periods,* London 1967.

R. BIANCHI BANDINELLI and Others, *L'arte dell'antichità classica,* I-II, UTET, Turin 1976.

D. MANACORDA, *Un'officina lapidaria sulla via Appia,* «Studia Archeologica» 26, Rome 1979.

The Middle Ages

VIOLLET LE DUC, *Dictionnaire raisonné dell'Architecture française du XI et XII siècles,* Paris 1865.

J. von SCHLOSSER, *L'arte del Medioevo,* G. Einaudi, Turin 1961.

M.S. BRIGGS, *Costruzione di edifici,* from «La Storia della Tecnologia», II-III, Boringhieri, Turin 1963.

R.H.G. THOMSON, *L'artigianato Medievale,* from «La Storia della Tecnologia», II, Boringhieri, Turin 1962.

D. TALBOT RICE, *L'arte Bizantina,* Sansoni ed., Florence 1966.

M. BACKES e R. DOLLING, *L'arte in Europa (VI-XI secolo),* Rizzoli, Milan 1970.

E. POLEGGI, *Santa Maria di Castello e il Romanico a Genova,* Sagep, Genoa 1973.

The Post-Middle Ages

P. CATTANEO, *I quattro primi libri d'architettura,* Venice 1554.

F. RODOLICO, *Le pietre della città d'Italia,* Le Monnier, Florence 1965.

A. BLUNT, *Le Teorie Artistiche in Italia dal Rinascimento al Manierismo,* G. Einaudi, Turin 1966.

E. POLEGGI, *Strada Nuova, una lottizzazione del Cinquecento a Genova,* Sagep, Genoa 1972.

C. KLAPISCH ZUBER, *Carrara e i maestri del marmo (1300-1600),* Historical Deputations for the Ancient Provinces of Modena, Massa 1973.

N. DAVEY, *Storia del materiale da costruzione,* Il Saggiatore, Milan 1975.

A. PAMPALONI MARTELLI, *Museo dell'Opificio delle pietre dure di Firenze,* Arnaud, Florence 1975.

S. ROSSI, *Dalle Botteghe alle Accademie,* Feltrinelli, Milan 1980.

General

«Marmo, pietre, graniti», Periodical Review 1930-1939.

«Il Marmo», Periodical Review 1941-1943.

P. BARGELLINI, *Belvedere,* Vallecchi, Florence 1959.

AUTORI VARI, *Capolavori nei secoli,* Enciclopedia di tutte le arti, Fratelli Fabbri ed., Milan 1963.

AUTORI VARI, *Architettura nei secoli,* A. Mondadori, Milan 1965.

AUTORI VARI, *Momenti del Marmo. Scritti per i duecento anni dell'Accademia di Belle Arti di Carrara,* Bulzoni ed., Rome 1969.

«Marmo», Periodical Review 1962-1971.

P.L. NERVI, *Storia universale dell'Architettura,* Electa ed., Milan 1972.

Enciclopedia Universale dell'Arte, Sansoni, Florence 1972.

A. HAUSER, *Storia sociale dell'arte,* G. Einaudi, Turin 1975.

Chapter Four

The Roman Age

L. BRUZZA, *Sui marmi lunensi,* from «Dissertazioni della Pontificia Accademia Romana di Archeologia», II series, tome II, Rome 1884, pp. 389-448.

C. DUBOIS, *Étude sur l'administration et l'exploitation des carrières de marbre... dans le monde romain,* Section I, Italie, Luna, Paris 1908, pp. 3-17.

L. BANTI, *Antiche lavorazioni nelle cave lunensi,* from «Studi Etruschi», V (1931).

L. BANTI, *Luni,* Institute for Etruscan Studies, Florence 1937.

U. FORMENTINI, *Monte Sagro. Saggio sulle istituzioni demoterritoriali degli Apuani,* from «Atti del I Congresso Internaz. di Studi Liguri», Bordighera 1956.

G. TEDESCHI GRISANTI, *Un rilievo romano delle cave di Carrara: i «Fantiscritti»,* from «Atti e Memorie della Deputazione di Storia Patria per le Antiche Provincie Modenesi», X (1975).

A.C. AMBROSI, *Sul culto della «Mens Bona» a Carrara,* from «Economia Apuana», III (1977).

AUTORI VARI, *Scavi di Luni,* I, II, Bretschneider, Rome 1973, 1977.

E. DOLCI, *Carrara Cave Antiche,* Commune of Carrara, 1980.

COMUNE DI CARRARA, *Mostra Marmo Lunense,* Pacini, Pisa 1982.

L. e T. MANNONI, *I porti di Luni,* in «Il porto di Carrara», Genoa 1983, pp. 9-64.

The Middle and the Modern Ages

G. SFORZA, *Bibliografia storica della città di Luni e suoi dintorni,* from «Memorie dell'Accademia di Scienze di Torino», LX, 1910.

A. BERTOLOTTI, *Artisti modenesi, parmensi e della Lunigiana in Roma nei secoli XV, XVI e XVII,* Modena 1882.

U. MAZZINI, *Luni e Carrara,* from «Dante in Lunigiana», Milan 1909.

M. LUPO GENTILE, *Il Regesto del Codice Pelavicino,* from «Atti della Società Ligure di Storia Patria», XLIV (1912).

G. VOLPE, *Lunigiana medievale,* Florence 1923.

A. ANGELI, *Carrara nel Medioevo. Statuti e ordinamenti,* from «Atti della Società Ligure di Storia Patria», LIV (1929).

F. SASSI, «Carraria de supra Luna», from «Raccolta di scritti storici in onore del Conte C. del Medico Stoffetti», Pescia 1942.

C. PICCIOLI, *Gli Agri marmiferi del Comune di Carrara,* C.I.A.A. Chamber, Carrara 1956.

P.M. CONTI, *Luni nell'Alto Medioevo,* CEDAM, Padua 1967.

M. LAPINA, *Popolazione, economia e società a Carrara: le origini dell'Industria del marmo,* Degree Thesis, Faculty of Arts, University of Pisa, Academic Year 1972-73.

C. KLAPISCH ZUBER, *Carrara e i maestri del marmo (1300-1600),* Historical Deputation of the Ancient Provinces of Modena, Massa 1973.

C. PICCIOLI, *Atti preparatori della Legge sulle cave di Massa e Carrara del 14-7-1846*, Order of the Solicitors and Barristers of Massa, 1976.

E. MERCURI, *Marmora di Carrara*, Saving Bank of Carrara, 1980.

The Industrial Age

E. REPETTI, *Sopra l'Alpe Apuana e i marmi di Carrara*, Badia Fiesolana, 1820.

C. RONCAGLIA, *Statistica generale degli Stati Estensi*, Modena 1849.

C. MAGENTA, *L'Industria dei Marmi Apuani*, Florence 1871.

T. CORSI, *Pareri sulla ferrovia comunale privata di Carrara*, Florence 1871.

V. SANTINI, C. ZOLFANELLI, *Della segatura del marmo*, Carrara 1874.

G. TENDERINI, *Delle segherie dei marmi in Massa e Carrara*, Carrara 1874.

C. LAZZONI, *Guida storico, artistico industriale*, Carrara 1880.

A. GIAMPAOLI, *I marmi di Carrara*, Pisa 1897.

G. BOTTIGLIONI, *Die Terminologie der Marmorindustrie in Carrara*, from «Wörter und Sachen», band VI, heft 1, Heidelberg 1914.

A. ANGELI, *Carrara. Aree del marmo*, monography from the series «Le cento città d'Italia», Sonzogno 1927.

C.A. FABBRICOTTI, *Alcuni cenni circa l'industria marmifera apuana*, Carrara 1928.

— *Il Consorzio per l'industria ed il commercio dei marmi di Carrara*, Carrara 1928.

G. LORSANI, *La produzione e il commercio dei marmi apuani*, S.E.T., S. Cassiano val di Pera 1933.

M. BETTI, *Quadro storico dell'escavazione del marmo di Luni-Carrara dal II secolo a.C. ai giorni nostri*, Massa 1934.

E. MAGNI, *Industria e commercio dei marmi apuani*, Rome 1934.

M. MAZZITELLI, *La lavorazione del marmo in rapporto alla salute degli operai*, Ist Exhibition of Marble, Carrara 1934.

A. BERNIERI, *Cinquanta anni di lotte operaie in Apuania (1901-1951)*, Chamber of Work, Carrara 1952.

V. DA MILANO, *Industriali e commercianti di marmo inglesi a Carrara fra il 1821 e il 1870*, from «Atti dell'Accademia di Lucca» (1952).

B. NICE, *Le Alpi Apuane. Studio antropogeografico*, C.N.R., Rome 1952.

G. CASALIS, G.A. RONCHI, *Studio per la riforma del sistema di trasporto dei marmi dai poggi al piano di Carrara*, Industrial Association of Massa e Carrara, 1956.

E. WALSER, *Les marbres de la région Apuane*, Gaugin et Laubscher, Montreux 1956.

R. MORI, *La lotta sociale in Lunigiana (1859-1904)*, F. Le Monnier, Florence 1958.

A. BERNIERI, *Cento anni di storia sociale a Carrara*, Feltrinelli, Milan 1961.

L. LAVAGNINI, *Carrara nella leggenda e nella storia*, Leghorn 1962.

L. CASELLA, *I cavatori delle Alpi Apuane*, La Nuova Europa Ed., Carrara 1963.

C. PICCIOLI, *Cento anni della Camera di Commercio Industria e Agricoltura di Massa Carrara*, 1963.

CAMERA DI I.A.A. DI MASSA E CARRARA, *Aspetti della industrializzazione nella Provincia di Massa e Carrara nell'ultimo trentennio*, from «Quadri di economia toscana», U.C.C.I.A.A.T., Florence 1972.

L. GESTRI, *Capitalismo e classe operaia in provincia di Massa-Carrara dall'Unità d'Italia all'età giolittiana*, L.S. Olschki, Florence 1976.

M. BORGIOLI, B. GEMINIANI, *Carrara e la sua gente*, Apuan Press and Publishers, Carrara 1977.

Periodical Publications

«Atti e Memorie della Deputazione di Storia Patria per le Antiche Province Modenesi» series I-X.

«Memorie dell'Accademia Lunigianese di Scienze Giovanni Capellini», I-XLII (1920-1972).

«Giornale Storico della Lunigiana», I-XXVII (1950-1976).

CENTRE OF STUDIES OF LUNI, «*Quaderni*», Luni 1-7 (1977-1982).

COMMUNE OF CARRARA, «Carrara Marmi», 1-11 (1975-82).

«Economia Apuana», I-III (1945-1983).

Chapter Five

AUTORI VARI, *Momenti del Marmo*, Bulzoni ed., Rome 1969.

Q. CAPUZZI, M. CARRIERO, S. FAILLA, *Ricerca coltivazione ed utilizzazione dei marmi apuani*, Carrara 1977.

Guida tecnica per l'impiego razionale del marmo, edited by the Italian Marble Industry, Milan 1972.

AUTORI VARI, *Marmi Graniti Pietre* (Guide and Atlas), Globo, Milan 1980.

Index